# WOMAN'S REALM

## Year Book

### FOR 1985

## ALL YOUR
## WEEKLY MAGAZINE
## FAVOURITES IN
## ONE BOOK

£2·35

# All Around

## Hello

**Richard Barber, Editor of Woman's Realm, introduces your Year Book for 1985**

I don't know about you, but if the Christmas had ever dawned in my childhood when I hadn't received the annual of my favourite comic I should have felt as disorientated as if the tangerine had been left out of the stocking-toe or the sixpences out of the Christmas pud ... It's all different now I'm an adult, of course. No annuals, no stockings and — now I come to think of it — no sixpences. Well, there's very little to be done about the last two, and anyway I'm happy to wait until my children are old enough to understand about stockings and Christmas puddings — and, yes, they'll have their annuals too. But, on reflection, why should they have all the fun? Why shouldn't adults have their own annuals? Why not indeed ... We call ours the *Woman's Realm Year Book*.

Regular readers of *Woman's Realm* will, I hope, agree that it is a jolly good read. So it is with the *Year Book* — our aim has been to give you a hearty measure of reading value, from superb original short stories, through lots of fascinating new features (from palm reading to family fun for free) to all your regular weekly favourites. Not forgetting our book-within-a-book, *Ring o' Roses* by favourite author Marie Joseph. For all of you who wrote remembering our serial and asking where you could re-read the story (and were met with, "Sorry, it's out of print!"), your wish is our command. And new readers are in for a real treat!

But the *Year Book* isn't all to do with sitting with your feet up — oh no! As with the magazine, its backbone is advice and inspiration for all the practical areas of your life, from cookery to craft. And that's where I hand over to the experts ... One last word, though ... Do tell me what you think of this, the second, *Woman's Realm Year Book*. You've let me trumpet its praises, but then I'm biassed. It's *your* opinion that really counts – so please let me hear it!

*Richard*

# the Year Book

Our Cookery Editor, CHRISTINE FRANCE, says: "Even keen cooks run out of ideas when they have families to feed day in, day out. So my first main *Year Book* feature concentrates on family fare — with recipes for super Sunday lunches, tea-time treats and weekday budget-beaters. And, at the other end of the scale, I've chosen easy-on-the-cook but impressive recipes for entertaining — whether you're throwing an informal party for a few friends or catering for a formal celebration. That way, you can enjoy the party quite as much as your guests!"

## YOUR KNITTING!

Our Knitting Editor, PEGGY GREEDUS, says: "From all the letters you send me, I am delighted to realise how many of you share my pleasure in knitting and the sense of reward it gives. For the *Year Book* I have chosen designs I think are particularly rewarding, both in the making and the final effect. They all have that special touch of luxury or originality that can't be bought — or only at a price. But what if you can't knit? Just turn to page 66 and we'll teach you, and then you can teach your children!"

## YOUR HOME!

Our Home Editor, **AUDREY HAINS, says:** "I've seen homes that cost a fortune to furnish, and I've seen those that have been put together with love, hope and charity-shop finds. And, believe me, money has very little to do with

creating a lovely home. For style and beauty come with the imaginative touches you bring to a house. I hope you find our 'Homely ways to live in style' a real inspiration for your own designs for living!"

## YOUR LOOKS!

Our Fashion Editor **CHRISTINE GRAY (right)** and Beauty Editor **ELAINE BENNETT (centre) say:** "So there are the bills to be paid and the kids need new shoes, and the last person you spend money on is you, right? Yet you don't really mind —

until the day you're just fed up with feeling long-term frumpy. Don't kick the cat — for we've got ways of making you look great fast! None of our ideas cost the housekeeping or hours to achieve: they're just new ways of using what you've got in your wardrobe or make-up bag, plus a few zizzy low-cost extras, to give you that fizzy, fashionable feeling again ... On the same principle, would you love a new hairdo, if only you could afford it? Well, we'll show you how to be your own hairdresser and give your locks just the boost they need ... Your wardrobe too, come to

that. You can make lots of lovely new clothes for next to nothing with our 'Fashion Workshop' feature ... For, in our book, your looks really are what you make them — and we're only too happy to help!"

# All Around the Year Book

## YOUR CRAFT!

**Our Craft Editor, DIANA SIMMONS, says:** "We may live in the computer age, but despite that (or perhaps *be-cause* of it?) more and more of us are taking soothing time out to learn new skills, to pro-duce something original that really is 'all our own work'. For the *Year Book* I have chosen three classic craft features for which I have had clamorous repeat requests: simple patchwork, a tapestry cushion and an enchanting rag doll. So why not get crafty?"

## YOUR TREATS!

## WHERE TO FIND US

Woman's Realm, King's Reach Tower, Stamford Street, London SE1 9LS

| | |
|---|---|
| Cookery: | 01-261 5640 |
| Knitting: | 01-261 6388 |
| Home: | 01-261 5655 |
| Craft: | 01-261 5655 |
| Fashion: | 01-261 6278 |
| Beauty: | 01-261 5773 |
| Fiction: | 01-261 5827 |
| Features: | 01-261 5708 |
| General enquiries: | 01-261 6244 |

7

# A short story by Margaret Wilkinson

"If you tread on a nick you'll marry a stick and the Kaiser will come to your wedding," my friend Maggie chanted as we made our way to school. I was careful to tread warily for I didn't want the Kaiser coming to *my* wedding.

Maggie ran on ahead, making sparks fly from her feet as she scraped her clog irons on the pavement. When I caught up with her, I asked, "Where do babies come from, Maggie?"

She stared at me, "You're the one who should know. It's your auntie that brings them, isn't it?"

That had never occurred to me, yet now that I considered it, I realised that each time Aunt Liz nursed a woman in the village, a baby miraculously appeared. I determined to ask Auntie about it and called at her cottage on my way home, only to discover that she was just on the point of leaving. She was enveloped in a snowy apron with linen cuffs protecting the sleeves of her dress and her carpetbag was on the table. I pulled it towards me and peeped inside.

"Now then, young lady, what're you seeking?" she asked.

"Maggie says it's you that takes the babies," I explained, "and I was looking to see if you had one in there."

"That lass knows more than is good for her," Auntie retorted, "and she's wrong. It's the doctor who takes the babies."

I passed the information on to Maggie later that day as we sat, legs dangling like black sausages, on the wall outside the Milloms' house, waiting for Auntie to emerge. Presently we heard the wail of a baby and Maggie said darkly, "There's been no doctor in there so it must be your auntie."

I had tea with Auntie the next day and as she carefully spread the remains of her butter ration on my toast, she said, "Have you heard from your dad lately?"

Proudly I pulled a postcard from my pocket. It bore a French stamp and was not the usual, embroidered silk card with a Flanders' poppy pressed inside it but a picture of a field of cabbages. Inside each cabbage a baby snuggled, while near by a young lady with a watering can watched over them and a leering soldier peeped over a wall.

"Look, Auntie, babies grow in cabbages in France," I said.

Auntie's lips pursed disapprovingly.

"They always did some funny things in France," she said.

I arrived home from Auntie's to find my mother in tears. I had never seen her cry before and the sight frightened me.

"Your dad's been wounded," she said, waving a piece of paper in front of me.

I hadn't seen my father for more than two years and I could only connect the news to a dimly remembered figure I'd waved goodbye to when I was much smaller than I was now. Mother dried her eyes and placed a plate of vegetables in front of me and suddenly I recalled my dad and the way he'd scoop up a forkful of cabbage off my plate and pop it into his own mouth. "You know I don't like cabbage," I said.

"Get it eaten. Little girls who don't eat cabbage stop growing." She always had an answer for everything and I believed them all.

That evening as Mother prepared me for bed, rubbing my chest with camphorated oil and putting a square of flannel on it (for I was subject to bronchitis), I asked, "Why don't you get a baby, Mum? It's lonely just us two." The familiar blush spread over her face and before she could change the subject I added, "Auntie will tell you how to get one."

"Say your prayers and go to sleep," she said.

One cold day in February, as Mother carefully placed a few pieces of our coal ration on the fire and we huddled in front of it, she told me that my father was being sent to a convalescent home in England and she was going to stay near by. "You will stay with your auntie," she said. "You'll like that, won't you, love?"

I certainly would. Staying with Auntie was like living in a fairy tale.

Every Saturday now, Maggie and I had the job of taking out two babies — the children of neighbours — and as we proudly pushed the

# THE DAY OUR

# BABY CAME

# THE DAY
# OUR BABY CAME

bassinettes through the village, we discussed procreation without ever having heard the word. My baby's mother gave me sixpence which I was saving for the day when I could buy a baby, if I could find out where the source was. Maggie said she didn't want any babies in their house as she had six elder brothers and sisters already. She was saving up for a pair of real silk stockings.

Just outside the village, she insisted, as she always did, that we change bassinettes because mine was in better condition than hers.

"It's only fair," she said, "because my baby's mother gives me a shilling so I should have the best bassinette."

She spoke with the authority of her two years' superiority in age, so I couldn't argue.

"Do you think it's Father Christmas?" I asked.

"What is?"

"Who brings babies."

Maggie raised her eyes heavenwards. "Don't tell me you still believe in him."

Then, in great detail, she told me how she had discovered who Father Christmas really was — her elder brother.

"Parson says we all come from specks of dust," she added, "but I don't believe that either."

"In France, they grow babies in cabbages," I said, pleased that I could tell her something, and I showed her the now tattered postcard.

She stared, wide-eyed.

"Ooh ... let's go and look."

We pushed the bassinettes across a field to an allotment where a few dejected winter cabbages still grew. Creeping between the rows, we examined each one until a window in a nearby cottage shot open and an irate voice shouted, "What are you two up to?"

"We're picking caterpillars off your cabbages for you," Maggie replied innocently.

"Well, go and pick them off your own!" the angry voice replied.

My mother returned from her visit to say that my father would not be coming home but was being sent to a camp in the south.

"I hate the Kaiser," I said.

Spring came with its bluebells and skipping-ropes. Boys rolled iron hoops along the footpaths and the girls had wooden ones which they twirled round their bodies.

One warm day Maggie and I walked through the lanes, pausing now and again to pick the harebells growing under the hedges.

"Our Bill gave me twopence for polishing his boots," Maggie said. "Let's buy two glasses of milk from the farm."

We watched as Martha, the farmer's poor relation who worked there in return for her food and bed, whisked the milk in a churn to distribute the thick cream. She filled two glasses and pocketed Maggie's pennies.

We sat with our backs against a hayrick and sipped the ice-cold milk. Maggie said through cream-moustached lips, "It can't be cabbages."

"Not here, but it is in France."

We pondered on the mystery a long time until the farmer's wife came out with two hot buns in her apron.

"Eat these, then go," she said. "Lassie won't stop barking while you're there and one of the cows is in calf — it upsets her."

Maggie glanced at me as we left. "I'll bet it's like being 'confined', being 'in calf'," she said.

"Shush," I murmured. For "confined" was like "in the family way" — words which were always whispered by adults if children were present.

We hung over the pigsty for a moment, watching the piglets suckling their mother.

"My mother says kittens come down the water spouts when it rains," I told Maggie.

She spoke scornfully. "They tell you these things until you're about fourteen." She pointed to the piglets. "That lot came from inside the pig. He lays them when he's got enough inside him. He must have wanted eight."

Whenever mother was talking to someone and she thought the subject not fit for my ears, she would inadvertently alert me by telling me to get on with whatever I was doing. When she did this while talking to Auntie one day, I immediately became all ears.

Their voices were so low I couldn't hear much, but Auntie was explaining something to Mother. I heard her say that Mum was to send for her as soon as she had a show. "Don't wait 'til the waters go. The second one is usually quick even though there's been a gap of eight years."

Mum glanced at me and said quickly, "Little pitchers have big ears..."

Auntie turned to me. "Come on, Dorothy, you can toast the pikelets." She stuck one on the end of the long fork and handed it to me, then to Mother she said: "This war's ruining my trade. I've only had two confinements in the past four months."

"Never mind," Mum said, "you'll be rushed off your feet when the men come home."

So men had something to do with it! Were all the soldiers in France picking babies from cabbages to bring home with them? I daren't ask. My mother's embarrassment was almost a tangible thing between us now and my curiosity had to be stifled.

Mum began to complain that the pikelets had given her indigestion but Auntie mixed some bicarbonate of soda in water, handed it to Mum and assured her that it wasn't the pikelets. "It's going to have a shock of hair, this one. It's the hair you see, that causes the indigestion."

I began to notice several odd things. The bassinette which I used to push Mrs Jones' baby in was now in my aunt's bedroom, covered with a sheet, and there were tiny garments at the bottom of a drawer I was forbidden to open.

Maggie too seemed secretive and mentioned several times that my mother was getting fat. Now I saw it was true. Could she lay a baby, I wondered, like the pig had? And if so, how many?

The days were shortening now and Maggie and I walked home from school, scuffling our feet through the brown leaves which filled the gutters. Mother was always knitting when I arrived home, but hurriedly pushed it out of sight as soon as I entered.

One foggy morning, she woke me early. She was clutching her back and looked dishevelled, with a coat over her nightie.

"Call at Auntie's on your way to school, love," she said, "and tell her to come quickly. Say 'the waters have broken'."

"Shall I get Mr Jones too?"

"Don't be silly. What for?"

I didn't wait to explain that Mr Jones was the man who mended the taps and put the water right. Instead I grabbed a piece of toast and raced through the village, the look on my mother's frightened face urging me on.

Arriving at my aunt's, I saw to my surprise that she was wearing her apron and the carpetbag was ready on the table. I didn't need to peep inside this time. I knew there was no baby in there, but I knew too that there was one somewhere on the way to us. And I knew for certain this was IT!

"She's started has she?" Auntie said, and we rushed out together to part at the end of the lane and go our separate ways.

I was immediately aware on entering school that a strange atmosphere pervaded the place. All the teachers were huddled together and seemed to be suppressing their excitement. None of us dared speak until the headmaster came in, but I was filled with pride. I knew what it was all about. They had heard that our baby was on the way.

The headmaster began to speak. "Your parents will have told you it's a special day today," he said, "so I'm going to let you go home early. School dismissed."

We flew out like bees from a hive. Some of the boys were wrapping tissue paper round combs and forming a band. Then they began to walk through the village playing *I'm the Head of the Army*. I thought *Rock-a-bye, Baby* would have been better, but already my attention was caught by the flags, which were beginning to flutter from windows, and the bunting across the the street. Everybody must know about our baby. I could hear people talking about having a street party as I raced through the village. I didn't even wait for Maggie.

"I know it's come," I cried, dashing into our cottage and grabbing Auntie round the waist.

"How did you know?" she asked.

"There's flags everywhere," I replied, rushing upstairs and glancing quickly round the bedroom. A drawer had been filled with a pillow and was on the foot of the bed to act as a cradle. Nappies and baby clothes were hung on a clothes maiden round the oil stove.

My mother's eyes were on me, waiting. She looked different: softer, younger, her hair spread round the pillow like a fan. She beckoned me to go nearer and turned back the sheet to expose a tiny face in the crook of her arm.

"A little sister for you," she said.

My heart was banging. I longed to hold the baby but was afraid — she looked so small.

"Why are you in bed, Mum?" I asked. "The pig wasn't lying down and he had eight."

Mum looked puzzled for a moment then, perhaps for the last time in her game of subterfuge, she avoided the issue.

"It's so that I can keep the baby warm. That's why doctors only bring babies to women who are ill in bed."

She put out a hand and took mine. "As soon as I've been churched, Dorothy, I'll be able to go out with you and you can push our own baby in the bassinet."

I could hear music and ran to the window. Soldiers from a nearby camp were marching past preceded by a band.

"Listen, Mum," I said, "even the soldiers know we've got a new baby — they've come to play for you! Dad must have told them!"

I raced downstairs to tell Auntie to thank them, but she gently caught hold of my arm and pointed to the calendar.

"Note the date, Dorothy, this is one you'll always remember."

It was ringed in red, November the eleventh. Higher on the page a circle enclosed the dates when Mum had stayed near my father in the Convalescent Home. February, 1918.

"Course I'll always remember it," I assured her. "It's the day our baby came."

THE END
© Margaret Wilkinson, 1984

11

*So you think you know your Britain? Then have fun testing your knowledge of the whos, the wheres and the whys of our home country*

**1.** In 1776, the first stately home was opened to the public. There was no admission charge but visitors were expected to slip the housekeeper a tip. The house was:
**a)** Longleat
**b)** Wilton
**c)** Belvoir

**2.** Ben Nevis is the highest mountain in the United Kingdom. Is it:
**a)** over 4,400 ft
**b)** over 5,400 ft
**c)** over 3,400 ft

**3.** Llanfairpwllgwyngyllgogerychwyrn-drobwllllantysiliogogogoch is the longest place name in the United Kingdom. What are the two shortest?

**4.** The first bus conductress worked in:
**a)** London in 1939
**b)** Manchester in the 1920s
**c)** Nottingham before the First World War

**5.** Britain's largest lake is:
**a)** Loch Lomond
**b)** Loch Ness
**c)** Lough Neagh

**6.** Match the place to the writer:

| | |
|---|---|
| Beatrix Potter | Doughty St, London |
| George Bernard Shaw | Burwash |
| Charles Dickens | Near Sawrey |
| Rudyard Kipling | Ayot St Lawrence |

**7.** Britain's longest river is:
**a)** The Thames
**b)** The Severn
**c)** The Spey

**8.** Where do people:
**a)** Chase cheeses on Whit Monday (Spring Bank Holiday)
**b)** Dance the Furry Dance on May 8
**c)** Claim Hocktide kisses

**9.** Which is the odd place out and why? Lancashire, Cheshire, Wensleydale and Lymeswold

# REALM QUIZ

**10.** Where would you find the following animal memorials?
**a)** one to: Foxhunter, Harry Llewellyn's showjumper and three times winner of the King George V's Gold Cup
**b)** one to: Bobby of Greyfriars, a faithful dog who never forgot his master

**11.** Where were the following buried: Charlotte Bronte, Winston Churchill, Karl Marx and Jane Austen

**12.** The first bicycle was built in Britain in 1839. Where did the inventor come from?
**a)** Oxfordshire
**b)** Caernarvonshire
**c)** Dumfries

**13.** Whose husband promised to reform the tax laws if his wife rode naked through a certain city?
Which city was it?
What was the name of the person who disobeyed the proclamation that no one should look at the rider?

**14.** Which Oxfordshire town figures in an equestrian nursery rhyme and what else is the town famous for?

**15.** What have the following in common:
**a)** Bath, Chelsea, Eccles
**b)** Portland, Purbeck, Cotswold
**c)** Buxton, Bath, Tunbridge Wells
**d)** Exeter, Durham, Southwark
**e)** Roxburgh, Cornwall, Gloucester
**f)** Uffington and Westbury
**g)** Hampton Court, Wyck Rissington, Hazlefield Park in Aberdeen

**16.** In what part of the country would you see the following, and what are they:
**a)** Pargeting
**b)** Oast Houses
**c)** Well-dressing

**17.** Which of the following palaces belong to the Queen:
**a)** Blenheim
**b)** Lambeth
**c)** Scone

**18.** Match the place to the product:
| | |
|---|---|
| Paisley | China clay |
| Harris | Porcelain |
| Nottingham | Shawls |
| Worcester | Lace |
| Northampton | Tweed |
| Parr | Shoes |

**19.** Here are the Christian names of some show-business personalities. All their surnames are place names. What are they?
| | |
|---|---|
| Richard | ...... |
| Susannah | .... |
| Charlie | ....... |
| Susan | ......... |
| Moira | ........ |
| June | ......... |
| Jill | ....... |
| Burt | ......... |

All done?
Now turn to page 188
for the answers
and your Realm rating

# Thanks a million!

"Without doubt, my late father deserves all the thanks for getting me into show business," says **Ken Dodd**. "A very funny man himself, he lived out his own desire to be an entertainer through me, and I just can't thank him enough!"

"I'd like to thank the serpent in the Garden of Eden," says fashion designer **Mary Quant** with a wicked twinkle. "Without him, we wouldn't be wearing clothes today!"

"I would like to say a public 'thank you' to Syd Little," says his other half, **Eddie Large**. "I talked him into packing up his job as a painter and decorator to entertain with me in the clubs. We've been together for 21 years and he's a true pal."

"Who would I thank? Why, my mother, no doubt about it! Without her, I wouldn't be here today," says singer **Patti Boulaye**. "No one else would give up everything and live for her children like a mother — or certainly like mine. She smacked the daylights out of me as a child — I'd have grown up very stubborn otherwise! And now that I have children of my own, I realise what it is to be a mum, and how much I owe to mine."

Says motorcyclist and TV presenter **Barry Sheene**: "I want to say the biggest possible thank you to Nigel Cobb, the surgeon at Northampton General Hospital, who saved my limbs after my crash at Silverstone in 1982. Without his skill and care, I'd be legless — in the worst possible way!"

"Though it's very difficult to think of one person to thank, it's certainly my son Thomas who brings more joy into my life than I ever thought possible," says yachtswoman turned bestselling author **Clare Francis**. "From the past, I would most like to thank my maths teacher — who made the whole thing comprehensible after years of mathematical darkness!"

"I'm not the easiest person to live with — I often find it hard myself — so I'd like to thank my wife Diana for putting up with me so well for so long," says TV film buff **Barry Norman**, married to Diana for 25 years. "When I get depressed, she just carries on as usual; when I'm working late, she never suspects 'another woman'; she understands me and my work; she's always there and she is *very* kind."

"I'd like to thank God, and I do every day, for all the good that happens in my life," says the actress and impressionist, **Janet Brown**

"I've played to 100,000 people since last autumn and I'd like to thank those fabulous fans," says King of the Comebacks **Gary Glitter**

"Sometimes I look at my husband Bruce and our children and think, 'Thank you, dog!'" says actress **Julia Foster**. "She's called Honey and when, years ago, she swallowed a balloon, I took her to the vet, and I met this young locum. After a week of him treating Honey I realised he was a terrific guy. The locum was Bruce, of course, and if it hadn't been for Honey bringing us together, would we be happily married today? Who knows?"

# The Sunday Best Lunch

Serve the roast-with-the-most, or a succulent casserole. Follow it with a perfect pud, and what have you got? Contentment, that's what!

## TRADITIONAL ROAST BEEF WITH YORKSHIRE PUDDINGS

*It's worth buying a large joint if you can, as it will serve at least two meals*
**Preparation time: 20 min. Cooking time: 1 to 2 hr. Serves 6**
**3 lb (1.4 kg) piece sirloin, boned and rolled**
**2 oz (50 g) dripping or lard**
*Yorkshire puddings:*
**4 oz (125 g) plain flour**
**Pinch of salt**
**1 egg**
**½ pt (300 ml) milk and water, mixed**
**Oil for tins**
Set oven at 425° F, 220° C (Mark 7). Weigh beef and calculate cooking time. For rare beef allow 10 min for every 1 lb (450 g) plus 10 min. For medium beef allow 15 min for every 1 lb (450 g) plus 15 min and for well done beef allow 20 min for every lb (450 g) plus 20 min.
Place beef in roasting tin, spread with dripping or lard and place in oven for calculated time.
*To make the puddings:* place flour and salt in a bowl. Make a well in centre and add egg. Gradually stir in milk and water, beating to a smooth batter. Allow to stand for 30 min. Place 1 tsp (5 ml) of oil in base of each hole in patty tin and heat in oven for 10 min. Fill each hole up to two-thirds with batter. Bake for 20 min or until well risen and crisp. Serve immediately around the roast.

## CARBONNADE OF BEEF WITH CROUTES

*This dish freezes well, but do add the croûtes on thawing as they are best freshly made*
**Preparation time: 40 min. Cooking time: 3 hr 20 min. Serves 4**
**1½ lb (700 g) shin of beef**
**Salt and ground black pepper**
**1 oz (25 g) flour**
**3 tbsp (45 ml) oil**
**4 oz (100 g) streaky bacon**
**1 medium onion**
**15.5 fl oz (440 ml) brown ale**
**1 tbsp (15 ml) demerara sugar**
**1 bay leaf**
**1 lb (450 g) baby carrots**
**8 oz (225 g) baby onions**
**3 oz (75 g) butter**
**4 tsp (20 ml) whole-grain mustard**
**French stick**
**1 oz (25 g) Cheddar cheese**
Set oven at 325° F, 170° C (Mark 3). Cube beef, coat with seasoned flour. Heat oil in flameproof casserole, fry bacon for 2 min, add meat and brown. Peel and chop the onion and cook until soft. Add ale, bring to boil, stirring. Add sugar and bay leaf, cover, cook for 3 hr. Peel carrots, cut into sticks; peel baby onions. Melt 1 oz (25 g) butter, fry veg for 10 min, add to casserole 1 hr before end of cooking. Combine butter with mustard. Slice bread, and butter. Sprinkle with cheese. Bake for 15 min. Serve with carbonnade.  ▷26

Below: Carbonnade of Beef with
Croûtes: Traditional Roast Beef
with Yorkshire Puddings
Right: Three Fruit Flan

# Tea As Mother Made It

It's the traditional round-the-fireside tea,
so put the kettle on and give them a treat!

Clockwise, from top right: Irish Soda Bread; Bara
Brith; Banbury Cakes; Spiced Chelsea Buns; Drop
Scones; Crumpets; Wholemeal Muffins
*(Turn to page 24 for the recipes)*

# For Everyday Appetites

Running out of interesting ideas for weekday meals that won't break the budget? Try our cheap and cheerful main meals — they'll soon be firm family favourites

## EGG AND HADDOCK SHELLS WITH PEAS AND TOMATOES

*You can substitute a cheap fish such as coley - or sardines - for the haddock*
**Preparation time: 20 min. Cooking time: 28 to 32 min. Serves 4**
**1 oz (25 g) long-grain rice**
**1 egg**
**Salt and ground black pepper**
**4 oz (100 g) smoked haddock fillet**
**1 oz (25 g) margarine**
**13-oz (370-g) pkt frozen puff pastry, thawed**
**Beaten egg to glaze**
**4 tomatoes**
**4-oz (113-g) pkt frozen peas**
Place rice in a pan with egg in its shell and cover with salted water. Cover with a plate and simmer for 12 min. Remove egg from pan, rinse, shell and chop. Drain rice and rinse. Rinse pan. Cut haddock into small pieces and place in pan with margarine. Cook over medium heat for 4 to 5 min until fish flakes easily. Add rice, egg and plenty of pepper, stir to mix. Set oven at 400° F, 200° C (Mark 6). Lightly flour work surface and roll out pastry to a 12-in (30.5-cm) square. Cut out 4 6-in (15-cm) circles. Spoon filling into centre of pastry, brush the edges with beaten egg and fold pastry over filling to make crescent shape. Press the edges to seal. Lightly score pastry with a knife to make a fan pattern. Brush with egg and place on

**Clockwise, top right: Corned Beef Pie with Spinach; Salami and Mushroom Pizza with Salad; Egg and Haddock Shells with Peas and Tomatoes; Lamb Stovies with Oatcakes**

baking sheet. Halve tomatoes, season with salt and pepper, place on baking sheet. Bake in top of oven for 12 to 15 min. Place peas in a pan of boiling salted water and simmer for 5 min. Drain and serve with pasties and baked tomatoes.

## LAMB STOVIES WITH OATCAKES

*Your butcher may have trimmings from chops which would be suitable for this recipe*
**Preparation time: 20 min (plus standing time). Cooking time: 3 hr 10 min. Serves 4**
**12 oz (350 g) boiling mutton or stewing lamb**
**Salt and ground black pepper**
**2 lb (900 g) large onion**
**2 oz (50 g) dripping**
**3 lb (1.4 kg) potatoes**
**4 triangular oatcakes**
**1 oz (25 g) butter**
Place mutton or lamb in saucepan, cover with salted water, cover with lid and simmer for 1 hr. Strain stock and reserve. Chill and remove excess fat. Remove meat from bones, discarding any fat, reserve bones for stock. Set oven at 350° F, 180° C (Mark 4). Peel onion and cut into rings. Melt dripping in frying pan and cook onion over a medium heat for 7 to 10 min. Peel potatoes and slice. Arrange half the onion in the base of a roasting tin, top with half the potato slices and season. Scatter half the meat over and repeat layers. Pour over ½ pt (300 ml) stock and cover with foil. Bake in centre of oven for 1 hr 30 min until potato is soft. Remove foil and cook for 30 min Serve with oatcakes spread with butter. ▷

## CAULIFLOWER AND MACARONI PIE

*Topped with breadcrumbs and cheese, this pie makes a substantial meal*

**Preparation time: 12 min. Cooking time: 25 to 30 min. Serves 4**

**5 oz (150 g) shortcut macaroni**
**Salt and ground black pepper**
**½ large cauliflower**
**8 oz (225 g) carrots**
*Sauce:*
**1 oz (25 g) margarine**
**1 oz (25 g) plain flour**
**1 pt (568 ml) milk**
**2 tbsp (30 ml) made English mustard**
*Topping:*
**2 oz (50 g) Cheddar cheese**
**4 oz (100 g) fresh wholemeal breadcrumbs**
**1 tsp (5 ml) paprika pepper**

Place macaroni in a saucepan, cover with salted water and bring to boil. Cover and simmer for 12 to 15 min. Break cauliflower into florets; scrape carrots and dice. Place in saucepan with macaroni 7 min before end of cooking time. Drain. *To make the sauce:* preheat grill to high. Melt margarine in a pan. Add flour and cook for 1 min. Gradually add milk, stirring, and bring to boil. Add mustard. Stir in macaroni and vegetables and cook for 2 to 3 min. Turn mixture into a 3-pt (1.7-l) ovenproof dish. *To make the topping:* grate cheese and mix with breadcrumbs. Scatter over macaroni. Sprinkle with paprika and grill for 4 to 5 min.

## HAM AND BEAN POT WITH CHEESE DUMPLINGS

*Choose cheese offcuts for this dish — they're cheaper than buying from the block*

**Preparation time: 25 min. Cooking time: 2 hr 30 min. Serves 4**

**1 lb (450 g) knuckle end of bacon**
**6 oz (175 g) dried haricot beans**
**15-oz (425-g) can tomatoes**
**4 sticks celery**
**1 tsp (5 ml) dried basil**
**Ground black pepper**
*Dumplings:*
**6 oz (175 g) self-raising flour**
**¼ tsp (1.25 ml) baking powder**
**¼ tsp (1.25 ml) salt**
**3 oz (75 g) shredded suet**
**1 oz (25 g) Cheddar cheese**
**Fresh parsley (optional)**

Place bacon in a saucepan with beans, cover with water, bring to boil, cover and simmer for 1 hr 30 min. Strain off stock and reserve. Remove meat from bone, trim off excess fat and discard with skin. Reserve bone. Cut meat into small chunks. Place with beans in a casserole with the tomatoes and 1 pt (550 ml) of stock. Wash, chop celery and add with basil. Cover and simmer for 1 hr. Season with pepper. *To make the dumplings:* place the flour, baking powder, salt and suet in a bowl. Add enough water to mix to a soft but not sticky dough. Coarsely grate cheese and roll dough lightly in it. Cut the dough into 8 pieces and roll into small balls. Drop dumplings into casserole, cover and simmer for 20 min without lifting the lid. Serve garnished with parsley if desired.

## CORNED BEEF PIE WITH SPINACH

*You can also serve this pie with baked beans cooked in the oven at the same time.*

**Preparation time: 20 min. Cooking time: 1 hr to 1 hr 10 min. Serves 5**

*Filling:*
**1 large potato**
**1 medium onion**
**1 medium cooking apple**
**12-oz (340-g) can corned beef**
**1 tsp (5 ml) salt**
**Ground black pepper**
**2 tbsp (30 ml) fresh chopped chives, optional**
*Pastry:*
**9 oz (250 g) plain flour**
**Salt and ground black pepper**
**3 oz (75 g) lard**
**¼ pt (150 ml) water**
**Milk to glaze**
**1½ lb (700 g) fresh spinach**

*To make the filling:* peel potato and cut into chunks; peel onion and cut into small pieces; peel and core apple and cut into chunks. Cut beef into chunks and place in a bowl with potato, onion, apple, salt, pepper and chives if used and stir to mix. *To make the pastry:* set oven at 400° F, 200° C (Mark 6). Place flour and 1 tsp (5 ml) salt in a bowl. Heat lard and water in a pan until lard melts and bring to boil. Add to flour mixture and mix to form a soft dough. Lightly flour a work surface and knead pastry until smooth. Roll out two-thirds of the pastry to a large circle and use to line base and sides of an 8-in (20.5-cm) round loose-bottomed Victoria sandwich tin. Spoon in filling and level. Roll out remaining pastry to an 8-in (20.5-cm) circle, and arrange over filling to make a lid. Trim edges of pastry and use trimmings to make leaves. Arrange on top of pie and brush with milk. Wash spinach and place in an ovenproof dish with salt and pepper; cover with lid. Bake pie in centre of oven for 30 min, then add spinach above it and bake a further 30 to 40 min, until pastry is golden and spinach tender.

# EGG CAKE WITH PARSNIPS

Vary the filling with vegetables, chopped bacon, slices of sausage or grated cheese
**Preparation time: 20 min. Cooking time: 20 to 30 min. Serves 4**
Parsnip chips:
**2 lb (900 g) parsnips**
**Salt**
**Oil for deep frying**
Egg cake:
**2 medium potatoes**
**1 leek**
**½ small red pepper**
**6 eggs**
**6 tbsp (90 ml) milk**
**½ tsp (2.5 ml) salt**
**Ground black pepper**
**1 tbsp (15 ml) oil**
To make the chips: peel parsnips and chip. Boil in salted water, then simmer for 5 to 7 min and drain. Deep fry parsnips for 2 to 3 min, until golden. Drain and keep warm.
To make the egg cake: peel potatoes and cut into chunks; trim root from leek and cut into rings; deseed pepper, cut into rings and halve rings. Crack eggs into a bowl, add milk, salt and pepper and beat. Fry potatoes in oil for 7 to 10 min. Add leek and cook a further 2 to 3 min. Pour egg mixture onto potato and leek. Stir. Arrange pepper over top and cook for 5 to 7 min until set.

# MINCE, MEALIE AND MASH

Mash and oatmeal stuffing make minced beef go further _and_ provide a filling meal
**Preparation time: 25 min. Cooking time: 1 hr 5 min. Serves 4**
Mince:
**1 large onion**
**1 large carrot**
**8 oz (225 g) minced beef**
**1 tbsp (15 ml) plain flour**
**1 tbsp (15 ml) oil**
**Salt and ground black pepper**
**½ pt (300 ml) beef stock**
Mealie:
**8 oz (250 g) medium oatmeal**
**4 oz (125 g) shredded suet**
**½ tsp (2.5 ml) salt**
**Ground black pepper**
Mash:
**1 lb (450 g) potatoes**
**1 lb (450 g) swede**
**Salt and ground black pepper**
**1 oz (25 g) margarine**
**2 tbsp (30 ml) milk**
To make the mince: peel and chop onion; reserve 4 oz (125 g). Scrape and slice carrot. Fry onion, mince, flour in oil for 5 min. Add seasoning, carrot, stock; simmer 1 hr.
To make the mealie: place reserved onion, oatmeal, suet, salt, pepper in a bowl and stir. Turn into a 1-pt (568-ml) pudding basin, cover with foil. Place in saucepan half-filled with water, cover, simmer for 1 hr.
To make the mash: peel and chop potatoes and swede, bring to boil in salted water, simmer 20 min. Drain, mash with marg, milk, pepper. Serve with mince and mealie.

# SALAMI AND MUSHROOM PIZZA WITH SALAD

Use processed cheese, loose from the slab — it's cheap and melts beautifully
**Preparation time: 20 min (plus standing time). Cooking time: 40 to 45 min. Serves 4**
Pizza dough:
**1 tsp (5 ml) dried yeast**
**½ tsp (2.5 ml) sugar**
**¼ pt (150 ml) tepid water**
**8 oz (225 g) strong plain white flour**
**1 tsp (5 ml) salt**
**1 tbsp (15 ml) oil**
Topping:
**1 large onion**
**6 oz (175 g) large mushrooms**
**1 oz (25 g) processed cheese**
**2 tbsp (30 ml) oil**
**14-oz (396-g) can tomatoes**
**½ tsp (2.5 ml) dried oregano**
**Salt and ground black pepper**
**3 oz (75 g) salami**
Salad:
**½ small lettuce**
**2-in (5-cm) piece of cucumber**
**½ small green pepper.**
To make the dough: place yeast and sugar in a bowl and blend with a little water until creamy. Allow to stand for 5 min. Place flour and salt in a bowl with yeast, remaining water and oil and mix. Lightly flour work surface and knead dough for 5 min. Return to bowl, cover with oiled cling film and leave in a warm place for 45 min.
To make the topping: peel and chop onion, wipe and slice mushrooms, slice cheese. Fry onion and mushrooms in oil for 5 min. Add tomatoes, oregano, salt and pepper and simmer for 15 min. Remove from heat.
To finish: set oven at 425° F, 220° C (Mark 7). Lightly flour a work surface and roll out dough to a 10-in (25.5-cm) circle. Lightly oil baking sheet and place dough on. Pinch edges lightly to give a raised edge. Spread tomato mixture over base, top with cheese and slices of salami. Bake in top of oven for 20 to 25 min until base is well risen and golden.
To make the salad: rinse the lettuce, wash and chop the cucumber, wash, deseed and chop green pepper and serve with pizza. ▷

## Tea As Mother Made It

Continued from page 18

### BARA BRITH

*This teabread is heavily fruited and will store well for 1 week in an airtight tin*
**Preparation time: 20 min (plus standing time). Cooking time: 1 hr**
**1 lb (450 g) strong plain flour**
**1½ tsp (7.5 ml) salt**
**1 oz (25 g) lard**
**1½ oz (40 g) caster sugar**
**½ tsp (2.5 ml) mixed spice**
**1 oz (25 g) fresh yeast**
**7 fl oz (200 ml) tepid water**
**2 eggs**
**12 oz (350 g) currants**
**4 oz (100 g) sultanas**
**1 oz (25 g) chopped walnuts**
**2 oz (50 g) chopped mixed peel**
Sieve the flour and salt into a bowl. Rub in the lard. Stir in sugar and spice. Blend the yeast with a little of the water. Stir in the remaining water. Stir eggs, currants, sultanas, nuts and peel into flour and add yeast. Mix well. Lightly flour work surface and knead mixture for 5 min until smooth. Shape into oblong and place in a lightly greased 2-lb (900-g) loaf tin. Cover with oiled polythene and leave in a warm place until doubled in size. Set oven at 350° F, 180° C (Mark 4). Bake, uncovered, in centre of oven for 1 hr until golden.

### WHOLEMEAL MUFFINS

*These buns will keep fresh for up to 3 days. Serve hot, split and buttered*
**Preparation time: 20 min (plus standing time). Cooking time: 10 min. Makes 12**
**6 oz (175 g) wholemeal plain flour**
**10 oz (275 g) plain flour**
**1 tsp (5 ml) salt**
**1 oz (25 g) fresh yeast**
**¼ pt (150 ml) tepid milk**
**7 tbsp (105 ml) tepid water**
**1 egg**
**1 oz (25 g) butter, melted**
Place the flours and salt into a bowl. Blend the yeast with a little of the milk. Stir in remaining milk with water. Pour into the flour mixture with the egg and melted butter. Mix to a soft dough. Lightly flour work surface and knead mixture for 5 min until smooth. Place in a lightly oiled polythene bag and leave in a warm place until doubled in size (about 45 min). Knead again and roll out until ½ in (1 cm) thick. Cut out rounds with a 3-in (7.5-cm) round pastry cutter. Lightly flour two baking sheets and place on rounds. Cover with oiled polythene and leave to rise until doubled in size. Set oven at 450° F, 230° C (Mark 8). Bake, uncovered, in top of oven for 5 min. Turn muffins over and bake for a further 5 min.

### SULTANA AND CIDER CAKE

*An energy-packed cake that can be frozen in slices wrapped in foil*
**Preparation time: 10 to 15 min. Cooking time: 1 hr 10 min to 1 hr 15 min**
**8 oz (225 g) self-raising flour**
**½ tsp (2.5 ml) ground cinnamon**
**½ tsp (2.5 ml) ground nutmeg**
**6 oz (175 g) butter**
**4 oz (100 g) soft light brown sugar**
**8 oz (225 g) sultanas**
**2 eggs**
**6 tbsp (90 ml) cider**
Set oven at 325° F, 160° C (Mark 3). Grease and line base and sides of a 7½-in (19-cm) round cake tin. Sift flour, cinnamon and nutmeg, add butter, cut into pieces, and rub in. Stir in sugar and sultanas. Beat eggs with cider and stir into cake mixture. Spoon into tin and level top. Bake in centre of oven from 1 hr 10 min to 1 hr 15 min. Leave to cool in tin for about 10 min, then turn out onto wire rack.

### IRISH SODA BREAD

*A quick-mix bread recipe, best eaten fresh. Cut into thick wedges to serve*
**Preparation time: 15 min. Cooking time: 25 to 30 min**
**12 oz (350 g) wholemeal plain flour**
**4 oz (100 g) plain flour**
**½ tsp (2.5 ml) salt**
**1 tsp (5 ml) caster sugar**
**2 tsp (10 ml) bicarbonate of soda**
**1½ oz (40 g) lard**
**4 tsp (20 ml) cream of tartar**
**½ pt (300 ml) milk or buttermilk**
Set oven at 400° F, 200° C (Mark 6). Grease and flour a baking sheet. Place the wholemeal and plain flour, salt, caster sugar and bicarbonate of soda into a mixing bowl. Rub in the lard. Dissolve cream of tartar in the milk or buttermilk and stir into

the dry ingredients. Knead until smooth. Flatten out to a circle about 7 in (18 cm) in diameter. Place on baking sheet. Cut a deep cross in top. Bake in top of oven for 25 to 30 min. Cool on wire rack.

## DROP SCONES

*Scotch pancakes are perfect for after-noon tea. Serve buttered and spread with jam*
**Preparation time: 20 min. Cooking time: 20 min. Makes 30**
**8 oz (225 g) self-raising flour**
**½ tsp (2.5 ml) salt**
**2 oz (50 g) caster sugar**
**2 eggs**
**½ pt (300 ml) milk or buttermilk**
**1 oz (25 g) lard**
Sieve flour and salt into a bowl. Stir in sugar. Add eggs and beat in milk or butter-milk. Heat a little of the lard on a grid-dle or heavy-based frying pan. Drop table-spoonfuls of mixture on griddle or pan, cook for 2 min on each side.

## BANBURY CAKES

*These flaky cakes have a fruity filling. Store in an airtight tin for up to 1 week*
**Preparation time: 35 min (plus standing time). Cooking time: 25 to 30 min. Makes 12**
**8 oz (225 g) plain flour**
**Pinch of salt**
**3 oz (75 g) margarine**
**3 oz (75 g) lard**
**1 tsp (5 ml) lemon juice**
**½ oz (15 g) butter**
**2 tsp (10 ml) caster sugar**
**3 oz (75 g) currants**
**4 oz (100 g) chopped mixed peel**
**½ tsp (2.5 ml) mixed spice**
**Pinch of grated nutmeg**
**Milk to glaze**
**1 oz (25 g) granulated sugar**
Sieve flour and salt. Dice fats, stir into flour with lemon juice, and enough water to make a dough. Lightly flour work surface and roll out to an oblong ¾ in (2 cm) thick. Fold into 3 (bottom ⅓ up and top ⅓ down). Give dough ¼ turn. Repeat 3 times. Chill 15 min. Set oven at 425°F, 220°C (Mark 7). Cream butter and sugar, beat in currants, peel, spice, nutmeg. Roll out pastry to ¼ in (0.5 cm) thick. Cut out rounds with 5-in (12.5-cm) cutter. Put creamed mixture in centre of rounds. Brush edges with milk, press together to seal. Turn cakes over so join is underneath, shape into ovals. Press with rolling pin. Brush with milk, sprinkle with sugar, make splits on top. Place on baking sheet, bake 25 to 30 min.

## CRUMPETS

*Toasted crumpets dripping with butter and honey are a welcome addition to any teatable*
**Preparation time: 20 min (plus standing time). Cooking time: 30 min. Makes about 15**
**12 oz (350 g) strong plain flour**
**½ oz (15 g) fresh yeast**
**½ pt (300 ml) tepid water**
**9 fl oz (250 ml) milk**
**½ tsp (2.5 ml) bicarbonate of soda**
**1 tsp (5 ml) salt**
**Oil for greasing**
Blend a little flour with yeast and water until smooth, cover and leave 10 min. Beat in remaining flour, milk, soda and salt until smooth. Grease a griddle or heavy-based frying pan and four crum-pet rings or plain 3-in (7.5-cm) cutters. Heat pan. Place rings in pan and pour 2 tbsp (30 ml) of batter in each. Cook over a low heat un-til set. Remove rings, turn crumpets over to brown other side. Cool. Toast on both sides.

## SPICED CHELSEA BUNS

*To serve, simply pull the buns apart. Keep the remaining buns in an airtight tin*
**Preparation time: 40 min (plus standing time). Cooking time: 22 to 27 min. Makes 9**
**8 oz (225 g) strong plain flour**
**Pinch of salt**
**2 oz (50 g) butter**
**½ oz (15 g) fresh yeast**
**4 tbsp (60 ml) tepid milk**
**4 tbsp (60 ml) tepid water**
**½ oz (15 g) caster sugar**
**1 small egg**
**2 oz (50 g) soft light brown sugar**
**1 oz (25 g) sultanas**
**1 oz (25 g) currants**
**1 oz (25 g) chopped mixed peel**
**1 oz (25 g) glacé cherries, chopped**
**½ tsp (2.5 ml) mixed spice**
**2 tbsp (30 ml) clear honey**
Sieve flour and salt into a bowl. Rub in 1 oz (25 g) butter. Blend yeast, milk and water. Stir caster sugar into flour, add egg and yeast liquid. Knead well. Place mixture in a lightly oiled polythene bag and leave in a warm place until doubled in size. Knead dough again and roll out to an oblong 12 by 8 in (30.5 by 20.5 cm). Melt remaining butter, stir in brown sugar, sultanas, currants, peel, cherries and spice. Spread over dough, 1½ in (4 cm) in from edges. Roll up and cut into 9 slices. Lightly grease a 9-in (23-cm) square cake tin and arrange buns closely together. Put in a warm place for 20 min. Set oven at 425°F, 220°C (Mark 7). Bake for 20 to 25 min. Turn out. Brush with honey.  ▷

## The Sunday Best Lunch

*Continued from page 16*

### CHICKEN ANDALUCIA

*Ring the changes with this delicious re-cipe. If you don't have a chicken brick use a heavy casserole dish with a lid*
**Preparation time: 25 min. Cooking time: 1 hr 25 min. Serves 4 to 6**
**4 lb (1.8 kg) chicken**
**2 large onions**
**1 red pepper**
**3 tbsp (45 ml) olive oil**
**1 tsp (5 ml) grated lemon rind**
**2 tbsp (30 ml) fresh chopped parsley**
**6 oz (175 g) cooked rice**
**1 oz (25 g) breadcrumbs**
**1 egg**
**4 sticks celery**
**2 tbsp (30 ml) plain flour**
**½ pt (300 ml) chicken stock**
**15-oz (425-g) can tomatoes**
**1 tsp (5 ml) mixed dried herbs**
**2 tbsp (30 ml) tomato paste**
**Salt and ground black pepper**
Wipe chicken with kitchen paper and re-move giblets, if necessary. Pre-soak chic-ken brick for 15 to 20 min. Set oven at 425° F, 220° C (Mark 7). Peel and chop onions. Wash, deseed and chop pepper. Place 2 tbsp (30 ml) oil in a pan and add half the onion with pepper and fry for 5 min. Stir in lemon rind, fresh chopped parsley, cooked rice and bread-crumbs, remove from heat. Add egg and mix until ingredients bind together. Use to stuff the neck end of chicken. Place chic-ken in brick and cook in the oven for 1 hr. Meanwhile, heat remaining oil in a pan and add remaining onion. Wash and chop celery and add to pan. Fry for 10 min, stir in flour and remove from heat. Stir in stock, tomatoes, herbs, tomato paste, salt and pepper. Return to heat and bring to boil, stirring, until sauce thickens slightly. Simmer for 10 min until vege-tables are soft. Put chicken on a serving dish and spoon sauce over it. Serve any remaining stuffing and sauce separately.

### LOIN OF PORK WITH GARLIC

*This is an impressive main course which is simple to serve as the meat is boned and easy to slice. The skin roasts separately to make pieces of golden crackling*
**Preparation time: 20 min. Cooking time: 2 hr 17 min. Serves 6**
**4 lb (1.8 kg) loin of pork**
**Salt and ground black pepper**
**1 clove garlic**
**½ pt (300 ml) dry cider**
**2 tsp (10 ml) cornflour**
Set oven at 325° F, 160° C (Mark 3). Remove skin from pork, cutting about ½ in (0.5 cm) fat with it, cut into strips about ½ in (1 cm) wide. Place in a roasting tin and sprinkle with salt. Using a sharp knife, carefully remove bones from pork. Flatten meat and season with salt and pepper. Skin the garlic and cut into thin slices, scattering them over the meat. Roll up the meat and tie firmly with string, sprinkle the fat surface with salt and pepper and place in another roasting tin with cider. Cook in preheated oven for about 2 hr 15 min, basting occasionally. Cook the pork skin in the top of the oven for the last hour of the roasting time, until crisp and golden. When the pork is cooked, drain off excess fat. Blend the cornflour with a little water and stir into the ci-der. Cook in a saucepan, stirring over a medium heat for 2 min or until the sauce has thickened. Serve pork in slices with the crackling and cider sauce as an ac-companiment. Serve with baked tomatoes and creamed potatoes.

### THREE FRUIT FLAN

*Make this mouthwatering flan as a dessert for Sunday lunch, or as an afternoon treat*
**Preparation time: 40 min. Cooking time: 38 min. Serves 6 to 8**
*Pastry:*
**8 oz (225 g) plain flour**
**Pinch of salt**
**2 oz (50 g) margarine**
**2 oz (50 g) lard**
*Filling:*
**1 lb (450 g) eating apples**
**2 tbsp (30 ml) honey**
**4 medium oranges**
**6 small pears**
**2 cinnamon sticks**
*Glaze:*
**4 tbsp (60 ml) apricot jam**
**2 tbsp (30 ml) water**
Set oven at 400° F, 200° C (Mark 6).
*To make the pastry:* sift flour and salt, rub in fats. Add water to mix to a firm

dough. Knead on a floured surface until smooth. Roll out and use to line a 10-in (25.5-cm) loose-bottomed flan tin. Bake blind for 25 min until crisp and golden. *To make the filling:* peel, core and chop apples. Cook over a low heat for 15 min with 2 tbsp (30 ml) water and honey, stirring occasionally. Cool. Slice oranges, place in pan with any juice. Peel, quarter and core pears, add to pan. Add 1 pt (600 ml) water and cinnamon, bring to boil. Simmer for 10 min. Lift out fruit and cinnamon, place in dish. Remove flan from oven. Cool. Bring liquid in which fruit was cooked to boil, boil until reduced to ¼ pt (150 ml). *To make up the flan:* spread apple over base. Place orange slices and pears on kitchen paper to absorb moisture, arrange alternatively in 2 rings inside flan.
*To glaze:* place reduced juice, jam and water in pan over a low heat until jam melts and mixes with juice. Brush over fruit.

## CHOCOLATE RUM CHARLOTTE

*Rum adds punch to this dessert, but if you're giving it to children use orange juice*
**Preparation time: 30 min (plus standing time). Serves 8**
**2 tbsp (30 ml) rum**
**2 tbsp (30 ml) water**
**About 27 sponge fingers**
**4 oz (125 g) plain chocolate**
**4 eggs**
**6 oz (175) soft unsalted butter**
**5 oz (150 g) caster sugar**
**¼ pt (150 ml) double cream**
**Maltesers or Chocolate Buttons to decorate**
Line a 2-lb (900-g) loaf tin with foil. Mix rum and water together on a teaplate. Dip each sponge finger, sugar-side down in rum mixture and arrange 9 or 10 fingers sugar-side down on the base of the tin. Cut remaining sponge fingers in half and dip, sugar-side down, in the rum mixture and stand, sugar-side out, around the tin. Break chocolate into pieces, place in a bowl over a pan of simmering water and allow to melt slowly. Separate eggs. Place whites in a clean, grease-free bowl and reserve. Place the yolks in a bowl with the butter and sugar and beat well until creamy. Stir in the cooled chocolate. Whisk the egg whites until stiff but not dry, using a rotary or small electric whisk. Fold gently into the chocolate mixture using a metal spoon. Spoon into the loaf tin, smooth the top and chill in the refrigerator overnight.
Turn out onto a serving dish, peel off foil. Place cream in a bowl and whisk until it just holds its shape. Place a large star nozzle into a piping bag and spoon in cream. Pipe rosettes of cream down length of charlotte. Place a Malteser or a Chocolate Button on each rosette.

## PAVLOVA

*Make the meringue in advance if you like and store in an airtight tin*
**Preparation time: 35 min. Cooking time: 1 hr 30 min. Serves 8**
**4 egg whites**
**9 oz (250 g) icing sugar**
**½-pt (284-ml) carton double cream**
**2 tbsp (30 ml) Grand Marnier**
**1 ripe mango**
**3 oz (75 g) green grapes**
**4 oz (100 g) frozen raspberries, thawed**
Set oven at 275°F, 140°C (Mark 1). Place egg whites in bowl over pan of simmering water. Whisk until foaming. Sieve sugar, gradually add to egg whites, whisking until all sugar is added and meringue holds shape. Spoon into piping bag with star nozzle, pipe onto bakewell paper to an 8-in (20.5-cm) circle, piping decreasing circles to fill base. Pipe whirls around top edge. Bake for 1 hr 30 min. Cool in oven. Place on plate. Whisk cream with Grand Marnier until just stiff. Spoon into pavlova. Peel and cut mango into chunks. Halve grapes, remove pips; drain raspberries. Mix fruit together and pile into pavlova. Chill.

## RHUBARB BRULEE

*A really smooth, custard-style dessert. Make in advance and serve with cream*
**Preparation time: 20 min. Cooking time: 55 min to 1 hr. Serves 6**
**1 lb (450 g) fresh rhubarb**
**3 oz (75 g) granulated sugar**
**½-pt (284-ml) carton single cream**
**¼ pt (150 ml) milk**
**1 oz (25 g) caster sugar**
**6 egg yolks**
**2 oz (50 g) caster sugar to glaze**
Set oven at 325°F, 160°C (Mark 3). Wash and trim rhubarb, cut into chunks. Place in pan with 2 tbsp (30 ml) water and granulated sugar. Cook over low heat for 15 min. Spoon into lightly buttered 2-pt (1.1-1) ovenproof dish. Put cream, milk and caster sugar in a pan and stir over low heat until hot but not boiling. Beat egg yolks lightly, whisk in cream mixture and pour over fruit. Stand dish in roasting pan half filled with water, place in centre of oven. Bake for 45 min until centre is firm. Allow to cool then chill. Sprinkle top with caster sugar, place under hot grill until lightly browned. Serve chilled.

# 'We should see ourselves as our children see us'

## says BRENDA CROWE, our childcare expert

Many years ago there was a *Punch* cartoon that has stayed indelibly imprinted on my memory. It showed a drawing-room where two middle-aged couples were chatting after dinner. One father was saying to the other, "At what stage are your sons now: the aggressive or the lofty condescension?"

This still puts it in a nutshell for many parents. But so may a very different picture, described by the mother of a troublesome 16-year-old son. She said, "One night last summer my husband and I stopped at a pub for beer and sandwiches. As we ate I watched a young lad standing by the bar — he couldn't have been much older than our son — and suddenly something hit me between the eyes. Why shouldn't he prefer being there, with the barman calling him 'Sir', than at home with someone like me endlessly saying, 'You're not going to sit down to a meal with hands like that!' "

At every stage we need to see ourselves as our children see us. But this is difficult if we only think of them as "children" and ourselves as "parents", for this can set up a mental image whereby we are forever right and in control, whilst they are forever fallible. It shouldn't be a power struggle.

These days there is a lot of talk about children, but not enough about childhood — which is a stage in its own right, and not something to be "got through". We never fully outgrow any stage: they are all still within us and come to the surface on occasion.

There are times when we all want to behave like babies, and our indispositions might be put behind us much more quickly if we could. When we are feeling physically or emotionally weak and dependent we long to sleep on undisturbed; and we don't want people to be impatient with us, or to be ministered to quickly, grudgingly or clumsily. Above all, we don't want to feel that we are a nuisance, preventing other people from getting on with their own lives. Neither do babies!

If we can learn to identify with babies as people, and credit them with feelings like ours, then the seeds of respect are sown. If we can't, then we may love them, dress them, feed them, tuck them up in bed, push them in a pram, and shout or scold occasionally — just as we did with our dolls when we were children. And the child/doll relationship can become a way of life. But if we see our babies as dolls, then we are in for a shock when the toddler stage arrives.

Real toddlers are just like us. Sometimes we get fed up with being watched, advised, criticised. We toe the line as best we can, for as long as we can — and then we blow our tops. And if we do, we want to be allowed to do it without too much fuss. But above all we want someone to take the time to try to understand what it really was that caused it in the first place — it's never the top being left off the toothpaste; that's only the final trigger.

The real cause is probably much the same as it is for our toddlers, which they might explain something like this: "I keep trying to do my best but no one thanks me, or praises me, or appreciates me. All I get is demands, grumbles and moans. I'm a person, I'm ME, I'm not just here to please you all the time." Or: "I get so sick of being good, quiet, sensible, careful — just sometimes I want to do what I want to do." Or: "I've only got one life to live, and today matters because it's not coming back again. Stop dragging me through it in a race against the clock!"

Sometimes we really do have to hurry, and so do our children — but if we are honest, a lot of rushing about is habit, and as bad for us as it is for them.

When our children first go to school, they need us to remember how we felt in our first job. Important, but apprehensive too. "Where's the loo? Where do I have to go? What do I have to do?" And when we arrived home we were exhausted to the point of being grumpy. Everyone wanted to know: "How did it go? What did you do?" It was all very kind and well-meaning, but we just wished they would let us flop in a chair and have a cup of tea.

So it is with children, and if we remember how a *person* feels in the early stages of a new chapter in their lives, we won't probe or question. Rather, we'll be comfortingly undemanding, but ready to listen if and when they are ready to talk.

As school becomes familiar, more energy is released for learning, but reading, writing and mathematics are skills to be mastered on a par with learning to drive. The fact that we go to (driving) school, already knowing quite a lot in general terms isn't a guarantee that we shall pick up the new skills quickly and easily. Some teachers are just right for some temperaments but not right for others. And some pupils' capacity to learn has already been blunted by the fear of making mistakes.

If we remember what we want from others when we make a mistake, then we can avoid programming our children to the expectation of failure. It doesn't help to be told, "Here, give it to me, I'll do it!" or, "Look what you've done!" or, "Who did this? Own up and I won't be cross..." It does help to be told, "Good, you've nearly got it!" or, "Never mind, it doesn't matter, let's mop it up!". At any age people need to be built up, not knocked down.

The suggestion is that we try to identify with our children, and to behave to them as we would like others to behave to us — but we also have to recognise that our children aren't exactly, or sometimes even remotely, like us. So, having identified, we then have to adapt, not only to our different children but to circumstances. For example, take homework. One child may rush in, sit down with her satchel still slung over her coat, and polish it off in 20 concentrated minutes. Another child may be so drained at the end of the day that homework is best left until after tea — or even the next morning. But sometimes it is our responsibility to say, in advance, "This is only supposed to take half an hour, and that's quite long enough at the end of the day. So I'll initial it at the end of that time and you can stop". This can lead to a burst of helpful concentration, in which the task is completed — but sometimes alerts the teacher to the fact that the task is too long, wasn't sufficiently prepared in general, or hasn't been understood by your particular child.

Teachers are people too, neither to be obeyed without question nor ignored without enquiry, explanation and responsible reasons — so are doctors, ministers, solicitors, friends, partners and parents.

But sometimes the person presented just isn't the real person at all — it is the mask put on to protect the private person hiding inside. Or it may be the person produced by over-dominant parents who cast the child in their mould very early on.

We neither have to "set" children in our own mould, nor wobble around them like half-set jellies ourselves. Given mutual respect, parents and children can set, and accept, limits within which both feel secure and free to develop. The children have a flying start and we are given a golden opportunity to outgrow some of our own restrictive habits.

# EVERY HAND TELLS A STORY

Palmists believe that your life is in your hands
— quite literally. So why not
try your hand at learning the basics of palm
reading? Who knows, it could
become your party piece! Mary Peplow reports ...

PINK ONES, PALE ONES, soft ones, square ones — no two hands are the same. And that's why, say palmists, our hands tell so much about our personality, ambitions, worries and emotions.

"I know at a glance whether someone is hard-working or lazy, selfish or kind-hearted," says Bettina Luxon, one of Britain's leading palmists. "My mother always used to say that it's your face that reveals all, but I look straight at a person's hands — the way they're held, their shape, colour, texture and the pattern of lines on the palm. Every hand has a fascinating story to tell."

People come to Bettina for help with emotional problems, advice about career decisions, travel plans, house-buying — you name it, Bettina can usually find the answer in their hands. "And after years of reading palms, I still get a kick out of being proved right!"

Bettina, with her motherly warmth and ready laugh, insists that she's no different from anyone else. "We've all got a sixth sense," she explains. "It's just that some people are more conscious of it than others. Anyone can learn to read hands. And if more people did master the art it could certainly save an awful lot of problems and mistakes. All you need to do is follow a basic set of guidelines."

The first thing to do, advises Bettina, is to study the way people hold their hands. So start now — look at your family over the meal table, watch other shoppers in the supermarket or passers-by when you're waiting for the bus. You can spot the bold, confident types who stride out, arms and hands swinging; then there are the nervy, finger-strumming, bone-cracking characters and the mean, "tight-fisted" folk who do, quite literally, clench their fists as they walk. The nail-biters tend to be rather jumpy and tense people, and those with long nails usually like everything to be "just so".

That may seem obvious, but it's also an indication of just how much hands can say about you. And indeed, in earlier times people feared the idea of their hands betraying their secrets. "Palmistry used to be considered evil," says Bettina. "Gypsies were driven from the country if they so much as mentioned palm reading, or burned at the stake as witches. Later, of course, palm reading came to be thought of as a bit of a laugh, a fairground thing. More recently, though, hand analysis and research has grown in importance. It's become a science."

OF COURSE, it takes years of practice, experience and a well-developed sixth sense to read hands in vivid detail. As Bettina explains: "I see pictures. The finer lines gel into images which seem to jump out at me. I'll see a car, for example, a blue car, or houses and scenery. I've travelled miles in people's hands — to India, America, far-flung places, and described views and buildings, though I've never stepped outside this country."

We might never see colours and images, indeed many of us may argue that we

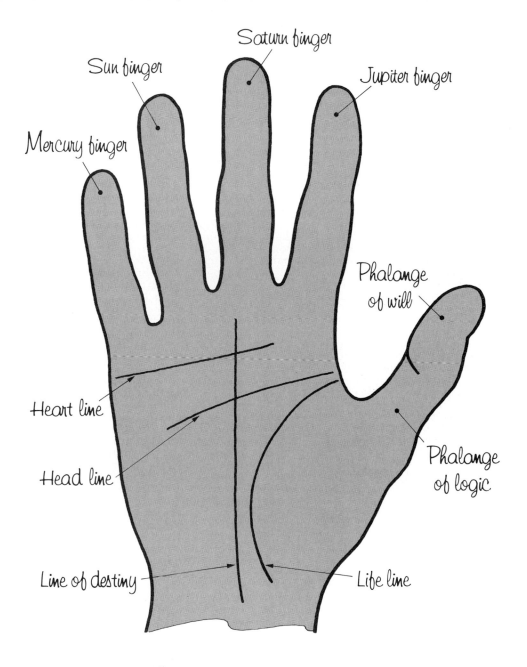

Sun finger

Saturn finger

Jupiter finger

Mercury finger

Phalange
of will

Heart line

Head line

Phalange
of logic

Line of destiny

Life line

The principal lines are common
to every palm. It's how they
interrelate that is so revealing

31

# EVERY HAND TELLS A STORY

never *want* to have such powers, but we can all have fun learning the basics of palmistry. First choose a willing subject — someone who doesn't mind sitting still while you study their hands. You can read your own hands, but to begin with it's usually easier to practise on someone else. The number one question is always "Which hand should I look at?" And the answer is "Both". You'll see that they look very different, and they are. On a right-handed person, the lines on the left hand show the traits of character that he or she was born with, and the right hand shows how they've been used. As you get more advanced, you'll be able to see the past in the left hand and the future in the right. On a left-handed person, this is reversed.

But before you start looking more closely at the lines, first try doing the "palm test" on either of your subject's hands. Put your thumb in the centre of the palm with your fingers stretched across the back of the hand and press to see how much "give" there is in the hand. If it's soft and springy, the person is enthusiastic about life and willing to learn. A hand that's hard and solid indicates an introvert, someone who is difficult to communicate with and probably stubborn. A hand with a little "give" shows a hard worker, someone who never shirks responsibility, maybe even takes on too much. There's a temper lurking there too!

NEXT LOOK at the fingers. First the colour: if they're pleasantly pink, the person is lovable and warmhearted. Pale fingers and nails show a cold, selfish character. The length of fingers is important too. If, for example, the Jupiter (the index) finger is long, as long as the Saturn finger, then the person is bursting with self-confidence and sure of success. In contrast, a short Jupiter finger shows someone with an inferiority complex. The thumb is split into two parts — the top phalange shows strength of will while the lower phalange indicates reason and logic. A well-balanced thumb shows someone who's sensible, reasoning things out before doing or saying anything. "Mind you," says Bettina, "well-balanced thumbs are few and far between!"

And now you come to reading the lines. But before you even begin, forget the old wives' tale that a hand with lots of lines shows a hard worker! "It's simply means that person is a born worrier!" Bettina explains. There are three main lines to look for in the palm: the Life Line, the Head Line and the Heart Line.

The Life Line encircles the thumb and goes round to the wrist. The quality of this line is important. A clear, long line is an indication of good health, whereas a weak line implies a poor constitution. If you see a "break" in the line, don't worry; there's usually a repair line behind it, which means any accident or illness will be overcome. Look to the other hand and if the Life Line is strong and clear, then that person will live to a ripe old age. Branches leading off the Life Line are important. If they lead upwards towards the fingers then it indicates both endeavour and achievement — a good sign. Holders of a double Life Line can count their blessings — theirs is a happy, healthy life!

But what happens if a palmist forsees serious ill-health, even death? "I never discuss a patient's health," says Bettina firmly. "Health and death are taboo subjects. I believe in being positive rather than negative. If I can see something nasty is going to happen, a miscarriage, for example, then I try to give a gentle warning. I might tell the person to take things a bit easier — avoid stretching and lifting heavy things. I can tell if someone has a tendency to depression, even suicide too, and again, I try to give a warning. I give them things to look forward to, emphasise the nice things that I see in the hand."

For, it seems, our fate is in our hands — in both senses. "One important thing tc remember in palmistry," Bettina explains, "is that our lives are not predestined from birth. We can change our fate. So even if I see an event such as an accident in someone's hand, if I warn them in time, they can change the course of their lives."

The next line to look for is the Head Line. This is the key to how the person copes with his or her life. It can show talents and skills and also how they're being put to use. An experienced palmist can also detect hidden talents waiting to be revealed. The Head Line starts near the beginning of the Life Line and travels across the palm. If the Head Line and Life Line are joined at the start then it shows a closeness to the family, someone who had a rather sheltered childhood. If they run together for some way, it's a sign that the person is rather shy and reserved. A small gap between the start of the two lines shows someone who's not afraid to stand alone while a larger gap usually indicates someone who tends to be too independent for his or her own good.

A HEAD LINE which slopes down shows a dreamer who finds concentration difficult while a Head Line travelling straight across the palm, even to the other side, belongs to someone with a clear-thinking, excellent and logical brain, but probably lacking imagination.

"But these are only pointers," Bettina is quick to explain. "You might see, for example, the mark of a dreamer in the left hand, but that could be cancelled out by indications in the other hand. That's where experience pays. You learn to assess the importance of the different signs in the hands and build up a complete picture."

The third important line is the Heart Line, which starts just below the Mercury finger and travels across the palm. The strength, direction and stopping point of this line are the things to look out for. These give clues to the person's emotions. If the line crosses the palm and then rises to the Jupiter finger then that person is kind and loving, sometimes too loving, but would make a wonderful marriage partner. If the line ends just below the Saturn finger then the person might not be romantic, but he or she is trustworthy. The person to be wary of as a friend or partner is someone with a Heart Line which travels right the way across the palm to the other side. There's an indication here of being out for what he or she can get!

There are many, many other lines too, such as the Line of Destiny, the Sun, Marriage, Children, Travel, Affection — which by virtue of their strength, length and position, complete the story. "And," says Bettina, "the lines that are not on a hand are just as revealing as the ones that are. Take the Line of Destiny, for example. This is the line which shows how people use their drive and initiative to make the most of their talents. What's the point of having artistic skills, if you don't use them? But someone who doesn't have a Line of Destiny isn't necessarily a 'waster'. It usually shows that the person has had difficulty in recognising his or her talents and finding a place in society. And that's where I can help. I can point the person in the right direction."

It's these minor lines that take the time to learn, but without them the picture would be only half-complete. And these lines change too, from day to day, which adds to the fascination of palmistry. Bettina gives an example: "A lady came to me for advice on whether or not to set up her own business. I looked at her hand and saw financial hardship and emotional heartache too so I told her that it would be best to postpone her plans for a few years. The next time she came to me, the lines in her hand had changed and I could see security and happiness. She told me she'd taken my advice and was glad because she'd been offered a new job with exciting opportunities."

The way to learn to read hands seriously is by studying books* and looking at as many hands as you can. "Over the years I've read millions," says Bettina. "And every one is different. Every one is a new challenge. A foreign lady asked me to read her hand the other day and I've never seen a hand like it before. The lines seemed to form a really strange pattern. I asked her for a photocopy so I could keep a record."

You might find that friends and family, although keen at first, grow bored with sitting for you, so why not ask for a print of their palms? But do remember the images are reversed so mark the palmprints "right" and "left". Then you can study them at leisure, weighing up the importance of the different lines and noticing the huge variance between hands.

But it's only when you see friends putting their hands in their pockets whenever you're around that you know you've learned how to read between the lines!

*We recommend Your Hand—Simple Palmistry for Everyone by Bettina Luxon and Jill Goolden, published by Heinemann

# WHAT WILL YOU BID

*Follow Alan Bond's keep-your-wits-about-you guide to auctions and you could find a hidden treasure going for a song*

**E**verybody loves a bargain and most of us rightly think of auctions as good places to find one. Whether we're competing for a masterpiece in a West End saleroom or for a rusty lawnmower in the village hall, we have every chance of picking up something we want at well below its usual price.

But what exactly is a bargain? Where are we most likely to find one? How can we hope to beat the dealers at their own game? What happens if we find ourselves landed with rubbish?

**It pays to advertise**

All auctions are battles of wits... Those who run them are in business to get the best possible price for the seller and a bumper commission for themselves. To make sure that their salerooms are packed with excited buyers, they · advertise widely through posters, in local quality newspapers and in specialised magazines. They send out thousands of catalogues to dealers and anyone else whom they think might be interested. If you are a keen auction-goer, it's worth paying a small sum to be put on their mailing list.

The top London houses will have all items examined by their staff experts before they are entered in the catalogue. Equally expert buyers will examine them before the sale. So your chances of picking up an unknown Turner for £5 are, frankly, pretty remote!

Outside London, the odds are slightly higher. Valuable pieces will occasionally go unnoticed, especially in places where no one expects to find them. Not so long ago a marble bust of Pope Gregory XV was knocked down for £85 at a modest country house sale. It turned out to be the work of the 17th-century Baroque sculptor Bernini and worth a cool half million!

Keen amateurs might sometimes strike fairly lucky in their own field. If you have made a lifelong study of some fairly obscure subject — say, Japanese netsuke (ornamental fasteners) — you might well know more than the auctioneer and pick up a gem which he has failed to recognise.

Luck comes into it too. Just before an auction at a small seaside town, my wife and I noticed an exquisite porcelain box in a job lot of kitchen junk. It wasn't mentioned separately in the catalogue and for some reason no one else saw it. Our bid of 50p was unopposed — and we walked off with a treasure worth as many pounds.

**On the grapevine**

Normally, of course, dealers are a force to be reckoned with, and not just local ones. "They have a grapevine," said one auctioneer. "A book man may come in on viewing day to see a set of Dickens. He spots an escritoire that looks interesting and tips off his friends in the furniture trade. Before you know where you are, half a dozen of them are after it." Yet

34

# FOR A BARGAIN?

bidding long after your commonsense should have told you to drop out.

Protect yourself by sticking to a simple drill. As soon as you see a sale advertised, send for a catalogue and tick off any items that interest you. On viewing day, examine them carefully, looking for cracks, woodworm and other signs of damage. Use a torch for lighting up dark corners and a tape-measure to ensure that furniture will fit into where you've planned in your home.

## Oh! Mr Porter...

The porter or receptionist can usually give you an estimate of what items may fetch. If you're still interested, decide how much you're prepared to pay and write it down in your catalogue.

Arrive for the sale in good time. If you're nervous, you can usually ask the auctioneer to bid for you. Otherwise bid for yourself by raising your hand, waving your catalogue or nodding your head. But you have to be quick. In small auctions, 140 lots may be sold in an hour.

If you get flustered or feel you can't bear to miss an item, you may be tempted to keep on bidding when it has gone beyond its true value. Stick rigidly to the limit marked in your catalogue. Show the auctioneer that you have stopped bidding by standing still or shaking your head.

Any item becomes yours as soon as the hammer falls and you may be expected to stump up part or all of the price before leaving. You may also have to pay VAT, a buyer's premium and also transport charges. Find out about these from the catalogue before the auction.

You will probably also find that your normal consumer rights have been taken away. (This is legal with auctions.) The goods sold are not guaranteed "fit for their purpose", "of merchantable quality" or "as described". Usually you are deemed to have examined them. You buy them "as seen", so it's a case of "buyer beware". If you end up with rubbish, it's your own fault. But don't let that put you off. In December 1983 Hans Kraus paid a world record £7,400,000 for the 12th-century Gospels of Henry the Lion. He said, "We got a real bargain. We would have gone to £10,000,000." A saving of £2,600,000 is well worth having — by any standards!

even when the saleroom is packed with dealers there are still bargains to be found — if you have your eye on something that is out of fashion or ahead of current trends.

## The Cinderella syndrome

You may pick up for a song the Cinderellas of the antiques world: items that are dull, dirty, verdigrised or need minor repairs, but which, with a bit of effort, could be transformed into highly desirable pieces.

Also, dealers have to make a profit, so their highest bid must be a good bit less than the price they expect to get when they sell. You can outbid them all and still end up paying between a quarter and a half less than you would have to pay for a similar piece in the shops.

You could, of course, make a disastrous mistake, especially if you become a victim of auction fever. In the excitement worked up by the auctioneer, you may buy something you never intended or carry on

# Romantically Yours...

With a picture-pretty trellis-and-flowers
sweater, you'll really be
wearing your art upon your sleeves!

**MATERIALS** Hayfield Grampian Perle DK,
10 [11:11] 50-g balls. Oddments in 2 con-
trasting colours for embroidery. One pair
each of 3¼ and 4mm OR nos. 10 and 8
knitting needles. A 3¼mm OR no. 10
circular knitting needle 60cm long. A cable
needle.
For best results it is essential to use the
recommended yarn.
For stockists send SAE to:
Hayfield Textiles Ltd, Hayfield Mills,
Glusburn, Keighley, West Yorks BD20 8QP.
**MEASUREMENTS** To suit bust 86 [91:97]cm
OR 34 [36:38]in, length from shoulder 56·5cm
OR 22¼in, sleeve seam 40·5cm OR 16in.
**TENSION** 22 sts and 31 rows to 10cm OR 4in
measured over rev st st on 4mm OR no. 8
needles.
**ABBREVIATIONS** K = knit; P = purl; st(s) =
stitch(es); rev st st = reversed stocking
stitch; beg = begin(ning); rem = remain(ing);
alt = alternate; patt = pattern; sl = slip; rep
= repeat; tog = together; inc = increase;
dec = decrease; cn = cable needle; C4 =
cable 4 worked as follows: sl next 2 sts on
cn and leave at front of work, K2, then K2
from cn; Cr3L = cross 3 left as follows: sl
next 2 sts on cn and leave at front of work,

P1, then K2 from cn; Cr3R = cross 3 right
worked as follows: sl next st on cn and leave
at back of work, K2, then P1 from cn; cm =
centimetres; in = inch(es).
**NB** Instructions for the larger sizes are in [ ];
where one figure is given, this applies to all
sizes.
**Back**
*With 3¼mm OR no. 10 needles cast on
96 [102:108] sts. Work 6·5cm OR 2½in K1,
P1 rib.
**Inc row** Rib 2 [5:8], inc in next st, (rib 6, inc in
next st) to last 2 [5:8] sts, rib to end.
110 [116:122] sts.
Change to 4mm OR no. 8 needles.
Beg P row, work in rev st st until work
measures 35·5cm OR 14in from cast-on
edge, ending wrong-side row.
**Shape armholes** Cast off 5 sts at beg of next
2 rows. Dec one st each end of every row
until 84 [88:92] sts rem, then each end of
every following alt row until 76 [80:84] sts
rem *.
Work straight until back measures 56·5cm
OR 22¼in from cast-on edge, ending
wrong-side row.
**Shape shoulders** Cast off 11 sts at beg of
next 2 rows and 10 [11:12] sts at beg of ▷

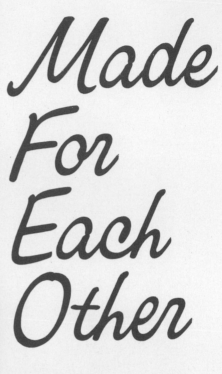

# Made For Each Other

With him in handsome
Fair Isle and you
in lacy, ladylike luxury,
what a well
matched couple you'll be!

*(Turn to page 43 for instructions)*

She'll just love this White Rabbit, fluffy bob-tailed jumper. And when she turns her back —he's disappeared!

# *It's Magic!*

**MATERIALS** Pingouin Pingolaine or Pingo-fine, 2 [2:3:3] 50-g balls in main colour, A; 1 [1:1:1] 50-g ball each in 1st and 2nd contrasting colours B and C. Oddments for embroidery. One pair each of 2¼ and 3mm OR nos. 13 and 11 knitting needles. A medium size crochet hook. 3 buttons.

**MEASUREMENTS** To suit chest 46 [51:56: 61]cm OR 18 [20:22:24]in, length from back neck 28 [32:35:37]cm OR 11 [12½:13¾: 14½]in, sleeve seam 17 [19:20·5:21·5]cm OR 6¾ [7½:8:8½]in.

**TENSION** 30 sts and 41 rows to 10cm OR 4in measured over st st on 3mm OR no. 11 needles.

**ABBREVIATIONS** K = knit; P = purl; st(s) = stitch(es); st st = stocking stitch; beg = begin(ning); rem = remain(ing); alt = alternate; rep = repeat; patt = pattern; tog = together; m1 = make one by picking up loop lying between needles and working into back of it; inc = increase; sl = slip; dec = decrease; dc = double crochet; cm = centimetres; in = inch(es).

**NB** Instructions for the larger sizes are in [ ]; where one figure is given, this applies to all sizes.

**Front**

* With 2¼mm OR no. 13 needles and B, cast on 70 [76:84:92] sts and work in K1, P1 rib for 4cm OR 1½in.

**Inc row** Rib 7 [8:8:10], m1, (rib 14 [15:17:18], m1) 4 times, rib to end. 75 [81:89:97] sts *.

Change to 3mm OR no. 11 needles and working in st st throughout, work 4 rows. Joining in and cutting off colours as required (twisting yarns tog when changing colour to avoid making a hole and using separate balls of yarn where necessary) place motif from chart as follows:

**Row 1** K32 [35:39:43] B, K11C, K32, [35:39:43] B.

**Row 2** P30 [33:37:41] B, P15C, P30 [33:37: 41] B.

Continue as set until row 6 of chart has been completed.

**Row 7** K25 [28:32:36] A, K25C, K25 [28:32: 36] A.

**Row 8** P25 [28:32:36] A, P25C, P25 [28:32: 36] A. Continue as set until row 49 of chart has been completed. Continue in A, until front measures 17[20:22:23]cm OR 6¾ [8:8¾:9]in, ending wrong-side row.

** **Shape raglan Next row** Cast off 3 sts at beg of next 2 rows. Dec one st each end of next and every following 4th row until 61 [67:77:87] sts rem, then each end of every following alt row until 43 [49:49:51] sts rem. Work 1 row **.

**Divide for neck Next row** K2 tog, K14 [17:17:17], turn and leave rem sts on a spare needle. Work on first set of sts as follows:
*** Continue to dec one st at raglan edge on every alt row as before *and at the same time* dec one st at neck edge on every row until 3 [5:5:5] sts rem.

Dec one st at raglan edge only until 2 sts rem. Work 1 row. K2 tog and fasten off ***.

Return to sts on spare needle.

With right side facing, sl first 11 [11:11:13] sts on a holder, join in yarn to inner end of rem sts, K to within last 2 sts, K2 tog. Now work as first side from *** to ***.

**Back**

Work as front from * to *.

Change to 3mm OR no. 11 needles and st st 10 rows. Join in A and work until back measures same as front to beg of raglan shaping, ending wrong-side row.

Now work as for front from ** to **.

Continue to dec one st at raglan edge on alt rows as before, until 31 [33:33:35] sts rem. Work 1 row.

Cut off yarn and leave rem sts on a holder.

**Sleeves**

With 2¼mm OR no. 13 needles and A, cast on 38 [42:46:48] sts and work 3cm OR 1¼in K1, P1 rib.

▷

◁ **Inc row** Rib 4 [3:2:3], m1, (rib 6 [7:14:14], m1) 5 [5:3:3] times, rib to end. 44 [48:50:52] sts.

Change to 3mm OR no. 11 needles. Work in st st, but inc one st each end of 3rd [3rd:3rd:5th] and every following 6th [6th:6th:5th] row until there are 60 [66:70:76] sts. Work straight until sleeve measures 17 [19:20·5:21·5]cm OR 6¾ [7½:8:8½]in, ending wrong-side row.

**Shape raglan** Cast off 3 sts at beg of next 2 rows. Dec one st each end of next and every following alt row until 14 [18:14:18] sts rem. Work 1 row.

Dec one st each end of every row until 6 sts rem. Cut off yarn and leave sts on a holder.

**Neckband**

Join raglan seams, leaving left back seam open. With right side facing and using a 2¼mm OR no. 13 needle and A, K across sts of left sleeve, K up 12 [13:14:14] sts from left front neck, K across sts from front neck, K up 12 [13:14:14] sts from right front neck, then K across sts from right sleeve and back neck. 78 [82:84:88] sts.

Work 2·5cm OR 1in K1, P1 rib. Cast off.

**To complete**

Leaving an opening of 8cm OR 3¼in at top of raglan, join rem raglan. With crochet hook and A, work one row of dc along edges of opening. Mark positions for 3 buttons. Work a 2nd row of dc making 3 buttonloops to correspond with button markers. With C, make a small pompon and attach to bunny. Using contrasting oddments of yarn embroider flowers, using bullion st, lazy daisy st and stem st, as photograph. Join seams.

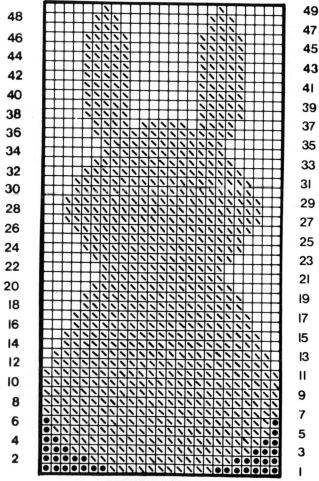

**25 PATT STS**

**KEY** ☐ MC A ⦿ lstC B ◹ 2nd C C

42

# Made For Each Other
Continued from page 39

## LADY'S LACY SWEATER

**MATERIALS** Jaeger Wool-Silk 14[15:16] 20-g balls. One pair each of 2¾ and 3¼mm OR nos. 12 and 10 knitting needles.
For best results it is essential to use the recommended yarn.
For stockists send SAE to:
Jaeger Handknitting Ltd, Consumer Liaison Department, Alloa, Clackmannanshire.

**MEASUREMENT** To suit bust 81[86:91]cm OR 32[34:36]in, length from shoulder 58[58:59]cm OR 22¾[22¾:23¼]in, sleeve seam 42·5cm OR 16¾in.

**TENSION** 28 sts and 36 rows to 10cm OR 4in measured over st st on 3¼mm OR no. 10 needles.

**ABBREVIATIONS** K = knit; P = purl; st(s) = stitch(es); st st = stocking stitch; rep = repeat; tog = together; patt = pattern; yfd = yarn forward; sl = slip; psso = pass slipped st over; yrn = yarn round needle; yon = yarn on needle; MB = make bobble, worked as follows: K into front, back, front, back and front of next st, turn and P5, turn and K5, turn and P2 tog, P1, P2 tog, turn and sl 1, K2 tog, psso; beg = begin(ning); alt = alternate; rem = remain(ing); inc = increase; dec = decrease; m1 = make one by picking up loop lying between needles and working into back of it; cm = centimetres; in = inch(es).

**NB** Instructions for the larger sizes are in [ ]; where one figure is given, this applies to all sizes.

**NNB When decreasing in patt count sts after rows 8, 9, 10, 11 and 12.**

**Back**
*With 2¾mm OR no. 12 needles cast on 119[127:135] sts.
Work 6cm OR approx 2¼in K1, P1 rib, beg alt rows P1.

**Dec row** Rib 7[8:9], work 2 tog, (rib 15 [16:17], work 2 tog) to last 8[9:10] sts, rib to end. 112[120:128] sts.
Change to 3¼mm OR no. 10 needles and work in patt as follows:

**Row 1** (Right side) K2, (yfd, sl 1, K1, psso, K4, K2 tog, yfd, sl 1, K1, psso, K4, K2 tog, yfd, K7[9:11] sts) to last 18 sts, yfd, sl 1, K1, psso, K4, K2 tog, yfd, sl 1, K1, psso, K4, K2 tog, yfd, K2.

**Row 2** P9, (K1, P21[23:25] sts) to last 10 sts, K1, P9.

**Row 3** K2, (yfd, sl 1, K1, psso, K3, K2 tog, yrn, P1, yon, sl 1, K1, psso, K3, K2 tog, yfd, K7[9:11] sts) to last 17 sts, yfd, sl 1, K1, psso, K3, K2 tog, yrn, P1, yon, sl 1, K1, psso, K3, K2 tog, yfd, K2.

**Row 4** P8, (K3, P19[21:23] sts) to last 11 sts, K3, P8.

**Row 5** K2, (yfd, sl 1, K1, psso, K2, K2 tog, yrn, P3, yon, sl 1, K1, psso, K2, K2 tog, yfd, K3[4:5], MB, K3[4:5] sts) to last 17 sts, yfd, sl 1, K1, psso, K2, K2 tog, yrn, P3, yon, sl 1, K1, psso, K2, K2 tog, yfd, K2.

**Row 6** P7, (K5, P17[19:21] sts) to last 12 sts, K5, P7.

**Row 7** K2, (yfd, sl 1, K1, psso, K1, K2 tog, yfd, K2 tog, yfd, MB, yfd, K2 tog, yfd, sl 1, K1, psso, K1, K2 tog, yfd, K7[9:11] sts) to last 17 sts, yfd, sl 1, K1, psso, K1, K2 tog, yfd, K2 tog, yfd, MB, yfd, K2 tog, yfd, sl 1, K1, psso, K1, K2 tog, yfd, K2.

**Row 8** P9, (K into front and back of next st, P21[23:25] sts) to last 10 sts, K into front and back of next st, P9.

**Row 9** K2, (yfd, sl 1, K1, psso, K2 tog, yfd, K8, yfd, sl 1, K1, psso, K2 tog, yfd, K7[9:11] sts) to last 18 sts, yfd, sl 1, K1, psso, K2 tog, yfd, K8, yfd, sl 1, K1, psso, K2 tog, yfd, K2.

**Row 10** P.

**Row 11** K2, (yfd, sl 1, K2 tog, psso, yfd, K10, yfd, K3 tog, yfd, K3[4:5], MB, K3[4:5] sts) to last 18 sts, yfd, sl 1, K2 tog, psso, yfd, K10, yfd, K3 tog, yfd, K2.

**Row 12** P.
These 12 rows form the patt.
Rep them until back measures approx 39cm OR 15¼in from cast-on edge, ending patt row 12.

**Shape armholes** Keeping patt correct, cast off 4 sts at beg of next 2 rows. Dec one st each end of next and following 10 alt rows. 82[90:98] sts*.
Work straight until back measures 58 [58:59]cm OR 22¾[22¾:23¼]in from cast-on edge, ending patt row 8[8:12].

**Shape shoulders** Keeping patt correct, cast off 7[8:9] sts at beg of next 2 rows, then ▷

43

◁ 8[9:10] sts at beg of following 4 rows. Cut off yarn and leave rem sts on a holder.

**Front**

Work as back from * to *.

Work straight until front measures approx 52cm OR 20½in from cast-on edge, so ending patt row 10.

**Divide for neck Next row** Patt 31[34:37], turn and leave rem sts on a spare needle. Work on first set of sts as follows:

** Dec one st at neck edge on next 8 rows.

Work straight until front measures same as back to beg of shoulder shaping, ending armhole edge.

**Shape shoulder** Keeping patt correct, cast off 7[8:9] sts at beg of next row and 8[9:10] sts at beg of following alt row.

Work 1 row.

Cast off **.

Return to sts on spare needle.

With right side facing, sl first 20[22:24] sts on a holder, join in yarn to next st, patt to end of row.

Now work as first side from ** to **.

**Sleeves**

With 2¾mm OR no. 12 needles cast on 56 [60:64] sts.

Work 6cm OR approx 2¼in K1, P1 rib.

**Inc row** Rib 5[3:5], m1, (rib 5[6:6], m1) to last 6[3:5] sts, rib to end.

66[70:74] sts.

Change to 3¼mm OR no. 10 needles and work 12[8:12] rows in patt as given for back.

Keeping patt correct as set, but inc one st each end of next and every following 12th [10th:8th] row until there are 84[92:100] sts, taking inc sts gradually into patt.

Work straight until sleeve measures approx 42·5cm OR 16¾in from cast-on edge, ending patt row 12.

**Shape top** Keeping patt correct, cast off 4 sts at beg of next 2 rows. Dec one st each end of next and following 14[10:10] alt rows, then each end of next 13[21:25] rows. 20 sts.

Cast off.

**Neckband**

Join right shoulder seam.

With right side facing and using a 2¾mm OR no. 12 needle, K up 25[25:27] sts from left front neck, K front neck sts from holder, but inc 3 sts evenly, K up 25[25:27] sts from right front neck, K back neck sts on holder, but inc 7[7:8] sts evenly.

116[120:128] sts.

Work 10 rows K1, P1 rib.

Cast off in rib.

**To complete**

Join left shoulder seam.

Set in the sleeves, then join side and sleeve seams.

Keep the ball bands for washing instructions.

# MAN'S SLEEVELESS SWEATER

**MATERIALS** Patons Clansman 4-ply, 3 [3:3:4] 50-g balls in 1st colour (Fawn Beige), A; 2[2:2:2] 50-g balls in 2nd colour (Baltic Blue), B; 2[2:2:2] 50-g balls in 3rd colour (Laburnum), C; 1[1:1:1] 50-g ball in 4th colour (Dusky Pink), D. One pair each of 2¾ and 3¼mm OR nos. 12 and 10 knitting needles.

For best results it is essential to use the recommended yarn.

For stockists send SAE to:

Patons & Baldwins Limited, Consumer Liaison Dept, Alloa, Clackmannanshire.

**MEASUREMENTS** To suit chest 91[97:102: 107]cm OR 36[38:40:42]in length from shoulder 64[65:66:68]cm OR 25¼[25½:26: 26¾]in.

**TENSION** 32 sts and 32 rows to 10cm OR 4in measured over "block" Fair Isle patt as worked immediately above welt.

**ABBREVIATIONS** K = knit; P = purl; st(s) = stitch(es); st st = stocking stitch; rep = repeat; patt = pattern; beg = begin(ning); inc = increase; dec = decrease; rem = remain(ing); alt = alternate; tog = together; tbl = through back of loops; cm = centimetres; in = inch(es).

**NB** Instructions for the larger sizes are in[ ]; where one figure is given, this applies to all sizes.

**NNB** When working Fair Isle strand the colour not in use loosely across the wrong side of the work, linking it in with last stitch of row.

**Back**

* With 2¾mm OR no. 12 needles and A, cast on 133[141:149:157] sts.

**Rib row 1** K2, (P1, K1) to last st, K1.

**Rib row 2** K1, (P1, K1) to end. Rep these 2 rows for 7cm OR 2¾in, ending rib row 2.

**Inc row** Rib 9[4:8:2], inc in next st, (rib 5 [6:6:7], inc in next st) to last 9[3:7:2] sts, rib to end. 153[161:169:177] sts.

**Next row** P.

Change to 3¼mm OR no. 10 needles.

Joining in and cutting off colours as required and beg K row, work in st st in patt as follows:

**Rows 1 to 4** 1C, (3B, 1C) to end.

**Row 5** 1B, (3A, 1B) to end.

**Rows 6 and 7** 2B, (1A, 3B) to last 3 sts, 1A, 2B.

**Row 8** As row 5.

**Rows 9 to 28** Rep rows 1 to 8 twice more, then work rows 1 to 4 again. Change to 2¾mm OR no. 12 needles.

**Rows 29 and 30** Work with C. Change to 3¼mm OR no. 10 needles.

**Row 31** 1D, (1A, 1D) to end.

44

**Row 32** 1A, (1D, 1A) to end.
Change to 2¾mm OR no. 12 needles.
**Rows 33 and 34** Work with A.
**Rows 35 and 36** Work with C.
**Rows 37 to 56** Rep last 4 rows 5 times.
**Row 57** Work with B.
**Rows 58 and 59** Work with C.
**Row 60** Work with B.
**Row 61** Work with A. Change to 3¼mm OR no. 10 needles.
**Row 62** 2A, (5D, 3A) to last 7 sts, 5D, 2A.
**Row 63** 1A, (2D, 3A, 2D, 1A) to end.
**Row 64** 1A, (1D, 5A, 1D, 1A) to end.
**Row 65** As row 63.
**Row 66** As row 62. Change to 2¾mm OR no. 12 needles.
**Row 67** Work with A.
**Row 68** Work with B.
**Rows 69 and 70** Work with C.
**Rows 71 and 72** Work with A. Change to 3¼mm OR no. 10 needles.
**Row 73** 4C, (1D, 7C) to last 5 sts, 1D, 4C.
**Row 74** 3C, (1D, 1C, 1D, 5C) to last 6 sts, 1D, 1C, 1D, 3C.
**Row 75** 2C, (1D, 3C) to last 3 sts, 1D, 2C.
**Row 76** 1C, (1D, 5C, 1D, 1C) to end.
**Row 77** 1D, (7C, 1D) to end. Change to 2¾mm OR no. 12 needles.
**Row 78** Work with C. Change to 3¼mm OR no. 10 needles.
**Rows 79 to 82** 1D, (1B, 1D, 3B, 1D, 1B, 1D) to end. Change to 2¾mm OR no. 12 needles.
**Rows 83 and 84** Work with A. Change to 3¼mm OR no. 10 needles.
**Rows 85 to 88** 1C, (1D, 1C, 3D, 1C, 1D, 1C) to end. Change to 2¾mm OR no.12 needles.
**Rows 89 and 90** Work with A. Change to 3¼mm OR no. 10 needles.
**Rows 91 to 94** As rows 79 to 82. Change to 2¾mm OR no. 12 needles.
**Rows 95 and 96** Work with C, then change to 3¼mm OR no. 10 needles.
These 96 rows form the patt which is repeated throughout.
Continue in patt until work measures 39cm OR approx 15¼in from cast-on edge, ending wrong-side row.
**Shape armholes** Keeping patt correct, cast off 10[11:12:13] sts at beg of next 2 rows *.
Dec one st each end of every row until 115 [117:123:125] sts rem, then on every following alt row until 101[105:109:113] sts rem.
Work straight until work measures 25[26: 27:29]cm OR approx 9¾[10¼:10½:11½]in from beg of armholes, ending wrong-side row.
**Shape shoulders** Cast off 9[10:10:10] sts at beg of next 4 rows and 10[9:10:11] sts at beg of following 2 rows.
Cut off yarn and leave rem 45[47:49:51] sts on a holder. ▷

## SLICK KNIT TIPS

For a good finish to your garment, it's important to use the right seam for the job.

**Back stitch seam**
As this is a strong, firm seam, it should on the whole be used for shoulder, side and sleeve seams (for exceptions, see below. A back stitch seam is particularly not suitable for baby clothes, because of the firm ridge which forms on the wrong side, which could be uncomfortable for the baby). To sew a back stitch seam, place the right sides of the work together and work with the wrong side facing from right to left (as shown in the illust-ration), keeping the line of stit-ching as straight as possible.

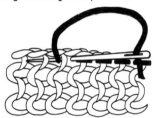

**Flat seam**
Flat seaming should always be used for joining ribbed welts, cuffs and front bands, and for the seams of Fair Isle and patterned garments, to ensure that the pattern is con-tinuous. It is also ideal for baby clothes. To sew a flat seam, using a wool needle threaded with match-ing yarn, weave on the right side of the work alternately from side to side for every stitch. Draw the thread up loosely as you sew, taking care not to pucker the work.

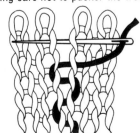

◁ **Front**
Work as back from * to *.
**Divide for neck Next row** K2 tog, K64[67:
70:73], turn and leave rem sts on a spare
needle.
Work on first set of sts as follows:
** Dec one st at armhole edge on next
8[10:10:12] rows and *at the same time* dec
one st at neck edge on every K row. 53[53:
56:56] sts.
Dec one st each end of every K row until
39[41:42:44] sts rem.
Dec one st at neck edge only on every
following 4th row until 28[29:30:31] sts rem.
Work straight until front measures same as
back to shoulder, ending at armhole edge.
**Shape shoulder** Cast off 9[10:10:10] sts at
beg of next and following alt row. Work 1
row. Cast off **.
With right side facing join yarn to inner end
of sts on spare needle, cast off one st, K to
last 2 sts, K2 tog.
Complete as given for first side from ** to **.
**Neckband**
Join left shoulder seam.
With right side facing join in A and, using a
2¾mm OR no.12 needle, K the sts of back
neck from holder decreasing 2 sts evenly,
then K up 72[76:80:84] sts from left front
neck, one st (and mark this centre st) from
base of 'V' and 72[76:80:84] sts from right
front neck. 188[198:208:218] sts.
**Row 1** (K1, P1) to within 2 sts of centre st, K2
tog, P centre st, K2 tog tbl, P1, (K1, P1) to
end.
**Row 2** Rib to within 2 sts of centre st, P2 tog
tbl, K centre st, P2 tog, rib to end.
Rep these 2 rows 3 times more. Cast off in
rib.
**Armbands**
Join right shoulder and neckband seam.
With right side facing join in A and, using a
2¾mm OR no. 12 needle, K up 150[160:170:
180] sts evenly all round armhole.
Work 8 rows K1, P1 rib.
Cast off in rib.
**To complete**
Press work on wrong side with a warm iron
over a damp cloth. Join side seams.
Keep the ball bands for washing instruc-
tions.

*Romantically Yours...*
Continued from page 36

following 2 rows.
Cut off yarn and leave rem sts on a holder.
**Front**
Work as given for back from *to*.
Work straight until front measures 49cm
OR 19¼in from cast-on edge, ending
wrong-side row.
**Divide for neck Next Row** P29 [31:33], turn
and leave rem sts on a spare needle.
Work on first set of sts as follows:
** Dec one st at neck edge on every row
until 21 [22:23] sts rem.
Work straight until front measures same as
back to beg of shoulder shaping, ending
armhole edge.
**Shape shoulder** Cast off 11 sts at beg of
next row. Work 1 row. Cast off **.
Return to sts on spare needle.
With right side facing, sl first 18 sts on a
holder, join in yarn to next st and P to end of
row.
Now work as given for first side from **to**.
**Sleeves**
With 3¼mm OR no. 10 needles cast on
50 [52:54] sts. Work 10cm OR 4in K1, P1 rib.
Change to 4mm OR no. 8 needles and
continue in rib until work measures 20 5cm
OR 8in from cast-on edge.
**Inc row 1** (Rib 1, inc in next st) to end.
75 [78:81], sts.
**Inc row 2** K14 [17:20], (inc in next st) to last
14 [17:20] sts, K to end. 122 sts.
**Foundation row 1** (Right side) K3, (P16, K4),
to end, ending last rep K3.
**Foundation row 2** K1, P2, (K16, P4) to end,
ending last rep P2, K1.
Now work in patt as follows:
**Row 1** K3, (P16, C4) to end, ending last rep
K3. **Row 2** K1, P2, (K16, P4) to end, ending
last rep P2, K1.
**Row 3** K1, (Cr3L, P14, Cr3R) to last st, K1.
**Row 4 and every following alt row** K1, (then
K all P sts and P all K sts of previous row) to
last st, K1. **Row 5** K1, P1, (Cr3L, P12, Cr3R,
P2) to end, endling last rep P1, K1.
**Row 7** K1, P2, (Cr3L, P10, Cr3R, P4) to end,
ending last rep P2, K1. **Row 9** K1, P3, (Cr3L,
P8, Cr3R, P6) to end, ending last rep P3, K1.
**Row 11** K1, P4, (Cr3L, P6, Cr3R, P8) to end,
ending last rep P4, K1.

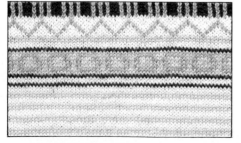

**Row 13** K1, P5, (Cr3L, P4, Cr3R, P10) to end, ending last rep P5, K1.
**Row 15** K1, P6, (Cr3L, P2, Cr3R, P12) to end, ending last rep P6, K1.
**Row 17** K1, P7, (Cr3L, Cr3R, P14) to end, ending last rep P7, K1.
**Row 19** K1, P8, (C4, P16) to end, ending last rep P8, K1. **Row 21** K1, P7, (Cr3R, Cr3L, P14) to end, ending last rep P7, K1.
**Row 23** K1, P6, (Cr3R, P2, Cr3L, P12) to end, ending last rep P6, K1.
**Row 25** K1, P5, (Cr3R, P4, Cr3L, P10) to end, ending last rep P5, K1.
**Row 27** K1, P4, (Cr3R, P6, Cr3L, P8) to end, ending last rep P4, K1. **Row 29** K1, P3, (Cr3R, P8, Cr3L, P6) to end, ending last rep P3, K1.
**Row 31** K1, P2, (Cr3R, P10, Cr3L, P4) to end, ending last rep P2, K1.
**Row 33** K1, P1, (Cr3R, P12, Cr3L, P2) to end, ending last rep P1, K1.
**Row 35** K1, (Cr3R, P14, Cr3L) to last st, K1.
**Row 36** K1, (then K all P sts and P all K sts of previous row) to last st, K1.
These 36 rows form the patt. Rep them until sleeve measures 40·5cm OR 16 in from cast-on edge, ending wrong-side row.
**Shape top** Keeping patt correct, cast off 5 sts at beg of next 2 rows. Dec one st each end of next and every following alt row until 62 sts rem. Cast off 5 sts at beg of next 4 rows, then 4 sts at beg of following 2 rows.
**Next row** (K2 tog) to end. Cast off.
**Neckband**
Join shoulder seams. With circular needle cast on 35 sts for tie, then beg at front neck K across sts on holder, K up 28 sts from right front neck, K across back neck sts on holder, K up 24 sts from left front neck to within 2cm OR ¾in of front neck sts, then cast on 35 sts for tie. 174 [176:178] sts.
Working backwards and forwards in rows, work in K1, P1 rib for 8 rows. K 1 row.
Work a further 8 rows K1, P1 rib. Cast off.
**Shoulder pads**
With 3¼mm OR no. 10 needles cast on 35 sts. Work 11·5cm OR 4½in K1, P1 rib, beg alt rows P1. Cast off in rib.
**To complete**
Set in sleeves, easing in extra fullness at top, then join side and sleeve seams. Fold neckband to wrong side, sew in position and tie. Using Lazy Daisy and Bullion Stitch, embroider motifs in diamond panels.

# HOW TO WORK BULLION STITCH

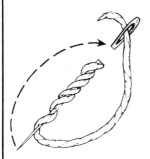

**A** Insert needle through garment and take a small stitch leaving needle still in fabric. Twist yarn round needle point about 9 times.

**B** Hold the left thumb on the coiled thread and pull needle through still holding coiled thread, turn the needle point back to where it was inserted (see arrow) and insert in same place. Pull thread through to wrong side so forming a loop.

**C** Continue as directed above until the flower petals have all been formed.

# The folk who live on the farm

**Drop in on our family of townees turned country folk — Steve Brown, his wife Gill and their daughters, Corrie, Suzie and Sammy — and hear tell of a day, and a night, to remember ...**

THE VILLAGE policeman places No Parking cones outside the church gate, a sure sign that something extraordinary is about to happen in our conspicuously uncongested setting.

Church bell-ringers work up a lather. People wait expectantly alongside the village green. Distant sound of hoofs! The immaculate ancient carriage, owned by the village and used only for special community occasions, is driven by a flowing beard in Victorian cloak and top hat. Face aglow, he whispers endearments to the gently trotting horse, glances at the church clock, and slows to a walking pace.

The bride, born in the village and known to everybody, looks endearingly shy, much too reserved to take all this attention in her stride. Eyes shining, overwhelmed by so much affection, self-consciously she smiles acknowledgment to shouts of good luck, waving like the princess she truly is for the day.

Minutes later, the flowing beard opens the carriage door. Church bells go festively crazy. Children throw flower petals prematurely. Cameras flash. The horse mounts the pavement, knocking a traffic cone flying, and both are hurriedly repositioned.

The church clock strikes three and the organ roars its greeting as the entire village rises to welcome the bride.

Gill pats the horse and chats to flowing

beard as bride and bridegroom sign the register, and emerge to a blitz of confetti. Eventually they drive away to a strictly family-only reception. Ah, yes, but that night the whole village focuses on the village hall for a celebratory barn-dance-cum-discotheque.

The happy couple circulate freely, receiving smiles of envy from the young and benedictions from elders of the village.

An old shepherd takes the floor by storm to perform what resembles a cross between an Irish jig and a Highland fling. Everybody claps, a few cheer, the red-faced octogenarian blooms. All the love this little community contains, never in doubt but often inhibited by natural reserve, suddenly breaks its banks and pours forth to envelop the newly-weds.

Loath to drag themselves away, Corrie and the twins get into the car for home. Shortly I turn off what we dignify by calling the main road to follow a rough track to our farmyard. Just beyond the third cattle grid, Sammy gets out to shut up her ducks for the night, while the car continues to inch its way forward as sheep and lambs reluctantly bestir themselves from favourite sleeping places.

First Suzie with her hens, and then Corrie with her angora rabbits follow Sammy's example; and then, still chattering on about the events of the day, they stagger into the kitchen and up to bed. I prepare bottles for a couple of orphan lambs bought the day before from a neighbouring farmer. Gill takes the warm milk, and I head for the cowshed. I've a vigil to keep there — for the best of reasons.

At last! Two tiny hoofs come into view. Confident that my best plan is simply to let the cow get on with it undisturbed, I lend Gill a hand with the lambs before together we retrace my steps. We gawp as the calf gently slips to the straw; and soon the proud mother is licking it clean.

Incredibly the calf starts to struggle to its feet almost immediately. The first few times it manages no more than to kneel before toppling over, but eventually, swaying

like corn in a soft breeze, it stumbles up, already searching for a teat, and begins to suckle. Again I'm reminded of my favourite quotation since coming here — to be honest, the only one by Aristotle I've ever known: "In everything natural there is something marvellous."

Gill nips to the farmhouse for a couple of coffees while I check the calf is receiving its full quota of colostrum, concentrated in the first flow of milk to assist protection from disease. Twenty minutes or so later, still intoxicated with magic, we ease ourselves wearily into bed; but all the excitement of the day, midwifery no less than wedding, makes sleep impossible.

MYRIAD STARS accentuate the blackness outside, blackness we never saw in the city. More soothing still is the silence that seeps into our very beings. True, owls hoot, bats squeak, a rabbit (victim of fox or, more likely, weasel) squeals, a dog in the distance barks ... yet such noises somehow emphasise the absolute silence below silence, as full of mystery as empty of fear.

"They'll miss the village," Gill suddenly whispers about the newly-weds, both of them unconsciously illustrating the glory and tragedy of our village: glory because any community whose children grow into such carefree responsible adults can't be bad; tragedy because the only way they can earn a living and set up home is to move far away.

In a flash I feel afresh the wonder of our coming here — the first lambing season for self-taught shepherds; Meg the horse licking some of the newborns clean; the first litters from our sows Pinky and Perky; the children beside themselves with handfuls of day-old chicks and ducklings; family haymaking; housecows queueing to unburden themselves of pints and pints of creamy milk, lots of it soon to become home-made cheese or butter; and only yesterday a rainbow whose beauty stopped me awestruck in my tracks, aching with happiness.

"We'll stay here for ever ..." I reach for Gill's hand. But she's already fast asleep.

# How to put the

# *spring*

## into
## cleaning

**With our home team's bright ideas for the great gleam-up, you'll be able to polish off the spring cleaning in no time at all!**

THE Victorians had a passion for spring cleaning. But then, the effect of open fires and gas lighting meant that a thorough overhaul each year was badly needed. Now, thank goodness, our homes are easier to look after.

Even so, when the first glints of spring sunshine show us dirty windows and grimy paintwork, most of us like to start a whole house freshen-up. There is, in fact, something quite therapeutic about it. There's no need for it to be back-breaking and it's a wonderful chance to clear out all the things you don't need. Good planning will help make the job less tiring.

**Everybody out**
Off-load children and pets, if possible. Though it's good to share day-to-day chores with the kids, a proper clean-up will be easier for you if they can be sent off to play or left with neighbours while you get on with the work. Try a spring cleaning swap. One mother cleans while the other baby-sits and provides lunch.

**Clean-up kit**
Cleaning cloths, brushes, spare bin liners for rubbish, extra vacuum cleaning bags, various cleaners (see over the page), a strong pair of steps, rubber gloves.

**Rooms for improvement**
Decide which rooms you want to tackle, remembering that energy and enthusiasm will flag as the day wears on. Wear old

clothes, plus an apron with large pockets for holding odds and ends.

## Take it from the top
Begin by removing small pieces of furniture, books and ornaments. Protect large pieces of furniture with old sheets or curtains. Work from the top of the room down, so that cleaned surfaces stay clean. Dust with a feather duster, or use the dusting attachment of the vacuum cleaner. Start with light fittings, lamp-shades and picture frames. Tackle mantelpiece, shelves and tables next, then the skirting. Move furniture around and vacuum thoroughly.

## Curtain calls
Dust curtains with the vacuum cleaner attachment, or take them down and hang them outside for an hour or two. Soak washable curtains in cold water before washing to help remove dust. Mark the positions of the hooks on the tape with clear nail varnish to speed putting them up again. Large, heavy curtains, or velvet ones, should be taken to the cleaners.

Wash curtain hooks in warm soapy water. Dust and wipe plastic curtain rails, then spray with a silicone polish to help the curtains pull more smoothly. Wipe metal rails with a metal polish. Rehang net curtains before they are completely dry — and you won't need to iron them.

## Glass conscious
Wash the windows, using about 2 tablespoons of vinegar to half a bucket of ▷

# TIPS OF THE TRADE

* *Use a cleaning caddy, or make one from a box. Put general cleaners, brushes, cloths etc inside and carry it around as you work.*
* *Scratches on plastic baths can be removed using a little silver polish on a cloth.*
* *Tackle black mould on tile grouting with an old toothbrush dipped in household bleach.*
* *Clean Venetian blinds speedily by wearing old cotton gloves and running your hand along the slats.*
* *Remove greasy marks from plastic using a little meths on a piece of cotton wool.*
* *Disguise scratches on wood furniture by rubbing with a matching wax crayon or shoe polish.*
* *Dust behind radiators using a cane with a sock fixed on the end.*
* *Vinyl flooring with a raised pattern is easy to clean with a plastic car-wash brush.*
* *Remove scuff marks on vinyl or lino with neat emulsion polish.*
* *Clean hairspray marks on mirrors with a little meths on cotton wool. Prevent mirrors steaming up by smearing with washing-up liquid.*
* *Replace washable loose covers on chairs before completely dry so that they stretch back into shape.*

# How to put the

*spring*

into cleaning

◁ warm water. Buff them up with crumpled newspaper to get a really good shine.

If the windows are very dirty, wash them first with hot water, to which you've added a little liquid detergent, then rinse with vinegar and water. On large window panes, a cleaning tool with a soft rubber blade will remove the dirty water cleanly and evenly. Always finish the inside of a window with crosswise strokes, and the outside with up and down strokes, then if there are any smears you will be able to tell instantly which side of the glass they're on.

**Paint fresh**
Paintwork often needs both dusting and washing. Wet dust is very sticky and hard to remove, so dust down ledges and door panels before you wash them, using a little washing-up liquid in hot water.

Work from the bottom up, in small squares side by side rather than dotting about like a crossword puzzle. If you work from the top down, little streams of dirty water tend to make tracks through the dirty area — and these can be very hard to remove.

Use two buckets, one for washing and one for rinsing. This is a great help as it cuts down the number of times you need to change the water.

If paintwork is very dirty, use sugar soap. This is sold in DIY stores for preparing paintwork for repainting. Use it in half-strength solution to wash painted surfaces. It's ideal for cleaning greasy areas above and around the cooker, or the sort of ground-in dirt that is caused by heavy smokers. Sticky marks around door handles and light switches are easily removed with a little neat cream cleanser on a damp cloth.

For large areas of paintwork high up, try using a squeeze mop. Before you begin, push the handle of the mop through a foil

# THE BRIGHT BRIGADE

*Most of the cleaners you need will probably be in the house already. You may like to stock up with a few useful extras, and your storecupboard should include:*
***Cream cleaner*** *for worktops, baths, sinks, basins, stained paintwork, worktops and machines.*
***Floor cleaner*** *for general cleaning, plus **water-based, dry-bright polish** for use on lino or vinyls.*
***A solvent-based polish*** *is good for waxed wooden floors and sealed cork tiles.*
***Washing-up liquid*** *is good for supplying hot soapy water for general cleaning — much better than using washing powders which often take a while to dissolve and can sometimes affect the colour of paintwork.*
***Bicarbonate of soda*** *is the ideal cleaner to use on the interiors of fridges and freezers. About 1*

plate so that you can catch the drips as you clean.

## On the carpet

Carpets need regular vacuuming or brushing to prevent dirt and grit working their way deep into the pile. If dog hairs are a problem in your home, try using a damp cloth and wipe it across the surface of the carpet to pick up the hairs. It works quite well, but you'll need to keep rinsing the cloth to remove the hairs.

Steam cleaning is the quickest and easiest method of carpet cleaning. The machines can be hired, usually from a dry cleaner, and it may well be worth getting together with friends to hire one for a week. But *do* organise the rota carefully! Preparations for treating stains and very dirty patches are usually included with the cleaner.

The machine is filled with water, and used like a vacuum cleaner, spraying a fine jet of steam into the carpet through

the nozzle and then sucking out the dirt.

But if you can't face cleaning carpets yourself, there are specialist cleaners who will do the job for you. Look in your local Yellow Pages for a list of addresses.

teaspoon mixed with 1 pint of warm water should be sufficient. You can also use it neat on a damp cloth to remove stubborn marks on worktops. **Household soda** is a good grease remover and ideal for sinks, or for soaking very dirty kitchen equipment. Do not soak anything made of aluminium in it, though, as it can cause pitting.
**Biological washing powder** for

soaking fabrics and tablecloths, which have stubborn stains on them.
**Vinegar** is ideal for removing hard water marks on ceramic tiles and getting rid of white patches on newly-laid quarry tiles. Wash these down with one tablespoon of vinegar in 2 pints warm water, but don't rinse them.
**Glycerine** is useful for softening old, ground-in stains. Mix with equal quantities of warm water, work into the stain and leave for about half an hour. When the time is up, wipe off the glycerine and, if necessary, treat the stain.
**Carpet shampoo** is very handy for spot-treating stains. The aerosol kind is probably the most convenient to use.
**Grease solvent**, in liquid, paste or spray form, is very good for use on carpets, upholstery and, in some cases, wallpaper.
You may well want to have **bleach**, **antiseptic**, a **cream polish** for furniture and a general purpose **spray polish** in your store cupboard too. Then you'll be equipped to tackle any cleaning!

# Where the Royals get

**The world really is their oyster. Yet, like every family, the Royals have differing ideas about holiday bliss. Join us, then, for a tour of some right Royal retreats! Ann Wallace reports ...**

*Balmoral Castle (above) for the Queen's favourite family holidays. Left: flying off on the crest of a wave!*

They may take to the tropics, or cut a dash on the ski slopes, or feel happiest just holidaying at home. But wherever individual Royals choose to get away from it all, one thing is certain. Each year —without fail—the Queen moves to her magnificent Scottish estate, Balmoral, for six weeks in August and September, and her family and friends join her throughout the stay.

Balmoral gives the Queen and Prince Philip the opportunity really to relax and enjoy their kind of holiday in country contentment. The Queen gets up early every morning—after tea and a read of the papers in bed — and has started on her official paperwork by 8 am. Meanwhile, the rest of the Royals and their guests drift down to a breakfast of eggs, bacon, kidneys, sausages, kippers, smoked haddock and ham, served buffet-style in the magnificent dining room.

Once the Queen has finished her work, days are spent walking, riding, playing tennis and golf and swimming in the enormous Balmoral pool. Picnics are high on the list of Royal pleasures and, when the weather is fine, the Queen selects a spot somewhere on the estate and supervises a feast of game pies, cold meats, pickles, salads, fruit tarts and puddings, all packed in traditional hampers along with crockery and cutlery, and transported by Land-Rover. Once arrived, the Queen plays "Mother"—there are no servants on these picnics—and hands round groaning plates of food. In fact, food plays a large role in the Balmoral holidays and the Queen is especially fond of tea at 5 pm with sandwiches, shortbread, scones and cream cakes. Dances are often held in the evening, and after all that exercise (not to mention food!) guests always sleep like logs.

Now that the family is grown up, the move to Balmoral is much simpler for the Queen. When the children were younger, however, lorries were needed to transport holiday necessities from Buckingham Palace—trunks, suitcases, holdalls, bicycles, go-karts, even Prince Andrew's pony and a horse for Princess Anne. But if the Prince and Princess of Wales continue the Balmoral tradition, it won't be long before their children will be wanting to take everything along but the kitchen sink for their holiday with Granny!

Another Royal tradition is to spend the Christmas and New Year holiday on the 20,000-acre Sandringham estate in Norfolk, where "The Big House" can accommodate with ease the largest Christmas party — it has some 250 rooms. The only year plans had to be changed was in 1974 when the Royal family were forced to squash into the six-bedroomed Wood Farm,

# away from it all

two miles away, because the house was being renovated. Wood Farm had been used by the Queen as a weekend retreat for 10 years; she enjoyed the more intimate setting for her Christmas holiday that year and took the opportunity to ring the changes with the choice of lunchtime venues for her shooting guests. They ate in a local pub, a village club and a corrugated iron village hall!

In the past, the Queen has enjoyed short holiday cruises along the Scottish coast on the Royal yacht *Britannia*, and she even took a holiday abroad with her family in 1969 when they cruised along the Norwegian fjords. But there's no doubt that when it comes to holidays, Balmoral is where the Queen's heart lies.

The Queen Mother's holiday heart certainly lies north of the border too. She has made Birkhall Lodge on the Balmoral estate her own domain. It's a stone-built house with a broad pine lodge porch, set in a dell carpeted with heather. Another favourite of the Queen Mother's is her beloved Castle of Mey, in Caithness. A turreted castle with six-foot-thick walls, it remains a very private Royal residence with only the gardens open to the public at certain times of the year.

Princess Margaret doesn't share her mother's and sister's love of holidaying at home. Her trips to Mustique in the Caribbean where she has a house, Les Jolies Eaux, are world famous, and her affection for the island is contagious: her cousin, Lord Lichfield, who originally owned one of PM's gatehouses

at Les Jolies Eaux, has now had his own five-bedroomed villa built for his own family holidays there.

The plot of land on which Les Jolies Eaux stands was a wedding present to the Princess and Lord Snowdon in 1960. The hill-top house, built by designer Oliver Messel, Snowdon's uncle, has cool stone floors and white-washed walls, open-sided terrace, swimming pool and a glass-roofed gazebo overlooking the private beach. Mustique gained most notoriety when Princess Margaret regularly took holidays there with her friend Roddy Llewellyn, and it was there that the Princess made her decision to divorce Lord Snowdon and, later, to end her relationship with Roddy. Yet despite its sad associations, the island and Les Jolies Eaux remain the Princess's own slice of paradise.

If Princess Margaret would hate to do without her holidays abroad, her niece, Princess Anne, couldn't be more different. She has never been keen on going away and even cut short a recent holiday at Balmoral to carry out engagements. She prefers to spend her time at home with her children, Peter and Zara, at Gatcombe Park, helping husband Mark Phillips on the farm and riding her beloved horses. She did try skiing on a New Year trip to Liechtenstein with Prince Philip and Prince Charles when she was 15 but the holiday was marred when she went down with gastric flu.

She holidayed again with Charles in 1969 in Malta, piloting their BEA Trident jet at 29,000 feet on the way there, and a few years later she took a six-day trip to Spain. Of course, there was her 1973 Caribbean honeymoon cruise on *Britannia* but, never one for the lazy life, Anne has steered clear of holiday trips since then. She always goes to Balmoral in the summer, and of course travels widely in her work as President of the Save The Children Fund. But a holiday to Anne means time on her own, with her family, at the house she loves. And who could find fault with that?

Like his sister, to whom he is very close, Prince Edward is not particularly fond of holidaying abroad, apart from skiing — he's a good skier and enjoys his trips to the slopes. But really Prince Edward likes nothing better than to spend his holidays at Balmoral, or with Princess Anne and her family in Gloucestershire.

Prince Andrew, on the other hand, has (not

# Where the Royals get away from it all

surprisingly) developed a real sailor's taste for travel. Yet one of his earliest — and happiest — holidays was at humble Bembridge on the Isle of Wight when he was nine years old. He stayed with the family of school friend Katy Seymour and spent an idyllic week building sand castles, swimming and fishing from the Seymours' boat — just like any normal little boy on holiday. But it was Mustique and his Aunt Margaret's house that really thrust the fun-loving Prince into the holiday limelight, when he took actress Koo Stark there in the autumn of 1982, after returning from duty in the Falklands. There they were heavily guarded and teams of security men kept sightseers and the Press well away. However, when the Prince and Koo visited the tiny island of Bequia, 10 miles from Mustique, where Princess Margaret has an away-from-it-all cottage, the attentions of the Press became too much and Prince Andrew flew back to London three days early.

He hasn't made the same mistake again. The following year he went on holiday to Canada on his own and spent three action-packed weeks shooting the rapids in a canoe, battling through the woods in the wild North West Territories and sleeping rough under the stars. He returned looking in the prime of health and happiness: could it be that action holidays suit him more than sun-soaking and lotus eating?

Prince Charles also has a liking for the unusual, and a secret holiday hideaway near Egilsstadir in the isolated north-east of Iceland was a favourite during the seventies. He stayed with friends in a fishing lodge on the banks of the River Hofsa and fished to his heart's content.

As for skiing — Charles first acquired the taste for it at 14 in Switzerland, and the appetite for winter sports has never left him. He stayed in the tiny village of Tarasp and, after his very first lesson, announced: "It was fine. I only fell twice!" Since then he's enjoyed many holidays in the snow, notably at Klosters, the Swiss picture postcard village where he has regularly stayed with ex-Olympic skier Charlie Palmer-Tomlinson and his wife in their chalet home. Charles was often accompanied by a girlfriend before his marriage, so inevitably his winter jaunts became a "must" for Royal watchers and photographers. Press interest reached new heights of lunacy, though, in January 1983, when Prince Charles and Princess Diana went to Liechtenstein for a skiing holiday. Their stay ended in tears when newsmen and photographers refused to leave the Royal couple alone and the strain proved too much for the Princess. She wept openly and refused to smile or even look up for photographers,

despite her husband's pleas that she was being "silly". The Prince and Princess clearly learned from that experience. A year later, they returned to Liechtenstein, announcing that they would allow one photograph and then expect the remainder of their holiday to be considered private. So Diana was able to brush up her skiing technique (learned at her Swiss finishing school) without the lenses of the world waiting to snap every slip.

But it's by no means all ice and snow for Charles and Diana. The Princess in particular loves the sun and is far happier holidaying on a golden beach than anywhere else. Since their Mediterranean honeymoon cruise after their wedding in July 1981, they have enjoyed sunseeking in the Bahamas: they stayed on Eleuthera when the Princess was almost six months pregnant, their last holiday together before becoming parents, and they treated themselves to a sort of second honeymoon — minus baby William — with a 10-day stay on Windermere, after the triumphant tour of Australia and New Zealand.

Naturally, the Prince and Princess join the rest of the family for traditional holidays at Balmoral and Sandringham, but they have made it clear that they need time to themselves and expect a degree of privacy from the family as well as from the Press. After Diana cut short a Balmoral holiday in 1982 and returned to London with William, Charles made sure that they have a chance for personal retreat by staying not in Balmoral Castle but in Craigowan, a small house on the estate. And, as often as possible, they drive up to the Highlands to spend weekends in a pretty fishing lodge by a loch, away from the crowds. For the New Year, the Prince and Princess prefer the intimacy of Wood Farm to the opulence of Sandringham House.

But when they really want to get away from it all, Charles and Diana take a helicopter to St Mary's in the Scilly Isles, where the headquarters of the Duchy of Cornwall is located and Charles has a three-bedroomed bungalow, Tamarisk. Ordinary and unpretentious, it sits in half an acre of lawns and is hardly noticed by the tourists. The locals guard their Royal visitors jealously and Charles and Diana can relax away from the glare of publicity that usually surrounds them.

And after all, that's what holidays are supposed to be — a time to unwind, away from the usual problems of work and the day-to-day chores. And in that respect, the Royal family is no different from the rest of us. When it comes to holidays, quite naturally they just want to be alone!

*Fairy-tale Vaduz in Liechtenstein, ski-scene for Charles and Diana*

*Left: the Prince and Princess catching a chair-lift up to the slippery slopes*

*Below: Prince Andrew paddles his own canoe on an action-packed Canadian trip*

# Where the Royals get away from it all

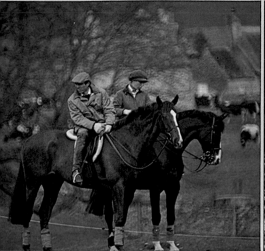

*There's no holiday place like home for Anne and Mark, and riding their beloved horses at Gatcombe Park*

*Charles shares his grandmother's love of fishing: here he's calmly casting a Scottish reel*

*Though Diana's heart may not belong there, Balmoral does have its idyllic moments – like a hand-in-hand walk across the heather on a sunny day*

*"Tamarisk", the Wales' modest retreat on the Scilly Isle of St Mary's*

*Left: a bracing stroll for the Queen and Prince Philip in the grounds of Sandringham House*

*And for sailing into the sunset, the Royal Yacht, Britannia!*

# Elena

**A short story
by Dorothy Cooper**

WHILE she polished the little cakeforks, Elena's thoughts went back twenty-six years to another hot July afternoon. Gibraltar, less than a week before her marriage, and the stuffy family parlour where the gifts were on display. And Bill, inspecting them, had stopped in front of the open leather case to ask, "What are these for?"

"To eat the pastries with, and not make sticky the fingers. They are from Señora Laredo, who has many like them, for when her friends come to tea."

"She should have given you a decent cheque, after the way you've slaved for her, instead of unloading some of her spares on you. She knows darn well that fancy tea parties aren't for the likes of us!" And then, seeing her expression, his arm went round her and he added, gruffly, "Never mind, Ellie love! You might get a chance to use them yet!"

Only she never had — until now. Sighing, she slotted three of the six forks into their velvet-lined grooves and closed the lid. She put away the rags and polish and, removing her apron, carried the remainder of the forks into the living room.

The table was covered with a linen cloth, freshly washed and

# Elena

ironed that morning. Though kept in tissue paper, age had yellowed it, but like the matching napkins it was hand-embroidered and edged with crochet. Placing a fork at each setting, she considered the effect.

Her best china. Sandwiches of cucumber, egg and tomato, ham. And in the centre, on a glass dish, the cake. A coffee-flavoured sponge with chocolate icing. The forks provided the ultimate touch of elegance and refinement.

Padding upstairs to the front bedroom, she glanced automatically at the framed photograph above the dressing table. The wedding group, taken after the ceremony at the Cathedral of St Mary the Crowned. Bill, looking stocky and self-conscious, and she incredibly slender in her bridal gown, with filmy veil lifting in a breeze from the sea. They were flanked by Carmen and Mercedes, clutching posies, and by her father and mother, while behind them clustered the relations, and some of Bill's mates from the Naval Dockyard.

Her eyes dropped to her reflection in the oval glass. Thick, dark hair coiled in a heavy chignon. Olive skin, almost unlined except for a worry-cleft between strongly marked brows. A generous mouth and rounded chin. But the lilac foulard with the white polka dots that had fitted perfectly last summer was uncomfortably tight.

"Dad wouldn't have wanted you to wear mourning for him," Tony had assured her.

"To show respect, son. It is the custom."

"Not nowadays. Not in England, Ma. Unless you're royalty or something."

So she had compromised with half-mourning. Lilac didn't suit her, but it eased a feeling of guilt.

KICKING off her house-slippers, she wriggled her feet into highheeled pumps, inserted the hooks of the Toledo earrings into the lobes of her pierced ears and tilted her head, making the hoops swing. For a guest, one must appear festive. And today Jenny, Tony's fiancée, was coming. They wanted, he'd said, to discuss their future plans.

Tony, engaged! Renewing her lipstick, she tried to marshal her thoughts. She had been pregnant when Bill returned to England, bringing her with him to the unknown country she had heard so much about. But she was unprepared for snow, and the bitter winter cold. Bill had no family to take her to, and the rooms they'd lived in were cramped and dingy. Shopkeepers found it hard to understand her and she was shy, and lonely.

Only days before her baby was due, she had tripped over a loose stair rod in their lodgings, and fallen. The child was born unharmed, but they told her she would never have another. And, though she had hoped the first would be a son, she had also wanted daughters.

"We name him Antonio, for my father," she'd said, gazing down at her only child.

"Make him sound foreign," Bill objected. "Why not Tony? And Bill, after me? Antony William Collins. All right?"

"All right."

Other dockyards. Other lodgings. And Tony growing up. A skinny, eager little boy with a mop of black curls and wide, alert brown eyes.

When he was a baby, she had talked to him in Spanish and sung him the lullabies she had heard her mother sing. It seemed to bring home nearer, but Bill said, frowning, "England's his home. And yours, now, Ellie. You'll get him all confused."

After they moved to London, she no longer told Tony stories about Gibraltar. He was growing fast, and filling out, and always needed new clothes. At seventeen, he was learning to be a computer programmer. Elena had no idea what it meant, though he did his best to explain it to her. But he was clever, and she was proud of him.

Another thing she never understood was why Bill, every week, did what he called the pools. But one evening she sensed his excitement, and, after supper, he told them the news.

"Not a big win, mind, when we share it out, me and four of the lads. But a nice little windfall."

"You'll put it in the bank, dear?" she asked. He earned good wages, and apart from an annual holiday at the seaside for the three of them, and a pint or two at the local, he was careful.

"We'll see," he said mysteriously.

A month later, she saw. The house was a semi, in a quiet street. He opened the front door and stood back for her to enter.

"Bought it, freehold!" He grinned at her. "Took most of my winnings, but I have the surveyor's report. Cheap at the price! Course, it needs quite a bit doing to it, but I can handle most of that in my spare time. Well, what do you think?"

"I ..." Standing in the hall, afraid that she was going to cry, she had put her arms round him and kissed him.

"Like it, love?" he asked.

"Of course!" But, as he led her through the empty rooms, her heart sank. Why hadn't he taken her to see it first? Asked her opinion?

She had only herself to blame. In her family, it

had been the men who made the decisions. And since marrying him, she'd never thought to argue. This was his country, and she felt a stranger.

So they had moved in. The walls were stripped of their ugly paper, and colour-washed. The curtains she had run up on her old machine, that had gone with them everywhere since her marriage, hung in the windows. The huge kitchen was bright with yellow paint, and geraniums flourished, bordering their patch of lawn.

When it was all done, and they had settled in, Elena felt curiously lost.

THE autumn Tony was twenty, disaster struck. Bill, coming home on a foggy night, was knocked down by a skidding lorry and killed instantly. She had attended the funeral, wrapped in her dyed black coat, and stonily received the condolences of Bill's friends and the neighbours. It was afterwards, in this bedroom, that the numbness of shock left her, and she had given way and wept.

But eventually the pain ebbed and as it did, restlessness took its place. Elena had never been idle, and necessity drove her back to her beginnings. Greatly daring, she answered an advertisement for a domestic help, and met Mrs Wilmot.

"But Ma, you can't!" Tony said, horrified. "What will people think?"

"They need not know. She is a very nice lady, with a small apartment in Kensington. I shall go to her on Tuesdays, Wednesdays and Fridays, in the morning. For working by the hour, the payment is a great deal. I shall enjoy to do it."

While Bill was alive, he and Tony had made up her little world. She had never been one to gossip with the neighbours, and had no close friends, but Mrs Wilmot was different. A widow like herself, but older, she had once been an actress and appreciated all Elena did, praising her work.

The days held variety now. Elena's confidence increased. Her horizons were widening and, listening to Mrs Wilmot, her English improved.

Tony was given a rise and, telling her, he added, "So you can stop charring, Ma."

"Stop? Oh, no! For why should I stop? Not see Mrs Wilmot? Not hear about the plays she acted in? Or about her daughter, who is married in Australia? And is our home neglected?"

"I didn't say it was. But you're doing too much."

"You talk as if I am an old woman! Old, at forty-three years?"

"I was only ... All right, Ma!"

He gave her the slow grin that reminded her of Bill's. "You certainly have changed, lately!"

She grudged the part of her earnings she spent on fares, but whether she travelled to work and back by bus or underground, the time was not wasted, because her knitting went with her. A sweater for Tony. A cardigan for herself. Patterns only half-remembered were recalled, and came to life under her flying fingers.

"But that's beautiful, Elena!" Mrs Wilmot said. "I wonder, could you make a twin-set for me?"

"With pleasure!"

And then, when she appeared one morning in a new summer print dress: "You made it yourself? Who taught you?"

"My mother." Elena crossed herself. "May she rest in peace!"

"I'm sorry." Mrs Wilmot had been told, months before, of Elena's second loss. She said gently, "Have you ever thought of taking up dressmaking?"

"No. It is cheaper to buy in the shops. The ready-made. I only do it for me. But I like best to knit and sew for the children. The very little ones," Elena said. "Only here ..."

"I wonder if you'd sew something for me," Mrs Wilmot interrupted. "I'd like to send something to Elaine, for the baby she's expecting in April. My first grandchild."

It was through Mrs Wilmot that the orders started to come in. She had a wide circle of friends and acquaintances, many of whom were grandparents. And carefully, Elena replanned her days.

The spare bedroom became her workshop and there, in the afternoons, she knitted baby clothes or lovingly sewed party dresses for little girls. "Take some samples to one of the big stores," Mrs Wilmot told her. "Build up a business."

"It would require more time," she explained, "and I would have to employ others. I prefer it like this. Personal."

"Then open a savings account."

Into the new account went the money she earned in the afternoons, at home. And gradually it mounted. It gave her a heady feeling of independence she had never known before.

A year passed, and then another. And one Tuesday, when she arrived at the Kensington flat, Mrs Wilmot asked, "Is anything the matter, Elena? You've been very quiet, lately."

"It's Tony," she confessed. "I am troubled about him."

"Why? Is it ... some girl?"

"Always there are girls, some very nice. But not

# Elena

a special girl, you understand? Not serious. I tell him he is a man now, and can support a wife, so he should marry."

"These days most girls support themselves, my dear."

"Yes, and Jenny does. Jennifer Green. She is a secretary where Tony works. An orphan and living with an aunt. He has presented her to me. She is pretty and modest. They are good with each other. But they do not speak of marriage."

"Well, they're probably looking for somewhere to live, and you know how difficult it is in London."

"But they could be with me, as Tony is now! Such a big house! Too big! I should be most happy to have them."

"Elena," Mrs Wilmot said gently, "have you thought this out? You've told me the house is in your name."

"Tony is helping with the rates."

"Yes, well, but it's yours, isn't it? He may feel it wouldn't work out. It's always better if young couples can start out together on their own, and not with in-laws."

Reluctantly, Elena agreed.

"Wait and see," her friend advised. "If the girl really loves him, and is willing to marry him even though it might mean sharing, you can get together and sort things out. Until then, just go on as you are."

NOW, the time of waiting was over. This was Saturday, and they would arrive in half an hour. And she still didn't know what their plans were, or what she would say.

Propped against the clock on the mantel was the letter she had written yesterday, and forgotten to post. It was addressed to Carmen, her youngest sister, in her sloping, childish writing. Before the parents died, it was Mama who wrote regularly, once a month, but now Carmen and Mercedes took it in turns to do so.

Putting their thoughts on paper was not easy for them. Nor for her, struggling to frame the Spanish phrases unfamiliar from disuse. Every time the airmail envelopes came, she felt her heart jerk. The flimsy pages, with news of their husbands and children, were warm with affection. With questions.

Would she never come to visit them? they asked. They had not seen each other for so long. They would have so much to tell. And she would be welcome. Most welcome.

Suddenly, Elena was swept with a wave of longing, an almost overwhelming homesickness. They were her sisters, Mercedes and Carmen. Her people. Closer, in many ways, even than Bill had been. She had remained in England for Tony's sake. Bill would have wished it, but Tony didn't need her now.

Light touched her bent head, burnishing the glossy hair. She tilted her chin, and the earrings glinted. On the wall facing her, a flight of ceramic swallows soared upwards. There were six of them. She had bought them when they first moved in, and Bill had put them up for her. She had bought them without knowing why, but now she knew.

The problems that had tormented her vanished. As if by magic, each piece of the puzzle fell neatly into place.

Once it was furnished, she had never cared for this house, and without Bill it meant nothing to her. If Tony and his Jenny wanted it, she would let it to them at a reasonable rent. Otherwise, it could be sold. She would take a flat, small and convenient and easy to run. Would continue with her knitting and sewing and even, perhaps, build up a little business as Mrs Wilmot had suggested. That, and her widow's pension, should be enough.

Tony had spoken of being married in the spring. Until the wedding there was much to arrange. But afterwards, she was going home. There was sufficient in the savings account for a return flight, and plenty to spare.

She pictured the reunion. Three middle-aged women, linked by ties of blood and memories of childhood. Pictured the bustle of Main Street, the crowded cafés. The relaxed atmosphere.

"Not Mrs Collins," she murmured, "Elena."

She straightened one of the silver cakeforks. Jenny could have them, too. And the dogeared copybook in which, as a teenager, she had copied Señora Laredo's recipes. The coffee-flavoured sponge was a special favourite of Tony's. But she would keep the ceramic swallows. Black swallows, forever flying towards the sun.

A car drew up outside. There would be protests, and objections to overcome. But she moved lightly, buoyantly, filled with a feeling of tingling excitement.

"It is not that I don't love you," she rehearsed, on her way to open the door, "but I have my own life to live."

She knew, at last, exactly what to say.

THE END
© Dorothy Cooper, 1984

# 'Trust is the key to friendship'
## says
## THE REVEREND ROGER ROYLE

SOME people collect friends as others collect stamps. I remember once being invited to a party. "It's only going to be for my most intimate friends," said my hostess. So you can imagine my surprise when I found 300 of us there. In the end it turned out that she did not know the names of half of them, let alone anything intimate about them. But then that is how some people look on friendship. The more names they can put in their address book, the merrier they are. That sort of friendship is about as deep as the veneer on a reproduction sideboard.

From that extreme you go to the other: the person who has one or two really good friends. They're never out of one another's houses; they know one another's thoughts. They have the same likes and dislikes in food, clothes and people. And Lord help the person who comes between them! The danger with this sort of friendship is that it can become very possessive. And there is no quicker killer of friendship than possessiveness.

You will not survive without friends, but the making of them isn't easy — at least not for adults. Children are far better at it. They just watch other children playing and gradually join in. Or they keep looking at one another until one decides to smile and a friendship is formed. Mind you, even their friendships can become complicated.

I shall never forget one childhood friend of mine, who fortunately still remains a friend, as I am Godfather to one of her children. Without Pat I would do nothing. She taught me to tie my shoe laces, ride a bike, go to school without crying — the lot. We were like those children who say to one another, "Now I want you to be my *best* friend". But sadly most "best friends" don't last too long. Soon someone comes along with a bigger and better toy and a new "best friend" is found to occupy the position.

Parents get concerned about the sort of friends their children make. "Why don't you go out with Wendy — she's such a nice girl?" And you can be sure, if their child goes off the rails, the reason that's given is, "He got into bad company". And yet young people have a greater sense of loyalty to their friends than many an adult.

The one type of friend that I can do without is the person who just uses you. Your friendship is deep, meaningful and relevant while you are of use to them. So long as you can lend them the Black and Decker, do the odd bit of baby-sitting or know someone who might be able to get their husband a job, they are all over you. But as soon as your usefulness runs out then you become scrap-heap material and they turn to someone new.

Some friendships are short term. Some holiday friendships are very strong for a while and then naturally fade. Although I must say that the friendships I see made on the *Woman's Realm* "Find a Friend" holidays seem to be longer lasting.

THE friends I truly value are those who stay with you through thick and thin. They will have a knees-up with you when all is going well and comfort you when your luck is not so good. They'll tell you to your face what they think and put it in such a way that it's not offensive. Even though you may not see them for weeks, months or years, you know that you can always call on them for support. With them you have no secrets and no fears. You can trust them. And that is the key.

Never mind what the adverts say. Perfume, deodorants or, in my case, aftershave will not help you find a friend or influence people — but trust will. So why not try it and see what a difference it makes?

# CALLING ALL NON-KNITTERS!

Wish you could knit, but don't know how? Or perhaps you can, but you're all fingers and thumbs when it comes to teaching your child? Either way, you're sure to find our beginner's guide to basic knitting a winner ...

## FIRST CAST ON

**1**

Hold yarn in the left hand and make a loop about 3 in (7·5 cm) from end of yarn (picture 1). Holding needle in right hand, place point of needle through centre of loop and draw the continuous yarn through the original loop, so forming a slip knot below the first stitch on the needle (picture 2)

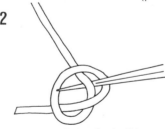

**2**

Holding the yarn from the ball in your right hand, place the right-hand needle point through the loop, then wind the yarn under and over the right-hand needle (picture 3)

**3**

**4**

Draw the yarn through the loop on left-hand needle (picture 4). Transfer the new stitch to the left-hand needle, which now holds two stitches (picture 5)

**5**

Insert right-hand needle between the two stitches on left-hand needle, wind yarn round point of right-hand needle. Draw a loop from between the two stitches on left-hand needle (picture 6), then place this loop on to left-hand needle. Continue to cast on stitches in this way until five have been cast on to the left-hand needle

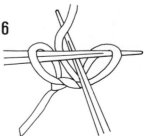

**6**

# NOW GET KNITTING

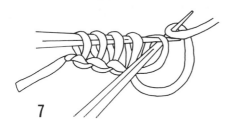

**7**

Hold needle with stitches in left hand. Keeping yarn at the back of the work, insert point of right-hand needle into the front of the first stitch on left-hand needle. Pass yarn under and over point of right-hand needle (picture 7). Draw a loop through this first stitch (picture 8), so making a loop on right-hand needle, then drop the stitch off left-hand needle

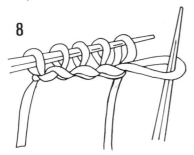

**8**

You have now worked one knitted stitch! Continue to knit each stitch in this way until all stitches have been worked off left-hand needle (picture 9)

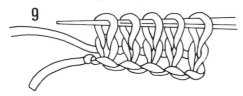

**9**

Now turn your work round so the needle holding the stitches is now in your left hand, with the wrong side facing you (picture 10). Now work another row as described above. Well done! You have now mastered plain knitting, which you'll find is abbreviated in knitting patterns as K. This stitch is called Garter stitch

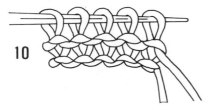

**10**

# AND CAST OFF

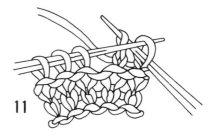

**11**

Knit two stitches; now with point of left-hand needle lift first stitch on right-hand needle over the second (picture 11) and off your needle. Now one stitch remains on right-hand needle. Knit another stitch from left-hand needle and work as for first cast-off stitch (picture 12) until only one stitch remains, which will be on your right-hand needle

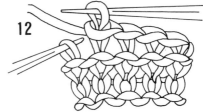

**12**

Cut off your yarn, leaving a small end, thread this end through the remaining stitch (picture 13) and pull tightly

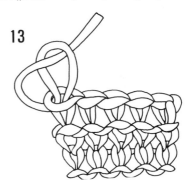

**13**

You can now knit, so why not put your new-found skill into making something wearable like a simple scarf? You'll need one pair of No.8 (4 mm) knitting needles and some double knitting wool in as many colours as you like. Cast on 48 stitches and work until required length. Cast off, then, with a wool needle (which is blunt with a large eye), weave in first and last tail ends of wool, and ends from knots. And there it is — your own hand-knitted scarf. Couldn't be simpler, could it?

## Some dream!

**Our dream holiday turned out to be a disaster. We were unable to stay in the hotel we had booked, and the one we ended up in was really dirty and the food was inedible. What can we do to get some compensation?**

I hope you complained to your holiday company rep or to the hotel manager while you were still there so they had a chance to put things right. To prove your case, you should have collected evidence — photographs, perhaps, and a record of your conversations with the rep or manager. Now you are back, you should take up your complaint with your travel agent. He is obliged to act on your behalf with the tour operator. If you didn't book through a travel agent, contact your tour operator direct. Again, keep a record of the steps you take and any letters you write.

If you are still dissatisfied, and the tour operator is a member of ABTA (Association of British Travel Agents, 55 Newman St, London W1 (tel: 01-637 2444), you can use the free conciliation service. Failing that, ABTA have an arbitration scheme (run by the Chartered Institute for Arbitrators) whose findings are binding. You may prefer to take action in the courts, although the Small Claims Court, where you can represent yourself, is only empowered to make awards up to £500, against £1,000 under ABTA's arbitration. If you need assistance, consult your local Trading Standards Officer or Consumer Advice Bureau.

## Clothes coach

**This summer I am going on a coach tour to California. Could you give me advice on the clothes I should take?**

The first rule is not to take too many clothes and don't bother with anything very formal. America is a very informal country and the only places which expect people to dress up are restaurants and hotels that are going to charge you far more than you will want to spend anyway.

The climate is tricky. California itself will be hot — in the 80°s on the coast and hotter still inland — but your bus will be air-conditioned and may get chilly. So have a sweater handy and avoid nylon. If you go into the mountains or visit San Francisco, both may be cool — which means sweaters again, particularly for the evening. In the city, I find shawls very practical. They look pretty and keep you warm. Generally, I'd opt for mix-and-match separates and one dress that won't crease. And do take comfortable walking shoes.

Finally, add a squashy shoulder-bag. Use it as hand-luggage on the long flight to the West Coast, and for your day-to-day clothes on the tour itself — then you won't need to unpack your case every night.

## Health wise

**I am going to Spain on holiday. Do I need to take any special precautions to protect my health?**

There are no compulsory vaccinations, but the DHSS recommend that everyone going anywhere in the Mediterranean should have a typhoid jab, which gives protection for three years. Around 200 cases of typhoid a year are reported in Britain. Most come from the Indian sub-continent but about 14 per cent are contracted by holiday-makers in Europe. The risks of typhoid in this country are minute: 0.4 people catch it per 100,000 population. Elsewhere they are greater: 53 cases per 100,000 in the case of Spain. So the jab *is* worth having.

There is also still a lot of polio in the world, and it can be caught at any age. The vaccination lasts five years and I think it is worth keeping up to date.

Otherwise take care with what you eat and drink. Beware of shellfish; ice cream sold by street vendors; unwashed salads; and, in unhygienic areas, ice in drinks.

To find out more, get leaflets SA30 and SA35 (Medical Costs Abroad and Protect Your Health Abroad) free from the DHSS.

## Budget breaks

**I read about all these glamorous holidays, but I just can't afford them. Isn't there anything for people like me?**

There are plenty of low-cost holidays, nearly all in this country. Caravans are not expensive and holiday centres are good value, especially for children because entertainment is included in the price. If you want a more energetic holiday, try

# Dear Judith...

youth hostels. In the Yorkshire Dales National Park, you can stay in converted field farms for £3 a night. Cycle-hire is inexpensive and there are a few companies packaging this with bed and breakfast in pubs. And do look at coach travel, before air or rail, both in this country and abroad.

Two tips which can be applied to just about all the holidays I've mentioned — take short breaks and go out of high season. Seaside hotels and a few guesthouses will now take people for a couple of nights rather than a whole week. The same goes for cabin cruisers on the rivers or the Broads. And even if you have children, you can avoid the top prices in the high season because you are entitled to take them out of school for two weeks a year for holidays.

For people with real problems, either financial or of health or handicap, there is an information centre which is run as a charity: The Holiday Care Service, 2 Old Bank Chambers, Station Rd, Horley, Surrey RH6 9HW (tel: Horley 74535).

## Shopping en famille

**I'm planning a family shopping weekend to one of the French Channel ports. Which should I choose?**
How much time do you have? Calais and Boulogne are only 75 minutes away from Dover by ferry, half that by hovercraft. Boulogne is more attractive with an old quarter and a number of good restaurants. There are good hypermarkets in both.

My favourite is Dieppe, four hours by Sealink from Newhaven. It has lovely shops and fish restaurants, plus a super market on Saturday mornings. Twice as far is St Malo, the great walled town rebuilt after the war. Brittany Ferries sail there from Portsmouth and Plymouth. A good guide to the French ports served by Townsend Thoresen — Calais, Le Havre and Cherbourg — is *French Entrée* by Patricia Fenn.

## Drive right

**I am taking my car abroad for the first time. What preparations should I make?**
It depends where you're going. For instance, in Spain you will need a bail bond; in Italy a translation of your licence. Both are available from the AA or RAC. In many European countries you should carry a warning triangle, in some a first-aid kit. French law requires you to carry a spare set of bulbs. In Germany, spectacle wearers should have a second pair in the car.

In general, get a Green Card Certificate from your insurance company. Although a British policy gives the minimum cover required in Common Market countries, you'd be alarmed to know just how minimal that cover would be!

Convert your headlamps for driving on the right. Your car instruction book may show you which part of the lens to mask, which will save you buying a kit.

Get the car serviced before the holiday and perhaps ask your garage to make you up a small kit of spares on a sale-or-return basis. And, please, *don't* try to drive too far in a day, particularly just after getting off a ferry.

## Worm in the Big Apple?

**My friend and I are thinking of going to New York, but just lately we have heard so much about it being unsafe. Would you and a lady-friend go alone?**
New York *is* a violent city. It is also one of the most thrilling places on earth. I've been there several times and never felt threatened. In fact, the humour and helpfulness of New Yorkers, particularly to the British, is one of its attractions.

But, I have never taken risks. I have avoided the "rough" areas; I don't walk at night. Above all, I have always taken the advice of the New Yorkers themselves.

*Need advice on where to go? What to pack, what to know? Whatever your problems, Travel Editor Judith Chalmers is here to help*

# My Secret Garden

Our gardening expert,
Kay Barton, has to be pretty
practical all year
round. So, just this once, we
thought we'd give
her the licence to dream: to create
— if only in her mind's
eye — the garden that is her
idea of paradise

THE trouble with dreams is that even the most realistic ones have a habit of galloping away with you.

Given thousands of pounds to spend on a dream wardrobe you'd probably find there weren't enough days in the year to wear all those clothes you yearn for — just as in my garden paradise I'd need about 48 hours in every day to look after it. But each part of it is a small dream in itself and could well become reality even in a tiny suburban patch.

So please, dream-maker, a modest request first of all for just two or three acres — enough to give privacy without pain and effort, and room to create within it an area to suit every mood. A breathtaking view that goes on for ever with magnificent, ancient trees on the horizon; some romantic woodland — haven for wildlife — and a pretty, trout-filled stream at the end of it; a cottage garden with well-stocked herbaceous borders, hollyhocks, lupins and a profusion of flowers for the picking; a stone terrace resplendent with fuchsia, pelargoniums, ivies and wisteria leading down to a sweetly scented herb garden; an old-fashioned kitchen garden, walled and sheltered with neat rows of abundant, healthy vegetables and fruit; and, best of all, a real secret garden…a magical place to relax and forget the cares of the world.

In the acres of my dreams, colours would be soft and subtle; scents heady and lingering to attract butterflies and bees. Even weeds would have their place. Life would be boring without a challenge and there's something therapeutically satisfying about pulling out weeds. But they'd be the manageable sort of course — or pretty enough to simply leave running wild!

But to get down to the delicious detail…

My *romantic woodland* would be planted with a carpet of snowdrops, bluebells and primroses for spring colour; everywhere there'd be wildflowers (to be left strictly alone) and, in the centre, a spectacular holly tree just like the one I came across by chance in the middle of a wood some 15 years ago.

The *cottage garden* would have old-fashioned hollyhocks and colourful lupins providing the backdrop to picture-postcard herbaceous borders. There'd be perennial flowers that bloom in spring as well as in summer and autumn to give a continuous display, and I would group several plants of one kind together to make attractive clumps rather than have odd ones dotted about. Tall ones like delphiniums and campanula at the back, medium ones like asters, phlox, coreopsis and aquilegia next, then low-growing plants at the front (ranunculus, potentilla, viola and armeria).

My cottage garden would have mature shrubs for shelter — a wealth of lovely, reassuring rhododendrons in mauves, pinks and white; and azaleas, honeysuckle, lilac and buddleia to attract butterflies and bees.

I'd leave a huge bed free for planting annuals and create a carpet of pinks and greens with bedding begonias, dianthus, ageratum, alyssum, gypsophila, lobelia, petunias, scabiosa.

Pink climbing roses would cover a side wall of my cottage garden — ones that bloom from June to October. They're so easy and rewarding for just a little judicious pruning in autumn and occasional spraying against black spot, greenfly and whitefly.

LARGE, weathered flagstones would make up the *terrace,* sheltered on one side with a screen of wisteria. I'd leave occasional gaps in the flagstones, fill them with soil and plant low-growing annuals like alyssum, or a "carpet" herb like camomile to provide scent and interest. Stone plant pots round the terrace would hold fuchsia, pelargoniums, trailing geraniums, ivies and lobelia. Experience has taught me to pack them with a mass of plants for best effect and to use a good soilless compost. I'd keep the compost from year to year but add a good handful of bone meal to it as well as extra fertiliser and peat to help it retain moisture.

To give interest at a higher level there'd be hanging baskets filled with flowers and greenery to match the pots below. I'd line them with sphagnum moss, fill them with a good potting compost and place the plants so that some trail over the edges.

The *herb garden* I see just below the terrace and not too far from the kitchen. I'd have it set out as a slightly smaller version of those traditional ones in ancient gardens of Elizabethan times, with triangles or squares of the different herbs separated by low-growing, neatly clipped box hedges or bricks between paving stones. Taller herbs would be in the middle, if the garden were an island bed — or at the back if against a wall or hedge. Most herbs like a sunny, south-facing position and well-drained soil, though mint and lovage will do quite well in partial shade. I'd keep the selection fairly simple and avoid the ones which have a tendency to take over. Parsley is a must, as are thyme, chives, marjoram, basil, sage, fennel and rosemary — and, of course, a bay tree. Different varieties of mint — ginger mint, apple mint, spearmint, pineapple mint — are lovely to have but I'd plant them individually in pots before putting them in the herb garden, to prevent them spreading like wildfire.

The nice thing about herbs is that they look so pretty as well as having endless practical uses in cooking, making your own cosmetics and medical

# My Secret Garden

potions, scenting drawers and storage cupboards around the house.

The *kitchen garden* would be well-stocked and orderly — and there'd be no finer sight! It would be like the one at a 15th century manor house I've stayed at in France: surrounded by huge stone walls that could tell a tale or two, but still getting plenty of sunlight. Sheltered, secure — a positive haven for pottering about amongst the peas and beans, cabbages and carrots! Part of the wall would face south — the perfect spot for luscious tomatoes and soft fruits like redcurrants and raspberries.

For sanity and to make life easier, I'd make sure that the plot was rectangular with straight edges (no fancy curved borders or fussy beds) and straight paths all the way round for accessibility.

"Five bean rows would I have there and a hive for the honeybee" — and, leading on from all this, a pretty little orchard of apple trees, pears, plums and damsons. (Dreams must include time for making

# Why Not Visit A Real-life Dream Garden?

Around the Realm gardens, full of creative ideas, are listed below. Admission charges vary from 50p up, with children half price.

**AVON**
**Crowe Hall**, Widcombe: beautiful trees, lawns, spring bulbs, walled gardens, Victorian grotto; old-fashioned shrubs and roses.
**Orchard House**, Claverton: herbs, alpines, ground cover and silver plants, rock gardens, herbaceous borders, lawns and shrubs.

**BERKSHIRE**
**Colnbrook Cottage,** Inkpen near Hungerford: 2½-acre garden with woodland on three sides; lots of shrubs, rhododendrons and azaleas; roses and herbaceous plants.
**The Old Rectory, Burghfield:** herbaceous borders, shrubs, roses, hellebores, plants from Japan and China; old-fashioned cottage plants.
**The Old Rectory, Farnborough:** unusual plants, fine view, herbaceous borders and old-fashioned roses.

**BUCKINGHAMSHIRE**
**Great Barfield**, Bradenham: bulbs, herbaceous borders, shrubs and young trees; lovely roses; ground cover in wood and shrub areas.

**CHESHIRE AND WIRRAL**
**Arley Hall**, near Knutsford: twin herbaceous borders, walled gardens, yew hedges, azaleas, rhododendrons, herb and scented gardens.

**CORNWALL**
**Trengwainton,** 2m NW of Penzance: shrub garden with stream and lovely view over bay; walled garden with precious plants.

**CUMBRIA**
**Levens Hall** near Kendal: topiary garden, formal bedding and herbaceous borders; fine trees.

**DEVON**
**Lower Coombe Royal,** Kingsbridge: historic woodland; rhododendrons, camellias, azaleas, magnolias and rare trees; terraces and herbaceous borders.
**Putsborough Manor,** Georgeham, near Barnstaple: old thatched house, herbaceous border and stream with waterside plants, primulas; walled garden.

**DORSET**
**Abbotsbury Gardens,** Abbotsbury: a magical place full of rhododendrons, camellias, azaleas and unusual trees and roaming peacocks.

**GLOUCESTERSHIRE**
**Barnsley House**, near Cirencester: old garden with shrubs and trees, ground cover plants, herbaceous borders, pond garden, laburnum walk; knot, herb and kitchen gardens; old summer house.
**Kingsmead**, Didmarton, near Badminton: huge variety of roses; old kitchen garden; topiary yew house.

**HAMPSHIRE**
**Field House,** Monxton: 2-acre garden with herbaceous borders and orchard; chalk pit garden with pond and kitchen garden.

**HEREFORD AND WORCESTER**
**Abbey Dore Court,** bordered by river Dore: herbaceous plants and shrubs,

endless pots of jam and delicious preserves.)

Finally my real *secret garden*…Reached through a door in the wall, a peaceful place for just grass, tall enveloping shrubs, sweet-scented roses and a summerhouse with soft cushioned seats. A private place for dreaming, reading, writing and getting away from it all. No cars or juggernauts can be heard. Nothing to do but a little gentle rose pruning and grass cutting occasionally, where only the birds sing and no bugs or beasties interfere with nature's nicest side. The very stuff that dreams are made of. "Tread softly for you tread on my dreams…"

ferns, circular herb garden, walled kitchen garden with orchard and vines.

## KENT
**Groombridge Place**, Groombridge: walled gardens, herbaceous borders and moated 17th century house.
**Hever Castle**, Hever, near Edenbridge: Italian and landscaped garden with statuary, sculpture, topiary and lake.
**Knole**, Sevenoaks: landscape garden, herb garden and deer park.
**Scotney Castle,** nr Lamberhurst: picturesque landscape garden surrounding 14th century, moated castle.
**Sissinghurst Castle** garden, Sissinghurst: famous and inspirational; spring garden, green and white garden, cottage garden, herb garden, romantic walks; Tudor buildings and tower. My real dream garden!

## NORTHAMPTONSHIRE
**Cottesbrooke Hall,** near Creaton: formal and wild gardens, herbaceous borders, old cedars, greenhouses and kitchen garden.

## OXFORDSHIRE
**Blenheim Palace,** Woodstock: original grounds and garden by Henry Wise; later additions by the famous Capability Brown.
**Dower House,** Stonor, near Henley-on-Thames: old garden refurbished, old-fashioned shrub roses, vegetable garden, clipped yew. — backed by Stonor Park.

## SHROPSHIRE
**Burford House Gardens,** near Tenbury Wells: flowering shrubs, herbaceous plants, rolling lawns.

## SOMERSET
**Orchardleigh Park,** near Frome: terraced gardens, attractive views over lake and park; old walled kitchen garden.

## SURREY
**Hascombe Court,** Godalming: originally conceived by Gertrude Jekyll; herbaceous border, sunken garden, terrace gardens, woodlands, azaleas, rhododendrons.

## SUSSEX
**Great Dixter**, near Northiam: topiary, huge variety of plants, and historic house.
*These and scores of other private gardens open in aid of the National Gardens Scheme (which helps many deserving causes) are listed in a booklet,* Gardens Open to the Public, *available from good booksellers.*

# The Holiday Diary of

# ADRIAN MOLE

## (aided and abetted by Sue Townsend)

**In which Adrian discovers that heaven and hell are but a pebble's throw apart, and that holiday romances cost a packet...**

*PEBBLECOMBE NEXT-TO-SEA CARAVAN SITE*

## SATURDAY:
## The First Day of My Holiday

We arrived here after a tortuous journey in the car. My father made us leave home at 3 am to try and beat the holiday traffic but it appeared that everyone else nad the same idea. By 5 am the roads were clogged with yawning drivers. My mother read two of her holiday books to fill in the time and I wrote a sixteen-page letter to Pandora. We've only been apart for one day but I am already longing for her. Haven't seen much of the camp site so far. It was dark when we got here.

## SUNDAY

So much for the brochure extolling the virtues of Pebblecombe-next-to-Sea Caravan Site! "The luxury mini-homes set in gently undulating parkland with full amenities and Kiddies Corner" are, in fact, plywood caravans on bricks set in severely potholed scrubland with a disgusting toilet block (cold water only). Kiddies Corner is a swing with a dirty sand pit. Stayed in caravan reading. Haven't seen the sea yet. It is two miles away and my father refused to take me in the car. He said, "You can walk and get some sea air!"

## MONDAY

Saw the sea. It looked cold, grey and horrible. A few people were swimming in it. They were pretending to enjoy themselves. I huddled behind a windbreak and read *Treasure Island*. My parents sat in the car in the car park staring at the sea.

## TUESDAY

Breakfast was late this morning because the gas bottle emptied before the bacon was cooked. Me and my father took the empty bottle back to the camp office and demanded a full one, plus a credit for nine rashers of back bacon at the camp-site luxury shop-around-the-clock. The camp commandant accused us of being "recklessly extravagant" with the gas and said that his shop anyway stocked only streaky. My father took the opportunity to have a big row about conditions of the camp site. The commandant said, "You can always leave, I've got people queuing up for a caravan!" And it was true! A line of cars was waiting behind the barbed wire enclosure. We carried the full gas bottle back and fitted it. My mother moaned that she wasn't having much of a holiday without her labour-saving machines or hot water. She said she wanted to be "spoiled in a hotel for a change".

## WEDNESDAY

Went to a model village. I trod on a church which had been carelessly positioned, so we had to leave before anybody noticed it.

## THURSDAY

The sun came out today. I couldn't take my shirt off because I've got twenty-one spots on my back. But it was quite pleasant to lie on a striped beach towel and watch girls and women in bikinis walking about fetching sand-wiches and jugs of tea, etc.

## FRIDAY 2 pm

My mother has gone on strike! She said she won't fetch any more water from the stand pipe and won't wash the clothes in the toilet block washbasins. But most serious of all, she said she won't do any more cooking on the mini cooker. Ate fish and chips for lunch but am dead worried about tonight's meal.

### GRAND HOTEL
### PEBBLECOMBE-NEXT-TO-SEA

## SATURDAY 7.30 am

My first stay in a proper hotel! I've got my own room (washbasin, H & C, black and white TV)! I have never known such luxury! My mother is dead happy. My father agreed to move here after he tried to cook a meal on the caravan stove. This hotel has got a disco so I might meet a girl and have a holiday romance. Must stop now — the breakfast gong has just sounded.

1.30 pm: I have just been told off by the manager of the hotel for keeping a starfish in my washbasin.

## SUNDAY

Went to the hotel disco last night, met a girl called Heidi. She is dead good looking but is a mere child of twelve, much too immature for a man of the world like me. I could tell she fell madly in love with me. My parents showed me up by doing old-fashioned dancing to modern records. I did a bit of body popping but hurt my head and had to retire early. My mother laughed and said it was less dangerous doing the Twist. Went for a walk along the beach today. Found a piece of drift-wood that looked like our dog so I brought it back to my room as a reminder. I hope the dog doesn't resent being at home with Grandma. It wrecks holidays so it's only got itself to blame. Wrote twenty-page letter to Pandora on the hotel's headed note-paper. I hope she will be impressed. I didn't mention Heidi.

## MONDAY

Tasted my first cocktail today. It was comp-letely yukky! Full of fruit and umbrellas and plastic sticks. I don't know why adults rave about them. My mother had three! She sat on a stool in the Waikiki Adventure Lounge and showed a lot of her legs. My father had a pint of bitter and talked to the barman about electric storage heaters. The barman look-ed dead bored. Perhaps he is more used to hearing tales of pillage and terror on the High Seas. Heidi was on the beach today. She doesn't look twelve in her swimsuit. She looked dead old. Fourteen at least! I wonder how old Pandora looks in hers.

## TUESDAY

I have spent all my holiday money in the am-usement arcades in a vain attempt to sec-ure a suitable present for Pandora. It just seemed to vanish into the slots. My father hit the jackpot. It's not fair. He's already got loads of money. It's true that the rich get richer while the poor get poorer.

## WEDNESDAY

My father relented and gave me five pounds today so I invited Heidi to join me on the fun fair. What a mistake! She wanted to go on all the fast rides (she was particularly vic-ious on the Dodgems). I was glad when the money ran out. Got back to the hotel to find that my parents had hung a "Do Not Disturb" sign on their door so I had nothing to do but write another long letter to Pandora and send cards to Bert Baxter, Queenie and Grandma. I chose a rude one for the Baxters and a scenic view for Grandma. I asked her to show it to the dog.

## THURSDAY

Had a picnic on the beach today. It was a disaster! Just as my mother had spread every-thing out on a bath towel a gang of rowdy girls ran by and kicked sand over the feast. My father blamed the upsurge of feminism. He said that years ago girls walked slowly and demurely. It's true that the girls stopped and apologised. But I couldn't help agreeing with my father — life would be a lot easier if girls and women were quieter. Even Pandora, I sometimes think.

## FRIDAY

Spent the day buying sticks of rock and pack-ing my six suitcases. Had some difficulty fitting the driftwood in. Then had a last walk around Pebblecombe. It does not have the flashy attractions of bigger re-sorts but I have enjoyed my second week here. When I am famous the hotel will have a plaque outside saying, "Adrian Mole slept here".

# HOMELY WAYS TO LIVE IN STYLE

**It's not money that gives your home that special something, but how you mix colours, adapt odd corners, display pretty things. It's combining flair and imagination to let your personality shine through**

Chances are that most of the people you know with a flair for furnishing don't spend a small fortune on their homes. It's the pictures they choose and the way they hang them ... their gift for mixing colour, pattern and texture ... the objects they collect and put on display ... the care they take over details ... that add up to that special something called style.

It's also having the eye to use old furniture and objects in new and unexpected ways.

It could be something as simple as transforming a pretty old teapot with a broken lid into a bulb or plant container, or turning the mirror of a discarded wardrobe into the focal point of a hallway by hanging it horizontally and adding new moulding or a wallpaper border.

In the living room pictured opposite you can see how easily junk or throw-away pieces can be adapted or restored.

The streamlined sideboard was originally a 1950s horror with spindly legs and an ugly shelf with sliding glass panels on top. We sawed off the legs, top, door and drawer handles, then added a new wooden top, round knobs and a few coats of paint to work the basic transformation. We painted an old frame to show off a modern print in matching colours for a super stylish finishing touch.

The dining chair near the window was a throw-away which we made a perfectly presentable part of our furnishing scheme by giving it a thorough clean-up and covering the seat in coordinating fabric.

As for the coffee table, our only expense was new timber for the top. The base is an old, once white, metal stand (taken with the owner's permission from a skip) with its legs cut down and painted dark blue.

Far too smart for the dirty washing now, the old linen basket — with two coats of paint — makes a perfect lamp and telephone table and doubles as a useful storage box.

With just a modest flair for DIY, you can renovate old furniture or build anew, copying designs that would otherwise cost the earth. The alcove shelving (right) for instance is much more unusual and interesting than ordinary shelves and brackets, and is simple for a handyperson to copy. A plank rests diagonally from the top of the skirting board to the outside wall of the chimney breast. (It's secured with screws to the wall above the skirting.) The shelves are supported on the left with battens screwed into the wall. The other end of each shelf is cut at a slant (with the aid of an adjustable square) to fit against the diagonal plank where it's secured with panel pins. What a marvellous place for showing off plants, a lamp, books or a charming collection of personal treasures!

Here the unifying factor is colour which pulls everything together to create one homely, restful room. We toned the cushion covers and the curtains to coordinate with our DIY renovations and choose a rug to echo the general theme.

Planning how to light a room is also well worth it. Yes, you want a good general light but you also need concentrated areas for reading or sewing or for illuminating special objects — such as a shelf arrangement or pictures. And you can add a soft mood light for background.

But there aren't any rules. If you live in a flat and pine for a country cottage, you can sand your floors and seal the boards with varnish. It's what you like that counts. Style means putting your own personality into every room of the house and it's a fair bet that the parts of the house which please you most were your own idea, perhaps inspired by pictures you've seen, but adapted by you to fit your home. So turn the page for more stylish ideas to suit yourself — and happy home-making!

Stylish budget-beaters are the converted coffee table, the new-look sideboard and smart telephone table, sanded floorboards and full-length curtains made up from pretty sheeting

Break away from ordinary shelving by adapting this elegant diagonal design

Even outdated 1950s furniture can be revamped with care — and a little paint

# HOMELY WAYS TO LIVE IN STYLE

## SAY IT WITH FLOWERS

In the nicest possible way, with tubs of flowers and pretty hanging baskets at your front door

## FRAME-UPS

Groups of pictures have more impact than a solitary print, which just gets lost in the middle of a wall. Here cards are set off by fabric and wallpaper mounts and frames painted with gloss car paint

## COLLECTORS' PIECES

Instead of arranging plates on shelves on a dresser, mount them on the wall to make a bright, eye-catching display. Start your own collection at jumbles or look out for "seconds"

## BORDER LINES
Stencilling is fun, inexpensive and produces charming and unexpected effects. Look how the pattern around the mirror extends its importance and gives a Spanish feel to the whole hall. The delicate tracery around the doors brings the garden inside all year round

## LOCAL COLOUR
For a lovely hint of nostalgia, cover a small round table with a floor-length cloth to match your decor then throw a lace cloth over the top. Notice how the blue and white theme is carried on through the wall colour, fabric, painted wicker chair and table ornaments and even the bric-a-brac on the alcove shelves

# SO YOU CAN'T DO A THING WITH YOUR HAIR?

Don't you believe it! For with our
tricks-of-the-trade guidelines you can make your hair do
pretty well anything you want.
So shape up and get set to be your own home hairdresser!

## STYLING YOUR HAIR

There are so many good home hairdressing aids on the market today that styling really is as easy as you want to make it.

Setting lotions, mousses and gels — applied to clean, wet hair — help protect it from excessive heat when drying it, prevent static, help give it body and add volume to your finished style.

Hairspray — used to help create an effect rather than as a fixative dressing after the event — can also achieve more volume and help hold a style without it looking too contrived. For up-to-date hair — whatever the style — should be worn au naturel.

Anna has fine, rather flat hair. We showed her two different, equally pretty, ways to give it extra body and movement with a bubbly roller set (below) or with a more casual, blow-dried style, overleaf.

**ROLLER SETTING**
Avoid roller marks on scalp by creating uneven sections with a tailcomb. You can adopt this technique whether you're using ordinary rollers, heated rollers, creating pin curls — or even using curling tongs. Wind rollers in alternate directions to prevent a "set" effect

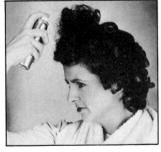

When hair is dry, remove rollers and backcomb curls at the roots to disguise any "tram lines" remaining and to give maximum root lift where you want it. Then spray each section at the roots with a little hairspray. This will help support the extra lift you have just achieved with your set

Finish styling by pulling wodges into shape all over the head, then by separating ends with fingertips to create curls

## BLOW-DRYING

Section the front (top right), then blow-dry the back with a round styling brush, twiddling it all the time that heat is being applied to avoid any brush marks on the hair. Repeat with the side sections. Apply a little styling mousse (bottom right) to the front sections, paying particular attention to the roots. Blow-dry with an upward movement. When hair is dry, toss head upside down and run your fingers through your hair. This will give your blow-dried style a much softer look (see below) and also help stop it looking too contrived

# TRIMMING YOUR HAIR

Obviously when it comes to a total restyle, there's no substitute for a really professional haircut. But it's very simple to keep an overgrown fringe looking tidy and prolong the life of your cut.

Firstly, remember to cut hair dry — it's easier to see how it wants to fall. Use thinning scissors — available from department stores — that have one straight blade and one serrated cutting edge. They trim fewer hairs in one snip than conventional scissors and give a more natural, graduated effect. Just remember to keep the blades horizontal (use your browline as a rough guide) and trim along two levels to prevent a hard cutting line. (But not more than twice, or you'll be taking off more than you bargained for!) Thicker hair will need more sections; there are no hard and fast rules as to how many, because hair thickness and texture vary so much.

Joy (above) had a layered style that had grown out much too far. We showed her how to tidy it by trimming the fringe.

Make a centre parting to ensure that the end result is even and grip your hair firmly on each side

Take a ¼-inch section halfway across fringe and, holding thinning scissors halfway up the section, cut right into hair, keeping scissors horizontal. Cut across section again, this time nearer the ends of the fringe. Thinning hair twice in this way gives a more graduated effect

Continue taking ¼-inch sections, further back into the fringe, being careful not to cut into hair at the sides. The thicker your hair, the more sections you'll need. Repeat with the remaining half of the fringe

Thin uneven sides — without sectioning off — by combing hair straight down, then using the thinning technique, first about two inches deep, and again nearer the tips of the hair. Repeat with other side. Style hair by combing an "extra hold" setting lotion through towel-dried hair, then tip head forward and dry off hair upside down for a tousled, natural-looking finish (left)

# PERMING YOUR HAIR

First of all, enlist a friend's help. You won't be able to manage the back. Both perming and our "taming" technique put your hair through chemical processes that work by altering its basic structure. So it's important that you take every precaution to get the best results! Always allow yourself enough time, and set out all your equipment before you start, so that you won't interrupt a critical timing stage. Follow any pack instructions to the letter and, as well as handling your hair as gently as possible throughout the processing, pamper it with conditioning treatments afterwards and dry using a low heat setting.

Our perming technique — using the new type of sponge permers on the crown — gives a soft, natural effect. These permers are more suitable for fine hair with a natural kink of its own — if your hair's straight, use conventional rods all over the head. Choose the larger type and take ¼-inch sections so that you get natural curl and maximum root lift. You can use any home perm kit — most of them have a version for curls and another for gentle waves. Carol (above) has good, thick hair; we showed her how to perm it for a chic style that balances bounce with control.

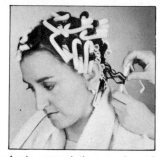

Section off bottom half of clean, damp hair and wind down with conventional perm rods, taking care to wrap each section with tissue end papers and then to roll up smoothly. This avoids buckling the ends, which can lead to frizz

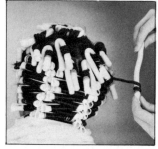

Wind top half in sponge permers, taking approximately 1-inch sections. Twist each strand, use end papers to hold in place, tuck ends neatly under near one end and wind up to scalp so that hair covers one half of the permer. When you reach the roots, bend the permer in half to hold in place

Apply perm lotion evenly with a sponge, making sure each section is saturated. Hair is ready for neutralising when it forms an "s" shape. Half unwind a perm rod and push hair gently back towards scalp to test whether it's ready. Check every 5 minutes. Rinse thoroughly with warm water. Blot with towel

Apply neutraliser generously to rods and permers only. Follow timing instructions on the pack. Before rinsing off, unwind hair gently and work neutraliser into curls with finger tips. Easiest styling? Apply hair gel while it's still damp, dry naturally, occasionally fluffing out with head upside down

# TAMING YOUR HAIR

If you have tried to give your hair a body wave, but the results have turned out too tight, you could try our "relaxing" technique a day or two after your disaster. Unlike conventional straightening methods that use two chemical processes, we are suggesting a much softer option to help you tame that unwanted frizz

Just comb through the neutraliser from a standard home perm kit and follow our instructions on conditioning your hair immediately afterwards. You will still have some natural movement in your hair — but it will be much easier to blow-dry, it will stay looking neat and tidy throughout the day, and see that you don't frizz up when it drizzles! When Linda

(right) had a perm the curl turned out far too tight for her liking. We showed her how to tame the frizz into gentler waves. She was delighted with the sophisticated result. Don't forget that there are also simple styling techniques that can "loosen up" hair that's too curly (naturally or otherwise!). Just take larger sections when using rollers and use the biggest ones you can find — to help give a more casual, but still bouncy and buoyant result.

Apply neutraliser to clean, towel-dried hair using a medium toothed comb. (Never use metal combs — they'll react with the chemicals and may damage hair.) Keep combing hair straight for about 15 to 20 minutes, taking care not to pull or drag it

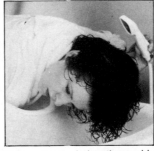

Rinse your hair thoroughly with warm water. Towel dry hair — gently, though — to remove the excess water

Apply a conditioning treatment pack without rubbing or stretching hair. Then wrap it in a plastic bag and keep in the warm for a further 20 minutes. Use a hood dryer, or else have a warm bath — the heat helps the conditioner to penetrate your hair and work more effectively

When your time is up, remove bag and work the conditioner into hair without rubbing scalp. Comb through so that it's well distributed and allow hair to cool off to help its outer protective layer — the cuticle — close up. Finally, rinse with cool water. Blow dry back from face, with gentle heat

# Ring o' Roses

**It's 1665 and the golden reign of Charles II is five years old. So, with the Merry Monarch on his throne is all well with the world? Not necessarily, and certainly not when you're just seventeen, headstrong and betrothed against your will ...**

Standing at the window of her chamber, a room jutting out over a cobbled street in the Holborn district of London, Jane Verney talked aloud to herself.

"I am fortunate indeed," she told the slanting roofs across the street, putting a deal of emphasis into each word. "I am seventeen years old, and at the end of this new year, which is but one hour old, I will be the blessed and well-loved wife of Samuel Reeves. By then he will have come down from Cambridge and be qualified to practise as a physician. We will live in a fine house, bought for us by his father, and furnished for us by my father, and Samuel will tend none but the rich who will pay him well for his services." She swallowed hard, feeling the ache of tears in her throat, and then continued with resolution: "Samuel is so very good and kind, and he loves me with all his heart, and I love him and will grow to tolerate him touching me." She raised her eyes with pious gratitude to the low ceiling. "And I am truly mindful of my good fortune, Lord. Amen," she added for good measure, then padded softly back to bed over the creaking floorboards. Turning her head into the softness of her pillow, she wept. And as Jane wept in the upstairs chamber of the Silver Still, her father's apothecary shop, in the early hours of the first day of 1665, her parents, William and Elizabeth Verney, were in the downstairs parlour, entertaining Samuel Reeves' mother and father. Celebrating both the betrothal and the coming of the New Year.

Still waiting and willing a sleep that would not

come, Jane winced as the sound of her father's booming laugh filtered up through the floorboards of her chamber. She could imagine him slapping a fat thigh, throwing his head back, laughing at his own jokes.

"Samuel Reeves?" she had said slowly when her father had first told of his plans for her. "The son of Mr Reeves with the big house in Lombard Street? I like him well enough, but liking is not loving, Father."

"*Love?*" William Verney's laugh had boomed out. "*Love?* Well, my dear, that will come when you are wed. Does it mean naught to you, Jane, that you have captured the heart of the son of a man with a house in Lombard Street and a property in Essex? Not counting his warehouse down by the river. You will worry your poor mother into an early grave if you persist in such foolishness."

"I haven't said I will *refuse* Samuel," Jane had said, "but I want..." Then she'd bit her lip and hung her head, not knowing what it was she wanted, but feeling, with a strange yearning in her blood, that it was something more than Samuel Reeves.

How could she tell her father that when Samuel kissed her, it made her feel physically sick? So sick that when she had pushed him away in disgust, he had interpreted her gesture as one of maidenly virtue, thinking he understood, when perversely she hadn't wanted him to understand.

Here in the privacy of her bedchamber, she could admit it to herself. She didn't deserve to be adored as Samuel adored her. She wasn't trying hard enough to love him back. But it was no good. His very kindness and patience irritated her, and his way of staring at her with his mouth half open made her want to laugh out loud. Or cry. Then ask herself why she was crying ...

Desperately Jane tried to bring to mind the image of his face. Round, pleasant, broad nose slightly flattened; a dumpling of a face, a lock of hair falling in a neglected wave over his forehead. Jane imagined him neglecting it deliberately in front of his mirror each morning.

It was no good. Now that she saw him clearly she wished him gone.

*P*ulling a blanket from her bed and draping it over her shoulders, she moved to the window again. In the adjoining room, with only a thin layer of lath and plaster separating them, her beloved younger sister Mary snored gently, recovering from a feverish cold. Laughing, rosy-cheeked, chatterbox Mary would never cause her parents to sigh with distress and bewilderment as they did on the many occasions when their elder daughter flung herself from the room in a burst of temper.

At the sound of a familiar voice in the street below, Jane hitched up her blanket and leaned further out of the window.

"Tom?" she called softly, and a tall young man, after a quiet word to his companions, left the shadows to stand beneath her window looking up at her.

Jane could sense that he was smiling even as he reproached her. As usual, when he talked to her, William Verney's senior apprentice teased without disrespect, making mockery of her moods.

"Mistress Jane! Fie on you! What are you doing, hanging halfway out of your bedchamber talking to one of your father's servants? Showing yourself off in your nightgown like a common tavern wench? I swear I blush with shame for you."

And at once Jane's black mood was gone, and she was herself again, her generous mouth curved into laughter, her blue eyes dancing with delight.

"Where have you been?" she whispered urgently. "To the Mitre? Tell me about it. Or have you been to the Playhouse in Lincoln's Fields again? Tell me *everything*. Stay and talk to me! Tom!"

Then at the sudden sound of her father's voice behind her, she gave a startled cry, and as she put a hand to her throat, the blanket slipped to the floor.

Swaying slightly from the effects of the wine he'd drunk, his eyes glittering with anger, William Verney faced his daughter, his whole body quivering with indignation.

"Get back into bed!" he ordered.

"It was only Tom, Father," Jane was saying, shivering as she pulled the bed sheets close round her neck. "He was coming down the street with some of his friends, and I heard them singing and talking, so I called out to them. Don't blame Tom, Father."

"I tell you, Jane, you anger me so at times I could take a stick to you right willingly. You might look like a woman, but 'tis like a child you behave. Why, even your little sister has a greater notion of what is right and wrong than you have."

Jane shrank further down into her mattress. Her father's anger frightened her.

"How many times do I have to tell you?" he was saying now, standing over her bed, the candle flame throwing his shadow on the white walls, beetle-like and grotesque. "How many times do I have to tell you that it is not seemly for you to be so ... so familiar with Tom Baxter?

"He's but an apprentice, even though he's been bound to me for more than his eight years. He has no ambition. But for me he'd have gone to the poor house and finished up as a street porter or a waterman. God knows he seeks their company often enough.

"And what would Samuel's mother and father think if they knew what you were about? Where is the *dignity* in your behaviour? Come the end of the year you'll be setting up house with Samuel and entertaining his rich patients. Isn't it time you started to fit yourself for such a position? Why can't you be more like your sister? Why must you always provoke me so? Not a moment's trouble has Mary caused your mother and me, nay, not since the day she was born. Why can't you accept things for the way they must be, as she does?"

"Oh Lord," Jane said piously, as her father left, "if I am to marry Samuel Reeves — and I do love him, 'tis just his touch I can't abide — help me to be a good wife. Amen."

Then she remembered something else.

"And let Mrs Doughty finish my new gown so that Samuel may see it when he calls."

It was halfway through February before Samuel Reeves left his chambers in Cambridge to see his beloved. Told of his coming by a long letter full of wild utterances of love, Jane had been so flattered that she had felt romantically obliged to carry the closely written sheets of paper tucked down the front of her bodice for a whole day.

And that morning she awoke to the sound of a bird singing its heart out in the back garden.

"'Tis far too early for birdsong," she told herself as she splashed cold water on her face and arms. She wanted to breakfast alone before her father was about, dreading the heavy-handed teasing he seemed to think was in order when Samuel was due to pay them a visit.

Besides this, she liked to talk to Prue, sensing that in the family servant she had an ally, even though Prue did have a tendency to tut-tut at everything she said.

No one could impart bad news with such relish as Prue, and even good news worried her with the surety that it could not last.

"Another spotted fever burial in St Giles last week," she was saying now. "My brother Edmund says there's a house in Drury Lane, and people cross over to the other side rather than pass it by. He says, Edmund does, that folks are saying 'tis the *plague* and not the spotted fever.

"He says the authorities are hiding the truth from the people on orders from the Lord Mayor himself. He says the truth is that the graveyards are full of corpses lying dead of the plague.

Jane widened her eyes in mock horror. She was used to pandering to Prue's morbid fancies. She got up from her chair, placed a hand on her brow and closed her eyes to add to the drama.

"Then if your brother is right and the sickness is fast creeping towards Holborn, it may well be that one day — maybe this very day — some poor soul suffering from it will enter my father's shop in search of medication."

"Oh, my Gawd!" said Prue, enjoying every minute of the impromptu performance.

Jane swayed as if overcome.

"Ah yes. I can see the wretch clearly, saliva dripping from his open mouth, the sores on his hands festering even as he stretches them across the counter for the lotion which will not do him the slightest good."

"Don't *touch* him!" squealed Prue, not sure now what was real and what was being imagined.

"Too late," Jane sighed. "There will be one more grave to be dug before this day is done."

Then, with a final anguished glance around her, she hurried from the parlour, leaving Prue staring after her.

"She's not ready for marriage, that one," she told herself. "Too flighty by half, and I knows who she's gone a-looking for now, and no good will come of that either."

Jane knew where Tom was likely to be at that time of a morning, and so she found him, rolling pills in the darkest corner of the still-room.

"Wouldn't it be better if you lit a candle?" she asked, leaning close to him. So close that he could see the growth of down on the lobes of her ears where her long hair had been looped back.

Didn't she *know* the effect she had on him?

"I can pill-roll in the dark, as well you know, Mistress Jane," he said, refusing to look at her. "And what brings you from your bed so early? Is it because that fine fellow you are to marry is coming a-calling today? He'll soon find out after you're wed what a lazy creature you really are."

"Oh, Tom," Jane said, laying a hand over his arm so that he was forced to stop what he was doing. "Why are you always so cross with me these days?"

How beautiful she was! Supposing he were to cover her hand with his own? Supposing he gave way to the intense longing to caress her wrist with his thumb, the underside where the blue veins ran, where her pulse beat? Slowly, slowly, whilst his eyes held hers and their heartbeats quickened ...

Closing his eyes for a moment and trying hard to shake the image from his mind, Tom opened them again to see what surely could not be a tear trembling on her long eyelashes. Oh, dear God, if she cried, he would take her in his arms and comfort her, even if she were Reeves' betrothed.

"This morning," she was saying, and her soft voice was unsteady, "as I dressed, just as dawn came, I heard a bird singing, Tom. I told Prue, but she seems to think it is an ill omen. It was singing as if it knew it was free; as if it knew it could spread its wings and fly away. And it could fly away, Tom. It could, and I cannot. And you can't fly away either, Tom. We are prisoners, both of us." She sighed. "I must marry because it is expected of me, and you must stay with my father although you have served your time and should have been turned over long ago. Does it not make you feel sad, Tom? Not sad all the time, but at moments like ..."

"Moments, Mistress Jane?"

"When a bird sings?" she said.

For a long moment they stood together, quite still, while from the cobbled street outside came the sound of London waking to another day.

Then, at a sound in the passage out side the still-room, Jane withdrew her hand, and left his side, her small feet in their slip-shoes making soft padding noises on the bare floor.

And after she'd gone, Tom Baxter, a man of

three and twenty, a nothing, a nobody, who but for William Verney's generosity would have been sent to the poor house, put his head in his hands and groaned aloud.

When the long awaited day was over, and Samuel had gone away again, Jane was able to tell herself that her deep despair of the morning had been completely unwarranted, mere fearful tricks of childish fancy.

Samuel, seen in the flesh, and not in the fevered imaginings of her mind, had been his usual good-humoured self. Sitting in the side parlour on a high-backed chair with the buttons of his waistcoat done up wrongly so that a left-over piece dangled down at the front, he'd listened avidly to her mother's non-stop rambling conversation. And while he'd listened, Jane had carefully observed him.

"I do love him really," she'd mused, as her betrothed was chatting cosily to her mother. "I love him because he is so kind. He must realise that my mother's views are never listened to in this house, and I do believe he is sensitive enough to sense her loneliness. It must be that, for he cannot be interested in the rapid rise in the price of seacoal, or in the fact that my aunt Henrietta has had three new gowns since Christmas."

But Samuel, she had had to admit, after another long hour had gone by, was apparently not feigning interest. His pale bulbous eyes were alight with it, and there was a look of complete concentration on his round face, as he smiled and nodded at all the right times.

As if he were another woman, Jane had decided peevishly, and a boring old woman at that, and wished she might make her escape to laugh and joke with Tom in the shop.

When Prue had shuffled in with a taper to light the tall candles, Jane had had to suppress a deep sigh of relief.

"The darkness is coming long before it has any right to do," the servant had grumbled, "even for the time of the year. And I swear we'll have snow. I can feel it a-coming in my big toe." Then, her task done she'd bobbed a plaintive curtsy in Samuel's direction. "I hope this cruel cold day finds you well, sir."

"Very well indeed, thank you, Prue," Samuel had said, only to be warned that whilst she was glad to hear it, she hoped he'd take great care on his journey back to Cambridge, as the road was infested by rogues and vagabonds of such ferocity that they'd kill you stone dead as soon as look at you.

Even Samuel was diverted.

"Is she always so brimming over with mirth?" he had asked as the door closed behind Prue.

Jane nodded. "Even her back looks sad, doesn't it? Only this morning she was telling me about the rumour that plague has broken out in St Giles. She has a brother Edmund, and last week he had a visitation in which everyone living in London died

of the plague, leaving the streets empty, with grass growing from between the cobbles."

She was smiling as she spoke, but then saw to her surprise that Samuel had taken her seriously.

A look of fear had clouded his pale eyes. "Only last week one of my tutors told us of a theory that the disease is passed on by tiny worms which lay their eggs on the skin or in folds of the clothing. 'Tis worse than the Black Death which eliminated one-third of England's population. Then they died quickly; this plague sends men mad with pain first."

To her astonishment Jane had seen that his eyes were wet.

"What is it, Samuel?" she'd whispered, and held out her arms.

And kneeling down awkwardly, he'd come into them, and she'd stroked his hair, conscious that for the first time she was holding him of her own volition. But there was nothing of passion in her embrace. Her impulsive gesture was the one a mother might make to her child.

"Tell me what distresses you, dear," she'd whispered.

"They brought a corpse for us to dissect," Samuel had said, and his voice broke. "I was so filled with horror, so afraid that if I went too near and breathed in that terrible smell, I would catch the sickness. So I hung back until one of them pulled me forward. 'Come closer, Reeves,' he said. 'Look at this!' And I looked and oh, God, will I ever forget what I saw? I am ashamed to tell you that I swooned."

"It was but a natural thing to do," Jane said softly.

He shook his head fiercely.

"Not a natural thing for a man in his final year of medicine to do, Jane. Oh, love, I was paralysed with horror. Me! Doctor Samuel Reeves soon to be. Soon to take an oath that I will help my fellow men. I was *afraid*, Jane — nay, more than afraid. Appalled."

Looking down at his bowed head, pity welling in her heart, Jane had been exultant. All doubts vanished as if they'd never been. Samuel *needed* her. And when his farewell kiss touched not her lips, but her forehead, Jane had told herself that it was not relief she felt, but maidenly gratitude at his concern for her virtue.

That night, Jane sat quietly for a long time, without moving, then she picked up her hand mirror, and holding the candle so that the light fell on her face, told herself she looked different.

"I love him," she said, then she said it again before taking up her comb and slowly, pleasurably running it through the length of her yellow hair.

When they were married, Samuel would perhaps do this. In the privacy of their chamber he would kneel by her side, and his hand would caress her neck beneath the soft weight of her hair. In the mirror she saw herself doing this. And saw the way her eyes dilated wide with apprehension.

And for no reason at all that she could fathom, she remembered the way the bird had sung its heart out that morning.

She had wanted to fly away then, and she had told Tom about it, and he had been angry. Why had he been angry?

She stared at herself, eyes questioning, mouth slightly open, hair sleek as sun-warmed butter.

She had told Tom about the singing bird. A pity she had forgotten to tell Samuel. He might have understood.

Then her eyes slid away from her own reflection as she faced the truth. In her heart she knew Samuel would *never* understand.

# Chapter 2

It was April before Samuel came again to the Silver Still, and then it was to help his parents move out of London to their house in Essex.

Jane was bewildered by the suddenness of it all.

"But you and I were to stay with your parents at Lombard Street until our own place was ready, Samuel, and now you say the house is to be sold?"

He nodded, avoiding her eyes.

"I wish you would go with them. You would be safe there, Jane," he said.

"Safe — from what?" she asked. "The war with Holland is to be fought at sea, not in the streets of London. Oh, Samuel, don't look so solemn!"

When he'd gone, kissing her absent-mindedly and promising to write more often, she went inside the shop.

"Father? Did *you* know that Samuel's parents are giving up their house in London to live permanently in Essex?" she asked.

"Only this morning, when Samuel told me before you came downstairs. It seems that Michael Reeves has taken it upon himself to retire prematurely." Pushing the round spectacles back to the bridge of his nose, he sniffed.

"I can't say I'm all that surprised. Michael Reeves is a frightened man. Ever since that Irish dockworker died of the spotted fever the day after he'd visited the Reeves' warehouse."

Jane felt her stomach tighten in a sudden convulsive knot of fear.

"And *was* it the spotted fever, Father? Prue says people are dying of the plague. Do you think the rumours are true, Father?"

"Of course it was the spotted fever, child. He was just a foolish ignorant man who spent most of his time, so they said, in Whetstone Park, consorting with prostitutes and the like."

"Do *you* think the rumours that the plague is spreading are true?" Jane asked her mother later when they were alone together.

Jane's question struck terror in her mother's very soul. She too had heard the rumours; whispers in the market place, women gossiping on street corners.

"Five dead last week. Fifty dead this week ..." Oh yes, she had heard them.

"I'll speak to your father about it this very day," she said.

But, after all, it wasn't necessary for Elizabeth to question her husband. He brought the subject up as they lay together in bed, with the curtains closed around them.

"Michael Reeves has *given* that warehouse of his away, not sold it. I have a feeling he's listened to too many of these tales about the plague being the spotted fever — or t'other way about. Though I told him often enough my special antidote makes light of the fever." He gazed into the middle distance, doing little sums in his mind. "Now that it's becoming so well recommended hereabouts, maybe I could charge more than the eight pence an ounce I'm charging now."

"I'm sure you could, dear," Elizabeth said.

She fidgeted herself into a more comfortable position, carefully so as not to disturb William. "Dear Lord, keep us safe ..." she prayed. "If the plague does come, dear God, keep it away from the children. From Jane, and from Mary — who is so infinitely precious to us all."

But the next morning, a sunny day as hot and dry as the one preceding it, the worry was still there, settling itself into a warm griping pain.

"Have you heard the rumours that the plague deaths are increasing daily?" she asked Tom, deliberately using the word plague instead of spotted fever.

For a moment he was so startled he almost dropped the armful of candles he was carrying, then he recovered himself and smiled at her. But the smile was frayed at the edges, and Elizabeth knew she was going to be soothed with words that meant less than nothing.

"Our Master has taken the precaution of placing a bowl of vinegar on the counter, Ma'am, so that customers may place their coins in it before we pick them up. And he has instructed me to smoke at all times in the shop, for tobacco is well known for keeping infection away. You need have no fear, Ma'am, the Master knows best."

Elizabeth nodded, the vinegar bowl causing her fear to be fanned into flame rather than soothed as Tom had intended. For Jane was in and out of the shop all day, and could breathe the air tainted by someone sick, in need of medication, and thus ... thus bring it into the house and to Mary.

Less than halfway reassured, she nodded again, and Tom made his escape before she could ask any more awkward questions.

For how could he soothe her when at times the fear festered in his own mind?

In the shop, a dour-faced man with a pock-marked face waited to be served.

"I have ridden from the village of Chelsea to

obtain Mr Verney's medication for spotted fever," he said.

Tom took a step backwards. It was only a matter of time before someone suffering from the plague came into the shop. He had known it, and his master knew it. And what good would their pesky vinegar bowl be then?

But the stranger from Chelsea was laughing, a hideous thin laugh with no humour in it.

"No need for alarm," he was saying. "My good wife saw a woman taken bad in the grocer's shop the day before yesterday, and has convinced herself 'twas the plague ... I mean the spotted fever, of course." Thin lips parted over long yellow teeth. "And Mr Verney's elixir causes sweating to sweat away the disease, so my wife has heard ... So, if you please?"

Handing over a bottle of the foul-smelling stuff, Tom nodded a thank-you as the man tossed his coins into the vinegar bowl. Then immediately the door of the shop had closed behind him, he told the young apprentice, Algernon, that he had urgent business to attend to and that if customers wanted prescriptions he would be back within the half-hour.

There was something he had to do. Something he had to find out for himself. For too long had he listened to what others had to say, closing his eyes and his ears to the rumours. Newton Street, they said. It had reached Newton Street now ...

And what he went to look for, he found.

In Newton Street, as quiet as the grave, four red ochre crosses on four closed and bolted doors. Down the doors the red letters dribbled as if they had a life of their own, and underneath four separate notices scrawled in ink:

"Lord have mercy on us!"

The rumours were fact, and the import of the facts was too terrible to contemplate ...

How *dare* William Verney allow his daughter Jane to walk abroad in the markets now that the plague was spreading?

*B*efore the beginning of May the grave-diggers in St Giles' Churchyard were hard put to it to find a space for one more grave.

And on a hot and humid evening, when Mary was a-bed, William Verney gathered his entire household together.

"In this house, at least, we are not going to give way to panic," William said. "But we must, until this enemy has retreated, take all precautions that are right and proper. Namely — you, my dear wife, and Jane, must keep to the house, taking the air in the garden, but not breathing of it too deeply. The same will apply to you, Prue, and to Algernon. Mary will of course stay away from school until I say it is safe for her to return. The child must not be frightened in any way. I am crossing the river at the end of the week to confer with my brother James, and should the sickness flourish — which I am sure will not be the case — I am going to arrange for her to stay with her aunt

and uncle for a few weeks until the danger abates."

Jane saw the way her mother was staring at her husband.

And she knew that her father had not thought it necessary to confer with his wife on the matter of sending Mary across the river.

"Never, never, will I tolerate such treatment from Samuel!" she told a sprouting sprig of rosemary as she tended the herb garden the next day.

"Do the herb plants talk back to you, Mistress Jane?"

So occupied had she been in her one-sided conversation with the feathery plants, that Tom had been able to walk along the worn brick path without her hearing him.

And so sad did he look that she gave up all pretence of trying to look dignified, or embarrassed at having been caught talking aloud to herself.

"Does anything ail you, Tom?" she asked him.

"I think your father should have arranged for you to stay with your uncle James across the river," he said, straight out, not mincing his words. "I am much afeared for you, Mistress Jane.

"The plague is spreading like an unwatered fire," he continued fiercely. "Almost every day now someone comes into the shop demanding a preventive for it. Not a cure, Jane because once they are stricken there is little we can do.

"Whether they fear they have the signs or whether a relative is stricken and they strive to keep it secret we do not know; we give them what they ask for and ask no questions." His voice grew bitter. "And because the price is high they imagine they will be saved, and your father grows rich."

For a moment Jane was so angry she could hardly speak.

"And so," she said, her colour high, "you are accusing my father of putting the safety of his family second to his greed for gold?"

"One thing can be said about your father. He is no coward," Tom replied. "The plague itself does not fill him with terror. What I am trying to tell you is that your father will not take time to establish his family in safety, because by closing his eyes to what is happening, he sees a chance to make a fortune far beyond his dreams."

"Out of poor people who seek a cure where there is none to find?" Jane did not want to believe it of her father.

Tom bowed his head, and was gone, walking back to the house along the brick path, a tall figure in his brown jacket with its leather lacing, his black hair curling over the white stock at his neck. And as he walked, his shoulders were bowed with the knowledge that what he had said was unforgivable. Unforgivable, but true.

And as Jane picked up the long brown skirt of her workaday gown and followed him, at that very moment, two houses in Lincoln's Inn Fields were being daubed with the dreaded red cross, and a brown rat, its coat furred with disease, was scampering on wobbly legs across the cellar floor in Jane's own house.

Then there were long days of heat; days of waiting for rain that never came, with the plague deaths mounting.

And through it all William Verney confronted his wife with what he believed was conviction.

"No need to give way to panic, my dear. A good friend of mine knows of a property in Westerham in Kent which is to come up for rent in a few weeks' time. I have authorised him to secure the tenancy on my behalf, and this he is arranging, this very week. So you see, my love, I am not quite the procrastinator that you accuse me of being."

"And after establishing us abroad, you will return to London, William?"

The wobbly chins settled themselves sanctimoniously over the white flowing stock, and she knew that another lecture was forthcoming.

"An apothecary is bound by his very undertaking to help his fellow man. And as a member of my own chosen profession I must help all I can, and if helping means keeping my shop open for both the tainted and those who only fear they are tainted, then so be it."

And so convincing were his ringing tones, so earnest his expression, that Elizabeth knew she had misjudged his motivations. How could this good man be thinking only of the moneys to be made at such a time of distress? She bent her head over her embroidery frame again.

But oh, how she wished they were moving to Westerham tomorrow. Or even this very day ...

The first week in June was the hottest the Londoners ever remembered. And Covent Garden was touched with plague ...

"One more week can make no difference," William Verney would tell himself, as the coins were tossed into his vinegar bowl so rapidly that Algernon was set to empty it four or five times a day.

He closed his eyes and ears to the hackney coaches, the carriages and the tumbledown carts as they rumbled along the street outside, carrying more prudent families to a safer place.

Just one more week, and he would spare the time to arrange the move. Just one more week and there would be enough money for him to stay with them for a while. Yes, he had earned that.

One more week. That was all ...

For Jane, the days had a kind of repetitive pattern that was soothing to her mind. A letter came from Samuel, but she was not to write to him, he said. Some stupid rule drawn up by his college, he explained.

"He's afeared lest you seal the plague in with your words of love to him," Tom Baxter said in the mocking tone he used whenever Samuel's name was mentioned. "He is afeared lest the sickness jumps out at him from the page. And as

for you not being able to write back to him — well, I've heard of no such law."

"You don't know *everything*, do you?" Jane retorted childishly before flouncing upstairs to her chamber to sit on her bed and read the closely written words again.

Now she could no longer bring Samuel's round bland face to mind, not even when she closed her eyes and concentrated.

There was so much she had to tell him. So much she would have told him but for the stupid rule.

They were moving to Westerham any day now. Her father said so. And then, when there was no danger of the plague lingering in her ink-pot, she would write a long letter to him.

*O*ne night the sticky heat sent Jane padding softly over to the window. She leaned far out. At once she drew back, her mouth a round O of startled surprise, her eyes wide with dismay.

No one had told her that plague had come to the house directly across the street. Not being allowed to enter the shop, she had not seen the dreaded red cross painted on the door, nor the watchman taking up his position in the street.

Now with a mounting horror, she heard the approaching clatter of iron-rimmed wheels on cobblestones.

It was a night of wisping clouds and slanting silvery moonlight, so that when the cart came closer she saw it with a terrible clarity ...

The man leading the horse, his face a blur beneath his black high-crowned hat. His companion, clanging the bell held in his hand.

The cart, tall-sided, with pick and shovel protruding from the tailboard, and the bodies piled high, a tangled heap of twisted limbs. The faceless man in the black-brimmed hat cried out in a rough voice, devoid of the slightest expression: "Bring out your dead! Bring out your dead!"

The door opposite opened and Jane saw the little huddle of the Tailor family grouped together in the doorway.

She knew them well, had known them all her life, but never with intimacy for the Tailors were quiet, God-fearing people of Quaker stock, keeping themselves to themselves and venturing out but seldom.

Then, as Jane watched, wanting to look away, but somehow mesmerised, the shrouded body of a child was passed out to the first man who tossed it to the second man as if it were no more than a log of wood.

The cart went on its way, the watchman laid his lantern down again on the cobbles by the side of his stool, and motioned to the sorrowing little group in the doorway to go back inside.

But before the door closed upon them once again, Jane saw the slight figure of Mrs Tailor take one step out into the street, saw her lift up her head and howl to the moon like a starving alley cat.

It was a terrible sound, made all the more

terrible because it came from so reserved and solemn a woman.

"Your father does what he considers to be best for us," her mother said the next morning.

"He still finds time to sit alone counting his money every evening," said Jane, ashamed when her mother's face stiffened with hurt.

"See," she said, "you are upsetting your sister." And Elizabeth went over to where Mary sat, and put her arm round the shoulders of the unusually pale little girl.

"'Tis this pesky heat, my lovey. Day after day and never a sign of rain. Just a few more days now, my pet, and you'll be able to run in the fields and make your daisy-chains."

Then, when Prue had taken the little girl by the hand, promising that she could help with the rolling of pastry for a herb tart, Elizabeth turned to Jane, her small dark eyes reproachful.

"Your father has hired a carriage, and is taking some of our good things to be stored by his friend Richard Gray at Marylebone for the time he will be with us at Westerham. He has a lot on his mind."

Jane clenched her fists in despair. "Good things! What do 'good things' matter now to people like the Tailors? Why must my father *always* put the wrong things first? Always?"

"You fill me with despair, Jane. What would Samuel think if he heard the way you shouted and criticised your own father?"

"Samuel wouldn't *care*!" Jane shouted louder than ever. "He doesn't care what is happening to us, otherwise he would ride over from Cambridge and find out. He is a coward. He admitted it himself. And I will tell you something else. I do not love Samuel Reeves, and I never have, and I would like to take the bride sheets I have been sewing, and dump them in the Thames!"

# *Chapter 3*

Was it true? Had her love for Samuel died, Jane asked herself later, reading the words of adoration penned in his meticulous handwriting?

Where *was* Samuel? She needed him. She was frightened, and he could have given her comfort.

An hour went by, then another. And so occupied was Jane by her melancholy thoughts that she did not hear the door of her chamber open.

Then, aware of movement, she turned round, startled. Framed in the doorway was Tom, holding Mary in his arms. A mumbling, incoherent Mary, with the vivid flush of fever burning on the cheeks which had been so unnaturally pale at breakfast time that morning.

"Keep away, Mistress Jane," he said. "Maybe 'tis nothing, but keep away."

With Elizabeth following behind, he walked

through Jane's chamber and into the smaller one adjoining and lowered the little girl gently on to her high bed.

Jane moved farther into the room, heedless of Tom's warning, and what she saw made pins and needles prick beneath her armpits and a sudden faintness make her stretch out a hand and touch the nearest wall.

For her sister's chest was covered with hard spots, each one encircled with a crimson ring.

Elizabeth was lifting her little daughter up in her arms, rocking her, moaning and whimpering.

"Oh, Lord, let me be stricken. Taint my flesh, but not this child's. Oh, Tom. 'Tis the tokens. I know it ... Oh, dear merciful Lord, have pity on us all!"

Over her mother's shoulder, Mary's dark eyes, glittering with fever, seemed to be staring straight at Jane, and she held out her arms and moved towards the bed.

But with a wide sweep of his arm Tom almost knocked her off balance.

"Get back!" he ordered. "Go downstairs and send Algernon to fetch your father, and pray he has not already left for Marylebone."

But even as he spoke, William Verney's loud voice could be heard from downstairs; demanding to know what in the name of thunder was going on.

Jane put a hand over her mouth to still its trembling.

"My father will know what to do," she told herself, speaking aloud as she did when troubled. "He knows the best potions. People come to him from far and wide. Father will know what to do for Mary."

But her heart pounded with sudden fear as the door between the two chambers was flung open to reveal William Verney, fat face and drooping jowls slack with shock, leaning on the wall for support.

"The Lord help us," he said, and his voice was ragged with emotion. "She burns with the fever, and already there are the swellings in her arm-pits and her groin. Fetch John Warren, Tom. He will let her blood ... he is the best man I know ..."

His voice tailed away as his wife put out a hand.

"Stay awhile, Tom," she said. Then she spoke quickly and quietly: "Think, Will. Think what it means if you send Tom for John Warren. You know he will inform the authorities at once, and we will be shut in, all of us and left to die. How often have you told me that your antidote can cure the distemper if it is taken early enough?

"So many times, when I've pleaded with you to remove Mary from here you have said you can treat the plague and that there was no need to fear it. Just this one night is all I ask. Mayhap Mary has vomited the sickness away, and if the fever leaves her we can take her to safety. *Please*, Will. I implore you."

Jane held her breath as she saw the anguish of

indecision in her father's eyes. She did not know the penalty for concealment of the plague, but she guessed it would be severe.

She glanced at Tom and saw how his dark eyes were fixed on his master's face, awaiting instructions. Jane knew that Tom would never give way to panic. Dear, dear Tom. If anything were to happen to him ... if he were to be the next ... if she herself were to be stricken? She felt the beads of sweat break out on her forehead.

Then, unexpectedly, she felt her hand held in Tom's warm clasp, and she relaxed as she felt his quiet strength flow from his fingers into her own.

William felt Mary's forehead again.

"She must sweat," he said. "She must sweat and sweat.

In the morning Jane woke to a stillness that filled her heart with dread. Along the passage and into the kitchen she crept, startled to see that the door to the garden was wide open. Then Tom appeared, carrying an armful of faggots, his black hair tousled and his eyes dark shadowed. He put his finger to his lips.

"I cannot find the courage to ask you how Mary is," she told him, lifting a strand of her long hair and tucking it behind an ear.

It was a familiar, childlike gesture, and it made his heart dissolve with love.

"The sickness runs its normal course with Mistress Mary," he said, "but now she sleeps, thank the Lord."

"And there's no doubt in my father's mind that it is the plague?"

"No doubt at all, Mistress Jane."

"What's to become of us, Tom, if my father sends for the physician? Even if Mary is much better we dare not open the shop and people will begin to ask questions."

She could not pretend to be brave in front of Tom. With Tom she could only be as she was: young and terrified.

"And we will die, Tom. We will catch the plague, one from another, and we will die!"

"Jane!"

Her father's voice, behind her, startled her into instant silence.

In differing circumstances William Verney would have looked ridiculous, swaying there before them, unshaven, his closely-set eyes bloodshot with weariness, and his considerable paunch hanging unfettered, but now he was just a pathetic shadow of the man he had been but a short time ago, in a different world where his little daughter skipped and laughed and sang.

"Your little sister is gravely ill, Jane." He swallowed hard. "I am going myself to fetch John Warren before he starts on his rounds.

"I should have taken you away weeks ago, my daughter. Your dear mother kept telling me the time had come, but I would not listen." He rubbed his eyes with the back of a clenched fist. "Yes, Jane. You see standing before you, a murderer; a man of such greed that he put the power of gold before all else."

And in spite of her terrible anxiety about her sister, Jane's uppermost emotion at that moment was shock.

Shock at her father's humility. Never in the whole of her life had she known him admit to being in the wrong.

"Now I want you to take Jane away." William Verney turned to Tom. "I want her away before I send for John Warren."

And everything Jane had said to Tom not five minutes before was forgotten.

"I cannot go away, Father," she said, catching at the table for support as her legs seemed to give way beneath her. "I cannot leave you ... Mother needs me ..."

But, completely ignoring her, Tom listened as his master gave instructions, issued orders.

"My brother, James, is a kindly man, and his wife not without some virtue, and I know they will take Jane in. You know his house down the river, over on the Rotherhithe side?"

Tom nodded.

"Tell ... my brother James that if it be the will of our Lord we will all meet again some day. And give this purse to him."

And from inside his open shirt he produced a soft leather purse and threw it down on the kitchen table. Tears rolled down his unshaven cheeks as he said softly: "Take good care of her, Tom. May the good Lord go with you, dear Jane."

"I won't go, Father!"

Jane was crying now, and would have embraced her father, but was held back by Tom's restraining hand.

William Verney looked long and lovingly into her face as if he saw her clearly for the first time, as if he would imprison the memory of her youthful beauty in his mind for ever.

Then, without another word, he turned and walked away.

Tom knew they must leave at once, before the early morning customers came pounding on the shutters demanding to know why William Verney's shop was closed.

Once the red cross was on the door they would melt away like snow in the sun's glare; once the red cross was painted there, William Verney and his family could be counted as dead.

Seeing that Jane hardly knew what she was about, he took her hand in his and pulled her towards the garden door. "This way. 'Tis safer this way."

"I cannot leave them, Tom. I won't run away."

She tried to pull away as Tom's fingers curled even more tightly round her wrist. "I will scream in the street, and people will come to my rescue."

"And when they find out who we really are they will send both of us to Newgate," Tom said levelly. "The penalty for leaving a plague house is death,

instant and on the spot! If you love your father, obey his wishes, just this time."

Jane glanced at him. His brown eyes were worried and filled with a terrible anxiety, no sign of the usual teasing laughter in their dark depths.

She saw for the first time that in his solicitude he had snatched up her long hooded cloak from the peg in the passage. And the small kindness made her weep, and convinced her more than words could have done that she must, at all costs, go with him.

"Put this on," he was saying. "I know 'tis too warm for the wearing of a cloak, but 'twill hide the brightness of your hair."

And so, on that sunlit morning, Jane Verney, with the hood of her everyday cloak pulled closely round her face, walked away from the house in which she had lived all her life.

In the haste of their departure she had forgotten that she was wearing her slip-shoes, fit only for indoors and the intimacy of her chamber. Now she felt each stone as she slipped and slithered over their greasy surface, and her brown workaday gown trailed behind her in the filth.

"You always wear your gowns too long," Tom said suddenly as if reading her thoughts. "Why don't you loop it over your arm, Mistress Jane?"

"Because I do not wish to," she answered childishly.

"So be it," he said.

"My feet hurt," she grumbled. "Why do you make me walk so quickly when you can see I am practically barefooted? Why was I not allowed even a few minutes to collect some of my things from the chest in my chamber? What will happen to my new gown? I've heard it said that all the clothes in a plague-stricken house are taken away and burned."

She was behaving like a child, and she knew it. But it was her only defence against the growing fear that filled her heart with dread. She glanced sideways at Tom, hoping for a reassuring smile, but, ignoring her, he walked on.

And she did not guess that he dared not look at her in case he weakened. Pity for her made him long to sweep her up into his arms; pity for her made him want to kick and curse the very cobblestones that dared to hurt her little feet. But they were passing a cross-marked house, and the watchman slumbering on his stool outside the door jerked suddenly awake and stared at them suspiciously.

"What will they do to my father when they find out he lied and allowed us to escape?" she was asking now.

"What your father has to fear now, Mistress Jane, is not the anger of the authorities ..."

Again Jane felt the sick clutch of fear in her stomach as she understood his meaning.

What her family had to fear now was death itself ...

But, half running, sliding and slipping as she went, she followed where Tom led her, down unknown alleyways, along twisting tributaries of shadowed streets, so narrow that even the bright sunshine could not penetrate. If she paused for breath he dragged her on.

She was almost exhausted when they came at last to the river, to a desolate stretch of broken seawall, with worn steps and a flimsy landing platform, and a narrow flat-bottomed little boat tethered there.

"I know the waterman who works this stretch very well," Tom said quietly. "I did him a favour once, and he'll get us across and no questions asked."

Jane crept back into the shadow of the wall, and watched as Tom approached a man — a huge bear of a man, with hair, beard and face of the same redness, and a neck so short and broad it seemed as if his massive head was hung there between his shoulders.

He seemed mightily glad to see Tom, and there was a lot of backslapping.

Then Tom set down a handful of coins atop a flat stone on the wall, and the waterman pulled at his fiery beard, held his enormous head to one side, and considered the amount with grave suspicion. Jane shivered with impatience.

If only they would hurry ...

Now the waterman was filling a pail with water and pouring it over the coins before he picked them up, spitting on each one for good measure before he stored them away in his belt. And at last Tom came towards her, holding out his hand.

"The rascal has charged me as much as if he planned to row us over to Holland," he whispered, "but I console myself with the thought that your father would consider it money well spent.

"You will never guess just who I told him you were," he whispered as he handed her down on to the rough seat in the small craft. "Little does he know that *she* is more than likely to be asleep in bed at this moment — more than likely with her head on the King's shoulder."

And in spite of her anxiety Jane was comforted. This was the Tom she knew, and because she wanted to make him proud of her, she returned the waterman's penetrating stare with what she hoped was the correctly haughty expression.

Smiling at her from beneath alarming red eyebrows, he jumped in after them, pushed off from the rotting platform with an oar and sculled into the middle of the river.

They were safe ...

The boatman's pendulous stomach rested loosely on his knees as he strained at the oars, and through his unfastened shirt she could see there was a luxurious growth of curling red hair.

Now and again as he rowed, he glanced first at Tom, then at her, and having come to some silent and private conclusion, his massive shoulders shook with laughter.

"Very little traffic today," Tom said, and the

waterman nodded and spat over the side of his craft.

"'Tis nothing to what it will be like," he told them. "I see the day not far hence when naught moves on this river but the ripples."

"Has much of the sickness reached the Rotherhithe side?" Tom asked him. And, first resting his oars and wiping the sweat from his face with a flapping shirt sleeve, the waterman gazed at them speculatively, then nodded.

"But only in the past weeks, and not much of it. Not yet. Aye, 'tis a hellish business and no mistake."

And he applied himself to the oars again ...

"Over there," Tom said, pointing to a short flight of green and slippery stairs. "You have done well, waterman."

Then, as the small craft glided silently towards the shore, and was moored with expert precision, he held out a hand to Jane, and whispered something to the waterman, who smiled at Jane appreciatively from beneath his wildly curling eyebrows.

"Watch your pretty step, milady," he said in his croaking voice, and was so overcome when she smiled back at him, that he almost toppled over into the river.

Tom urged her on once again, pulling at her hand until they reached the top of the hill overlooking the town.

"Oh, Tom," Jane whispered. "Why did my father not send us all away in time? He is greedy perhaps, but not wicked. He loves us so. You saw the way he was this morning, and the way he looked when he first knew that Mary was stricken. Why am I so certain that I will never be able to forgive him?"

To her surprise, as they stood together, Tom suddenly put out a hand and pulled back her hood, so that the light and most welcoming breeze lifted her long yellow hair. He spoke with a quiet gravity:

"When something as terrible as this happens, Mistress Jane, we are so afeared, we *have* to blame someone. Someone or something. 'Tis only nature helping to make it more bearable. If you did not blame your father, you would be blaming yourself, or God, or the ways of the world. So now you can stop tormenting yourself with thoughts that do not become you. So tidy your gown and smooth your hair. We are safely across the river, and all I have to do now is to deliver you to your uncle's house. Like a package."

He tapped the side of her nose lightly with his forefinger, smiling at her with the sun in his eyes. Tall and straight, and proud.

"And then I can make my way back to the shop," he added so casually that at first she thought she could not have heard him aright.

"Make your way *back*, Tom?" You are deliberately going back to where the sickness is?"

She was almost beside herself with dismay. "I will tell my uncle James you were ordered to stay with me. He will believe me ..."

But Tom was shaking his head at her; still smiling but shaking his head. And his will could be as strong as her own. She knew that well.

"Listen to me, Mistress Jane," he was saying. "I cannot cross the threshold of your uncle's house. I touched Mary, remember, when the tokens were on her, and so I could be tainted in my turn. But even if I knew for certain that I had not taken the sickness, I would go back. Your father is more than an employer to me, Mistress Jane: he took me in when I was a nobody, a poor and hungry orphan from the country, reduced to stealing so that I might live. How could I desert him now?"

And for once in her life, Jane was speechless. She wanted to shout at him, to beat her fists against his chest. To cry, to plead, to beg, even to order him to stay with her, but she knew it would have been to no avail. This was not the Tom who gave in to her, obeying her even as his dark eyes twinkled at her.

In the short time since they had left the shop, he seemed to have grown in stature, to have exchanged his teasing ways for the seriousness of a man who knew exactly what he wanted, and was determined to have his way. And she could only marvel at his courage. Wordlessly she stood on the hillside, head bowed, defeated, with nothing left to say.

"Come with me, Mistress Jane," he was saying now, holding out his hand to her and smiling.

"Dear Tom," she said. "Very dear Tom. Not Mistress Jane. Just Jane, please."

And there for a moment, the boy she knew was back again, as, his dark eyes sparkling with mischief, he grabbed her hand and pulled her after him down the long grassy slope.

"Very well, just Jane," he laughed, and hand in hand they started across the field path to her uncle's house ...

A substantial citizen like his brother William, James Rupert Verney lived in a fine four-storeyed house in a fine curving street. James was a London merchant, dealing mainly in spices, and his spoilt and pampered fat wife, Henrietta, felt that their move from overcrowded London had been a step in the right direction up the social ladder.

The fact that their house was a good four miles from London set it, in Henrietta's eyes, in the category of a country residence. From the moment she rose from her bed, Henrietta Verney was dressed in the height of fashion, and the ringlets dropping from the wires behind her ears were tortured into position each day by her maidservant Nelly, a trembling slip of a girl who wielded the curling tongs with such fear in her heart that her eyes had a perpetual haunted glaze of apprehension.

Henrietta did not like people very much. Some

of them she was forced to tolerate, but her brother-in-law, William, over in Holborn, and his wishy-washy wife, Elizabeth, were so beneath her contempt that she treated them extra graciously to show how low they really were in her estimation.

"I am not looking forward to living with Aunt Henrietta until the plague is over," Jane told Tom as they approached the house. "She is a lazy good-for-nothing who will summon her maid rather than pick up her kerchief from the floor. And she cannot abide me either."

"'Twill do you a world of good to live for a while with the likes of your aunt Henrietta," Tom teased. "She might just be able to turn you into a lady."

Jane stopped walking. "Oh, Tom, stay here with me. Please! You could be of great use to uncle James."

But Tom chose to ignore her.

Wordlessly he reached for the knocker and rapped three times on the ornate front door.

# Chapter 4

It seemed a very long time before they heard the quavery voice of old Adam, the manservant, calling out from behind the closed door.

"Who is it? Make your business clear."

"Tell your master 'tis his niece, Jane Verney, his brother's elder daughter."

From behind the door, they heard shuffling, followed by loud mutterings, and at last, with obvious reluctance, the door was opened.

And there, blinking in the bright sunshine, stood uncle James, pot-bellied like his brother, sparse of hair, the veins visibly tightening on his forehead as he looked upon his niece. And behind him, a kerchief held to her mouth, hovered Henrietta.

Her fashionably wired ringlets seemed to dance with disbelief.

"There is trouble," she said. "You do not need to tell me."

Tom spoke quickly and firmly:

"Good sir. My master, your brother, gave Mistress Jane into my charge, to deliver her safely into your care, knowing how close a family you are, and how you have always been ready to rally round in time of trouble. You will have heard how the dreaded distemper has, these past weeks, been approaching the parish where they live? This night past, Jane's sister, Mary, has been taken with what they fear is the plague ..."

Jane felt her heart sink within her as she saw the way her uncle James' eyes narrowed. He began to close the door against them.

"Oh, please, Uncle James, I beg of you ..." she began, then her heart began to pound in her breast

as Tom moved swiftly and put a foot inside the door, preventing it from being closed.

"My master begs you to give Mistress Jane shelter," he said. "There is nothing to fear. Since the tokens appeared on Mistress Mary's skin, her sister has neither touched her nor smelled her breath. My master told me to tell you this most particular." He held the purse out at arm's length. "He bade me give this to you. The money has been well soaked in water and vinegar, I promise you good sir. There is nothing to fear."

Surely they couldn't be refusing to let Jane in? Why, this flabby, paunchy man, this only brother of his master, loved Mistress Jane as if she were his own daughter. He had heard him say as much many times when he visited the Silver Still.

"My master asks you to pray for them in their plight, to cherish Mistress Jane in the name of love and compassion, and he prays that with the will of God you will meet again when this sadness is past."

Tom spoke directly to James Verney, ignoring his wife, but she appeared to be about to burst with rage.

"And how, pray you, can you be sure that you are not carrying the infection? How *dare* you bring the danger to our very door? And how dare your father think that we would endanger ourselves in this way? Take your foot from the door! Or I will set up such a screaming that the whole town will hear!"

Tom answered her with a quiet dignity that filled Jane with admiration.

"And if you do that, Madam, and if you make it known that the reason for your screaming is that you fear you have come into contact with the sickness, then your friends and neighbours will melt away like river ice in June. Your husband will be barred from his fancy coffee houses, and there will be no one to admire your fine gowns. Is that what you want? If so, then scream till your lungs burst. We are all waiting!"

Jane stared at him in horror. No one spoke to her aunt Henrietta like that. In spite of his blustering ways, her uncle James went in daily and obvious dread of her sharp tongue.

Jane felt a fleeting pang of pity for him. She drooped against the doorway, and her uncle mopped at his face with a purple kerchief. He felt ill, dammit. Short of breath and with a distinct pain in his chest. Drat that brother of his. Putting them in such an impossible position.

He wished they would just go away and that Jane would stop looking at him like that. There were tears trembling on her long eyelashes. She *knew* he loved her; dammit he had always loved her. And families were supposed to help each other in times of crisis ...

But not when their own lives were at stake ...

He spoke firmly.

"Your aunt is right, Jane. I know we must seem to be unfeeling, but we are not thinking merely of ourselves, but of our servants also. You must see we have a duty ..."

His wife interrupted him.

"The Lord be with you, Jane," she said, and then, with a nod to old Adam cowering in the background, she ordered him to close the door.

And when the door was closed to them, they heard the sound of bolts being shot into place.

They had reached the bottom of the sloping street where the houses thinned out into fields, before Tom could bring himself to speak. Then, looking back the way they had come, he raised his arm and shook his fist.

"And the Lord be with you, Mistress Henrietta, and with your apology for a husband! May He show you the same mercy that you have shown this day. May the plague rot your flesh! May your evil tongue swell and turn black!"

Then he looked down at Jane, a glint of the old teasing, good humour in his brown eyes. So gently that she scarce felt his touch, he lifted a strand of her long golden hair and tucked it behind her ear.

"And now what shall we do, my pretty Jane?" he said.

Jane knew then that the Tom she knew was back with her again. He was smiling at her as if it were just an ordinary summer's day and they were a man and his maid out for a stroll.

"Godstruth, but I feel better for that," he grinned, then he took her hand in his and started to walk quickly back along the field path which led to the river.

There was an urgency in his long strides, and a desperate wariness in the way he glanced back over his shoulder, as if he feared that someone might be following.

"We must make haste. I have heard it said that there are places on this side of the river which abound with rogues and felons. Would that I had thought to strap on your father's sword."

He was becoming more conscious with every step he took of the weight of the purse at his waist.

When they were well out of sight of the houses, he at last stopped and sat down on the grass, pulling an exhausted and grateful Jane down beside him.

"Rest awhile," he said. Then he smiled at her as if to reassure her that all would be well. "I crave your pardon for ranting and raving at your father's brother and his wife. We must remember that your aunt Henrietta would think we were bringing the plague right over her doorstep. Your father must have been well nigh demented not to have realised they would react as they did."

Jane rubbed at an ankle and grimaced with pain. "Aunt Henrietta would not have wanted me even if I had a certificate of health from the most eminent physician pinned to my chest."

"She has known wealth and comfort all her life," Tom reminded her, "and a woman like that finds it hard to come to terms with harsh reality." He sat up straight and made a mock bow in the direction from which they had come. "Dear Aunt Henrietta, I forgive you freely, and I wish you a most pleasant plague. May all your dreams be happy, and may you never lie awake in the night pondering on the misfortunes of those less fortunate than yourself. Long live dear Aunt Henrietta! So be it."

Jane laughed — a ghost of her normal merry laugh, but a laugh all the same. And it wasn't the first time, she realised with affection, that Tom had made her smile when she thought the world was tumbling round her ears.

"Oh, Tom. You really have forgiven Aunt Henrietta, I believe, even though you jest. Do you really never think ill of anyone?"

She put out a hand and shyly touched the white linen doubled into a cravat at his throat. "How can you be so forgiving when your own life has been so sad? My father told me once that when he brought you to the house there was little but skin

99

on your bones, and that you had been scavenging for scraps in the markets."

Tom propped himself up on an elbow beside her, and she raised her eyes and saw his face close above her, serious and intent.

"You ask me why I bear malice to no one, Jane? I think 'tis perhaps because I have known neither mother nor father and so have had to make my own judgement on matters. Or at least because I have learned through my own experiences never to judge. Hunger and fear make thieves and rogues of the best of us. That is why I can understand your Aunt Henrietta in a way. It was fear of dying that made her act as she did, not lack of affection for you, sweet Jane."

His face was so close she could feel the sigh of his breath on her cheek. If he leant but a fraction closer, he would be no more than a kiss away, and his mouth was softly curved, the lips mobile, but firm. Not fleshy as Samuel's were fleshy.

Her heart was beating with a quickening thud; and she parted her lips in anticipation of the kiss she felt must surely follow.

Then suddenly, and with a deep sigh, he rolled over and away from her. As if he had all at once read the plague in her eyes, Jane thought, or even worse — as if he had read an invitation in her parted lips.

"Rest a little while longer," he was saying. "I will keep watch, and then we will be on our way."

"To where?"

"To somewhere," he said. "I will find somewhere, never fear."

The soothing words were like a blessing in her ears. Of course she could not, and would not sleep. Her mind was too cluttered with terrors and anxiety. But Tom was there, by her side, and the sun was warm on her closed eyelids; she could see its golden light …

She awoke with a suddenness that startled her, to feel Tom's hand on her arm as he shook her far from gently. No more than a few yards away, three men were watching them with what appeared to be an air of evil calculation.

Helped by Tom's hand, and half dazed with sleep, she stood up, swaying as he bundled her cloak back round her shoulders.

"Good day, gentlemen," Tom said, the slight tremor in his voice betraying his nervousness to her. "I pray you do not come any closer to us. We greatly fear we may be tainted with the sickness."

The tallest of the three men stepped back a pace.

"You look well enough to me. And your good lady. I cannot see any signs of the distemper. Can you?"

And he turned to his companions and laughed, but it was a joyless sound that made Jane's blood run cold.

Tom held up his hand and spoke quickly: "I beg you, do not come any nearer to us. We are newly wed and have made our bond together, to die in the fields rather than on a lonely pallet in the attic of our lodging house."

"Well now …" the tall man went on, running his tongue over thin lips. "If you are to die in each other's arms of the distemper, the money you have tucked away in that purse at your belt will be of no further use to you. Whereas we, who are untainted and still have a long way to travel, will have great need of it."

"For your own safety, gentlemen, I pray you listen to what I have to say," said Tom. "I tell you, we are doomed. We cannot escape the disease, and neither will you if you come within touching distance."

At his words the smallest of the trio retreated a step.

"We bid you good day, gentlemen," Tom said suddenly, as suddenly as if he were come to a decision. Then, holding firmly to Jane's arm, he led her away.

No sound of footsteps behind them. Nothing. And yet she knew the three men were there; she could sense their presence, and guessed they were walking on the grass bordering the winding lane.

"They could murder us and no one would see, or come to our aid," she whispered. "Oh, Tom, have we escaped the plague only to be killed in this lonely place?"

Tom squeezed her hand. He tried to keep the terror he was feeling from his voice. "Please, dear Jane, keep on walking as if you were not afeared. Soon we will be at the wall, and the waterman will be waiting for us."

It was a day-time nightmare; Jane wanted to scream; but most of all she wanted to run, to run and run from this place, back to the comfort of the narrow streets with friendly houses leaning towards each other. Away from this walking silence in which nothing happened.

When the men did catch up with Tom and Jane as they hurried along the field path, it was with a suddenness that made Jane cry.

The tallest man, coming up behind them, knocked her to the ground with a single movement of a long arm, and she saw with horror that in his hand he held an axe, a butcher's axe.

Tom had seen it too, and with all his strength he grasped at the hand that held it, bending the tall man's arm backwards, trying to make him loosen his grip.

For a long moment he fought like a man possessed, and Jane caught the look of startled surprise on the man's evil face as he recognised Tom's strength.

He had the tall man on the ground now, with the axe loosed from his fingers.

"Run, Jane!" he called. "Run! The waterman! Run!"

But even as she scrambled to her feet, one of the watching men picked up the axe, and as Jane ran towards him, all fear for her own safety vanished, he brought it down with a sickening thud on

Tom's head, and she saw that the fingers he had spread wide to protect himself ran with blood. The second man, at a quick signal from his leader, turned Tom's lifeless body over with the toe of his boot, and wrenched the purse from his belt.

Then, between them supporting the tall man, who was half dazed from the fight, they made off across the fields.

Jane knelt down and cradled Tom's head in her lap, heedless of the blood which seeped slowly into a spreading stain over the skirt of her gown.

Never in the whole of her seventeen years had she felt so inadequate, so helpless.

She could not remember ever having to make an important decision. Her betrothal to Samuel Reeves had been decided for her, and she had never even walked the London streets alone. And yet here she was, with the river between her and her home, her uncle's door closed against her, alone with a Tom who would surely die. No one could lose so much blood and not die, she told herself aloud.

"Oh, God, what am I to do?"

If she ran for help, who would heed her?

Gently she covered Tom with her cloak, shielding his face from the sun with the hood. "Very dear Tom, I will be back soon," she whispered.

Then she gathered up her long skirts and started to run in the direction of the river, praying as she ran that she would remember the exact spot where they had climbed the hillock and left the waterman with his boat.

And suddenly there he was, the huge red-bearded giant of a man, patiently waiting, as Tom had ordered him to do, sitting on the grassy bank.

"Tom ... he ... he is hurt ... you must ... must ... come with me!"

The waterman shook his shaggy head.

"Steady, milady. Sit ye down and try to catch your breath awhile, but nay, I cannot leave my boat, not for all the spices in the Orient I cannot, milady."

"Three men," she said, her breath coming easier now. "Thieves. Rogues. Took all our money, and Tom — his head — he is bleeding, and I fear he will die."

She grasped the waterman by his arm, trying in desperation to drag him along the path.

Still he resisted, and then, from the depths of her distress she remembered that Tom had hinted she was ... what? One of the ladies at Court? One of King Charles' many mistresses?

"In the name of our most beloved King, I order you to come with me."

And immediately the look in the waterman's blue eyes changed from one of stout noncooperation to one of unwilling obedience. He got to his feet.

"Very well, milady," he said at last, and with a final lingering glance at his boat, he started off up the rough path, with Jane hurrying along beside

him, muttering little frantic prayers as she went.

As they came to the place where Tom lay, the waterman muttered an oath so foul that in differing circumstances Jane would have blushed all over her body. They knelt down on the grass beside Tom's corpse-like figure, and she saw that the bleeding had stopped.

The waterman carefully lifted Tom into a sitting position, talking softly to him all the while.

"Nah, then, listen to me, young Tom. We'as to get you to the boat. Right? Me and milady 'ere." He glanced at Jane. "Wot might be your name, beggin' your pardon, milady?"

"Jane."

"And Mistress Jane is 'ere wiv me, so for her sake you 'ave to try ..."

And with one almighty effort, bending his knees to take the strain, he hoisted Tom over his shoulder, as if he were no heavier than a sack of pullet feathers.

So slowly, very slowly, they managed to cover the distance from the field path and down the slope to the river, where, to the waterman's loudly expressed relief, the small craft waited, bobbing at its moorings.

"The Lord in his blue 'eaven be praised!" he said, then, as gently as a mother lowering her first-born into his cradle, he laid Tom down in the bottom of the boat.

Then, stopping only for a moment to wipe the sweat from his scarlet face, he rowed with powerful strokes out into the middle of the river.

With the far shore receding, Jane felt she could breathe freely again. Bending down, she lifted Tom's head on to her lap and saw that his wound was bleeding once more.

"I would we had some vinegar," she sighed, then as the waterman looked away with exaggerated, but quite sincere, modesty, she tore a strip from her undershift.

He groped around in the bottom of the boat, and from underneath a heap of rags produced a cask of ale. Pouring a quantity of it over the strip of cloth, he passed it back to Jane.

"Use this, milady. 'Tis a sight cleaner than that there water. I uses that fine brew for everything. You have a swig of it yourself, then sprinkle some of it on his face. I swears by it, that I do."

Lifting the cask to her lips, Jane felt the beer trickling down her parched throat, then she poured a little of the amber liquid over Tom's dry lips.

"He's taking it!" she said. "See! Oh, thank the Lord. He's drinking!" She smiled at the big rough man and gave the cask back to him. "You are very kind. I was beginning to think that never again would we meet with kindness."

The waterman smiled back at her, beaming through his whiskers like a benevolent father.

"There's good and there's bad, Mistress Jane, milady. Now see if you can lift young Tom a bit higher. I'll try and give you a hand, but I don't

want to capsize this 'ere boat. That's right. Hup you comes, laddo!"

And even as Jane struggled, Tom raised his head of his own volition, opened his eyes and, staring round him in bewilderment, thrust his hand inside his belt, in search, Jane knew, of the purse of money. Finding it gone, he moaned aloud.

"Oh, dear God ... All the money gone, and your uncle's door closed against you." He looked up at the sky, a vast expanse of blue with not a cloud in sight. "And still the sun shines on. Oh, why does the Lord not stop the sun from shining? I have failed my master and I have failed you ..."

His voice petered out, and she saw that tears of weakness were filling his eyes.

The waterman brought his boat into the landing stage and made it fast, his broad back towards them, and there, with the bright sunshine lighting up the scene as if it were some well-illuminated nightmare, Jane Verney held Tom, her father's servant, in her arms, whispering soft words of comfort into his darkly matted hair.

Never again when things were not going her way would she rebel and declare with a pout of her lips and a stamp of her foot that she was no longer a child. She *was* no longer a child. She was a woman, a woman so filled with tenderness for the young man in her arms that she would fight the whole world for him if need be.

"You'll get me out of this place yet," she whispered. "We'll get out of it together; you and me, Tom. You'll see."

The fall of yellow hair drifted across his face as she talked softly to him, hair as bright as the sun itself.

And comforted, and in a strange way filled with a languorous content, Tom sighed. And slept.

# *Chapter 5*

As the night passed and the stars grew pale and Jane at last fell into an uneasy sleep. Tom stirred fitfully and awoke.

"You are better," she told him, dragging herself back to wakefulness, and touching his forehead which, to her relief, was blessedly cool. "I told you you would be, and the waterman has gone; he stayed away all night. Try to drink a little."

During the long night, she had fastened the heavy weight of her long hair back with a ribbon torn from the front of her gown. There were blue shadows underneath her eyes, and a streak of grime down one cheek.

Tom watched her with the ache of love, and the anguish of knowing that he alone was responsible for her from now on.

He must try to shake off this terrible weakness which possessed him; he must grit his teeth and

bear the pain which dissolved into pricking lights before his eyes when he moved his head.

"Odsfish, but I could eat a horse, harness and all," he said, and Jane smiled. It was like hearing music when he spoke in his usual bantering tone, and as if in answer to his words, the waterman appeared, carrying a cloth tied at the four corners, holding it aloft as he climbed down into the boat.

Proudly he unwrapped the bundle, and there inside the cloth was a slab of cooked meat and a pot of pickles, together with a loaf of bread. And there was a little, jingling cloth parcel which the waterman slipped to Tom.

"Fit for 'is Majesty 'imself," he said, the colour in his cheeks challenging the redness of his beard, so immense was his delight in pleasing them. "I ain't arsking no questions, young Tom, but where are you a-going to? The woman wot let the room to me last night told me that the poor folks moving out of the city are starving on account of the country folk refusing to sell them victuals. I'm much afeared for you."

So genuinely worried was he, so concerned for their welfare, his broad forehead creased into deep lines of anxiety, that on impulse Jane leaned forward and planted a swift kiss on his cheek.

"We'll be all right, Tom and me, and some day we will come back and see you," she whispered.

When they had finished eating, Tom climbed out on to the stairs, swaying so that Jane feared he would fall into the river.

"I am well enough," he assured her, then as they stood together he adjusted the fastenings of her cloak, pulling the hood up round her face.

"In spite of all that has happened, do you trust me still?" he asked her gravely. "Do you trust me to take you away from this place to one of safety?"

Standing on tiptoe, Jane smoothed the black hair away from Tom's forehead in a gesture that moved him more than if she had embraced him and kissed him full on the lips.

"Dear Tom," she said. "I trust you with all my heart."

Tom appeared to be walking only because his brain told his feet to place themselves one in front of the other. His long black hair clung to his head, lank and matted with the blood he had lost, and with every tortured step he took, sweat poured down his ashen face.

Jane pulled at his arm. "Tom? Are you sure you feel strong enough to walk? Your head is bleeding again. You should have it attended to."

Tom shook his head, wincing with pain as he did so.

"Jane, listen well," he said. "I think you know that when I was a small boy I lived with a good man and his wife and their two sons, in the country, many miles north of here."

"Mother Benson," Jane said. "You went to see her last summer, and told us that her husband had died."

"She is very poor, but her heart is full of

kindness, and I have been thinking about her, and I am sure that she will take you in." He put out a hand and touched her cheek. "Do you think you can walk there, Jane?"

"Is it a very long way?"

"Far enough. I have always managed to ride there on a carrier's wagon, but we will have no choice but to walk." He looked down at her, an anxious frown creasing his forehead. "Do you think you could try, Jane?"

She caught at his hand as he stood there, swaying in the cloying heat. In his distress he had forgotten that her shoes hung from her feet in tattered ribbons.

"If you can walk there, then so can I, Tom Baxter." Her chin lifted in determination.

*B*ut every step she took was a small agony, and she saw that her slip-shoes were no more than a dusty tangle of matted silk. Each and every cobblestone seemed to be pushing its individual way into the tender soles of her feet. However, she would not, and could not, complain. If Tom with his poor, battered head could continue, then so could she.

"I prayed all night," she said. "For you."

But Tom was walking with head bent, his lips tightly clenched, and did not appear to hear.

Two houses in the street they now turned into were guarded by watchmen. As they drew near a window opened, and a woman's head appeared; a woman with eyes as sunken as if they had been gouged out of her face. Arms flung wide, she shouted her frantic grief to the vivid blue sky.

"Lord! Lord! Why hast Thou forsaken us? My first-born has gone! How can you let a little child feel such pain? Lord! Oh, have mercy on us! I beseech you!"

This was not London. This was the city of a thousand nightmares.

Tom gripped her arm so fiercely that she winced with the pain of it as his fingernails dug into her soft flesh.

"Do not draw attention to us, Jane," he whispered urgently. "The watchman is suspicious and the poor souls shut up in there are crying out in plague frenzy. They are doomed and there is nothing anyone can do."

Jane cast a despairing glance over her shoulder as the thin high wailing started again.

"My poor little mother," she murmured. "She will need me so much if ... if Mary should die. I have to go back to the house, Tom. If they are all to die, then I must die with them."

They were turned now into yet another alleyway, and suddenly Tom turned on her.

"Why must you talk so much, Jane? You always talk too much. Why must you always question the authority of those who know what is best for you? This day, you do as I tell you. You walk, then you walk again, and you say nothing. Do you hear me?"

In his anger and his alarm for her safety he stuttered over the words; in his anger his dark eyes flashed fire. Subdued now and not a little ashamed, Jane bowed her head and obeyed.

And still the sun rose higher, and still they walked, always going north, towards the open fields of Highgate. The houses were thinning now, and when they came to a rough path where the grass was toughened and burnt brown, as stubbly as twine. Tom tripped and would have fallen but for Jane's restraining hand.

At last, when Jane thought she must surely die if they did not rest, they saw an inn. "We will first creep past, behind those trees, then approach it as if we were coming *from* the country," Tom said, "but please, sweet Jane, say nothing. I have not forgotten how to talk as if I were born with a straw in my mouth, but your speech is not the speech of a country girl. You understand?"

"I understand," Jane said.

The taproom was empty of customers, just as Tom had hoped it would be. The inn-keeper, when he came, stood afar off, behind his counter, fat jowls wobbling with apprehension as he stared first at Tom, then at Jane.

"No horse to be hired here," he muttered, "and my tapster has fled. Sorry, sir." He turned away, dismissing them, his very attitude willing them to go away. But Tom, reaching inside the cloth bag given to them by the waterman, threw a few coins into the bowl of vinegar placed at the ready on the broad expanse of counter.

"Two pints of ale," he said, "and you need have no fear. My wife wishes to see how her parents are faring. They live out Ludgate way and, not hearing from them, she fears for their safety."

The jowls wobbled in a little dance of disbelief, but the inn-keeper relented enough to place two tankards of ale before Tom.

"You would be crazy to venture right into the town," he said. "You must have heard that London is doomed. They say there are parts where the red cross is on every door in the street, and the dead-cart calls in the daytime, there not being time to collect all the dead in the night. Tomorrow I am taking my inn sign down and going far from here."

"With your family?" Tom asked.

"No, good sir, I sent my family away weeks ago, and I miss them sorely, but how could I let them stay so close to the city which is as cursed as if the devil himself had laid his horny hand on it?"

"Not every man thinks as you do," Jane said bitterly, unable to curb her too-ready tongue.

"We cannot all be as noble as you are, Tom Baxter," she said, as the inn-keeper moved away.

"Judge not ..." Tom said softly. "You know the rest."

"Oh don't be so damned sanctimonious," said Jane, sounding so much like the young girl who used to drive him to distraction, that he laughed out loud.

The inn-keeper, hearing their laughter, was so

103

moved by it, fearing it would be the last time they laughed so merrily for a long time to come, that he refilled their tankards, refusing to take any payment.

The air inside the Silver Still was so warm, so sticky, that sweat broke out on foreheads and trickled down faces blotched with weeping. Mary's skin was as wet as if she had been immersed in water, and yet her teeth chattered as she grasped for every tortured breath.

Elizabeth put her hands over her face.

"Oh, if only I could be the one to be stricken, William. I would gladly bear twice, nay, ten times the pain Mary is suffering if only she could be well. She *will* be well, won't she? Say it will be so."

Had he answered? She could not remember. She only knew that somehow she found herself on her own bed, with the curtains drawn back and the door wide open to catch what air there might be. And to catch the slightest sound from Mary's room...

Jane was safe. She must keep telling herself that; hang on to that. And she must not let the thought even creep into the corners of her mind that she wished it were Mary. If Mary died, then she would not ... she would not care if she never saw Jane again ...

"Oh God," she cried in a broken voice. "I did not mean that! I am so weary I do not know what I am saying. Forgive me."

The city gates behind them, Jane felt the air fresh and clean. On either side of them were fields.

About two miles further down the deeply rutted road, Tom pointed to a stream, hardly more than a trickle of water, hidden by trees on both sides.

Jane plunged her arms into the stream, splashing the water over her face. And the feel of the clear water was so wonderful that, all embarrassment flown, she took off her tattered slippers then, unbuckling her garters, she rolled down her stockings, and with blue eyes half-closed in ecstasy, she dabbled her swollen feet in the stream.

"Have a care you do not fall in," Tom teased, then he saw her blistered feet, and with an exclamation of dismay, knelt down beside her.

"And to think you have walked all this way, and said nothing! Mayhap you are not the spoilt and pampered Jane I knew before. Oh, love, to think I shouted because you did not walk quickly enough ... and all the time ..."

Gently he patted her feet with his cast-off shirt, then he raised his head, and what she saw in his eyes made her heart leap.

"I am no longer a spoilt and pampered child, Tom," she said softly.

For what seemed an eternity they stared into each other's eyes, exhaustion and grief forgotten. Tom lightly touched the tip of her nose in a gesture grown familiar over the years, but this time the affectionate touch was the first tentative caress of a lover.

Slowly and with infinite tenderness he trailed his finger down her cheek, outlining the shape of her wide mouth.

Passion flamed like a lick of fire; her heavy-lidded blue eyes held his own with an expression of longing. Oh, Lord, it was true; she was no longer a child, and in another moment would surrender herself to him completely.

But she was his master's daughter, trothed to Samuel Reeves, given into his care by her father.

So, marvelling at his self control, he kissed her lightly on her forehead, a kiss of affection, promising nothing, regretting nothing, a kiss as fleeting as a brotherly caress.

"If Tom is not back by nightfall," William Verney told his wife, "I cannot say I blame him. I was selfish to expect him to come back to the house once he had got away."

Elizabeth imagined Tom striding along in the sunshine, laughing aloud at the narrowness of his escape. And although she had loved his merry teasing manners, and appreciated the way he had always treated her with respectful kindness, she found herself hating him.

"I wish him dead," she said slowly. "I hope he takes the plague and rots where he falls!"

The nurse-keeper brought by John Warren, Mollie O'Malley, came into the room and saw the look of horror on the apothecary's face as he stared at his wife.

Well, she told herself, with a shrug of plump shoulders, she had seen it all before. Days of seclusion turning love into active dislike; fear making murderers of ordinary decent citizens. Only the week before she had seen a mother covered in the tokens of death, take her baby son into her bed, holding him so that he too would take the sickness and die.

Tom pointed to a barn at the far end of a field.

"It belongs to the farmhouse you can see over there, over the brow of the hill. See the smoke coming from the chimney? I swear I can smell their meal cooking ..."

"I will kill you if you talk of food, but first let me sleep. Even my hunger pangs are weary," Jane muttered.

Tom put his finger to his lips and made Jane wait quietly until he had made sure the barn was deserted.

"No use looking wistfully at the farmhouse, sweetheart. The farmer would as soon give lodging to a scabby leper. Tonight your bed-chamber will be his old barn, and your couch a mound of hay."

And it seemed as if she had been asleep for no longer than a few moments when she awoke to the sound of angry, frightened voices.

Quietly she moved to the open door of the barn

where Tom stood, arms spread wide, arguing fiercely with a crowd of villagers, grouped a distance away.

"Why don't you be gone?" a thickset man in a slouch hat was bellowing at the top of his voice. "How dare you bring the plague to our farm? Be off with you! We have our wives and families to think about. Go back the way you came, if you know what's good for you!"

Jane moved closer to Tom and felt the reassuring weight of his arm about her shoulders.

"I give you my word that we have not the sickness on us. We are on our way to my mother's cottage, ten miles or so from here," Tom said quickly. "Force us to return the way we came, and I will not answer for this young maid's life. She is exhausted. Where is your Christian charity, my friend?"

"These days there is no room for charity!" a burly man shouted and raised his right arm.

And the moon, appearing from behind a drifting wisp of cloud, glinted on the barrel of a gun ...

Jane shuddered. Yesterday it had been an axe; now it was a gun, and something had to be done, and done quickly ... She moaned and slid to the ground in a perfect semblance of a swoon.

"Already she sickens with the plague," she heard one of the men shout, then, as Tom knelt down beside her, she opened her eyes briefly and whispered: "They surely will not kill me when I am lying down?"

And now when Tom's voice rang out, it vibrated with scorn. "'Tis not the plague that makes the maid grow faint, but simple hunger and weariness. All we ask is for a roof to cover our heads for the night, and in the morning I promise you we will be gone."

As Jane sat up, passing a hand wearily over her forehead, she saw that the men had drawn into a huddle. Then the man with the gun spoke again: "If you give us your word, pledged on the name of our Lord, that you will not approach the village, nor our hamlets, we will leave you and the young maid be."

"On the name of our Lord, I swear ..." Tom began, but the men were backing away, ultimatum delivered.

And now that the immediate danger was past, Jane started to laugh uncontrollably. Silently and with mounting hysteria, covering her face with her hands.

So, tenderly leading her back into the barn, Tom lay down on the straw beside her, pulling the cloak round them both, holding her close in his arms. Like a lover; like a husband, he thought, as with murmurings and gentle words of comfort, he soothed her into sleep.

And when she moved against him, sighing his name, he knew that she loved him. Or thought she loved him.

Too tired for passion, too tired to stay awake, but too afraid to sleep, he held her as the long dark hours slipped away.

Tomorrow, God willing, they would reach Mother Benson's cottage, and she would be safe. Tomorrow, or the day after, he would go back to London. He *had* to go back. To William Verney he owed his very life.

W hat is there to be gained if you go back to catch the distemper?" Jane asked when they had walked for almost an hour without her speaking.

Tom shook his head in mock despair. "For the last time, I tell you 'tis my *duty* to go back."

Jane would not lift her eyes, but he knew they were filled with tears.

"But I need you," she whispered. "This Mother Benson — she may not want me; she may not like me. If you, if you cared for me as a friend, and I thought you *were* my friend, then you would stay."

At that Tom tilted her chin with his finger, forcing her to look him straight in the face. Her mouth was trembling, and he ached to kiss her.

"I *am* your friend, sweetheart, and I do care for you. I have cared for you since I came to your father's house ... You are the sister I never had, the friend I always hoped I would have. And I am not going to kiss you so you can open your eyes ..."

So angry was she that she stamped her foot. Then she cried aloud with the pain, hopping around and nursing her toes so that Tom burst out laughing.

"I hate you!" she shouted.

His laughter, her weariness, and her anxiety made her want to hit out at him. Or to throw herself in his arms and cry away her fears.

He folded his arms.

"Good. In that case you will be glad to be rid of me, and my going back to London will relieve you mightily. Now stop shouting and waving your arms, and save your breath for walking. We have many miles to travel today."

Subdued now, Jane walked along by his side, refusing at first to hold on to his hand when the way grew rough. What was happening to her, she asked herself? How could she admire and like and violently dislike the young man at her side, at one and the same moment? Was *this* the love she had dreamed about, lying on her narrow bed in the hot summer nights? And how, at this awful time, could she feel this topsy-turvy kind of happiness, as if nothing mattered when he was near?

And again there was nothing but the road ahead; the effort of putting one foot in front of the other. On and on, until the sky grew dark.

And then at last they climbed a hillock, and there in the shadow of a great hollow Tom pointed out the flickering candlelight from the window of a cottage.

"We are safe, sweet Jane. May the Lord be praised."

"Amen," she said, with such a depth of feeling

that he laughed out loud, and held her for a long moment, close to his thankful heart.

Mother Benson was a tiny, bright-eyed woman, with greying hair. She held a candle aloft and peered at Jane and Tom with short-sighted eyes.

"Well!" she said. "'Tis Tom! Tom Baxter! Well! By all that is merciful. Come inside, both of ye."

Tom took Jane by the hand and pulled her forward.

"This is Jane Verney, the elder daughter of my master. We have walked from London and have already been turned away from one door, and she is afeared you might send her away again. Her young sister, Mary, was taken by the plague, and her father gave Jane into my keeping before their house was shut up."

Then, as the tiny woman showed none of the terrified reactions they had come to expect, he went on: "I can promise you that neither of us is tainted. If it were so, the symptoms would have shown themselves by now."

With a nod of her small head, Mother Benson dismissed the plague as if it were of no importance whatsoever.

And when Tom explained that he would be returning to London the next day, leaving Jane with her, she nodded again.

"I'll watch out for her," she said, "and Mistress Verney can have the boys' chamber up in the loft. I keep it ever ready in case they come home."

There was a wistful sadness in her voice, which Jane was quick to notice.

"Where *are* Christopher and John?" Tom was asking. "The last time I was here they were living not a stone's throw away."

Mother Benson tilted her small chin. "Gone, the both of them, to Oxford with their wives." The bird-like head lifted proudly. "They would have taken me with them, but I said I would not leave my home."

Tom smiled at her. "And you still walk across the fields and work in the buttery at the big house?"

"And will do for as long as I can. Folks who stop working just lay them down and give up," the old lady went on, talking too much and too quickly, the way the lonely do when unexpected company comes their way.

Jane was so exhausted that the murmur of voices from downstairs as Tom and Mother Benson sat up talking did not reach her. The sound of Tom climbing the wooden stairs to the tiny chamber partitioned off from her own left her undisturbed.

And yet, around mid-morning, when she opened her eyes, her first thought was of Tom, and her second that he might have gone without saying farewell to her ...

But, stumbling down the stairs, with hair uncombed and face unwashed, she found him waiting for her, tending the fire.

"Mother Benson has gone across the fields to the big house," he told her. "We talked long after you were abed, and it grieves me to see how old and frail she has become." Then, putting his arm round her shoulder, he kissed her cheek. "Sit down, love, and eat your breakfast, and when I get this pesky fire a-going I will sit with you and watch you eat." He knelt to his task again. "If I saw her two sons I would beat them out of their senses."

Jane stared at the bread on her plate. It was all very well for Tom to talk about Mother Benson's family, but they were strangers to her. It was her own mother she wanted now; wanted her as fiercely as she had when a child and a terrifying nightmare had tormented her.

What was she doing here? Miles from home, in the tiny cottage of an old woman with whom she was expected to live for how long?

"You must take good care of Mother Benson," Tom said, but his eyes were saying other things. "Be a daughter to her, the daughter she never had, and be careful to bolt the door at nights."

A terrible sadness engulfed her.

"You are going," she said, and he nodded.

He got to his feet again, and drew her up into his arms. And she clung to him.

"I love you," she whispered, and the saying of it brought a feeling of such relief that she snuggled closer to him, lifting her face in anticipation.

"I know," he said tenderly. "I know, sweet love. At this moment you love me because I am Tom, and because you know me so well, and because I have brought you away out of terrible danger."

"I love you because I love you!" she said loudly, raising her head, and then, as their eyes met, they smiled, then laughed, the easy laughter that had always come so readily to them.

And when he opened the door and the bright, inevitable sunshine flooded into the cottage, Jane cried out: "Come back for me, Tom. When all this is over — come back for me.'

Tom had been away from the city for a short time only, and yet in those few days it seemed to have died a little more.

Few were abroad, and those who had ventured out kept to the middle of the road, averting their eyes in case a friend or even a foe accosted them.

And the watchman outside the Silver Still slumbered on his stool, leaning on his halberd, but when Tom stopped and stood before him, he sprang to his feet in astonishment.

"You mean to say you wants to go in *there*?" he asked.

And as the watchman fumbled with the lock, Tom looked upwards, giving one last glance at the sky ...

"I am not the brave man you imagine me to be, my Jane," he told her silently. "I am so afeared my legs will scarce do my bidding ..."

The big front door clanged to behind him, and he stood for a few moments in the gloom of the darkened passage. "'Tis Tom Baxter!" he called softly, and from the door at the end of the passage, leading to the kitchen, Mollie O'Malley, the nurse, appeared, her eyes swollen and red with weeping.

"The prodigal returns," she said. "Well, well. They'd given you up, they 'ad." She jerked her thumb towards the stairs.

Keeping a firm grip on himself, for he knew what he was about to find, Tom lifted the latch of his master's bedchamber, following the direction of Mollie's pointing finger.

"In there," she whispered, "they put the little mite in there."

Mary lay on the canopied bed, her body wrapped in a bedsheet, swaddled round her as if in death her grieving parents sought to warm her.

Tom shut his eyes, forcing back the tears, knowing as he spoke gently to William Verney and his wife that despair had removed them to a place where they neither heard nor saw.

It was Tom who called through the shutters to the watchman and arranged for the cart to call that night; Tom who helped his master to carry the pathetic bundle down and out through the briefly opened front door.

"All for nothing," William Verney said, and leaning against the wall, sobbed and beat his fists against the plaster until his knuckles ran with blood.

And it was two whole days before Tom told him that Jane was not with her uncle James, but safe in the country with Mother Benson. Two whole days before the broken-hearted father was ready to listen.

"He is a good boy," Mother Benson told Jane. "It nearly broke my heart to let him go to be apprenticed in London. He was a wild boy, with notions of his own, but I loved him from the day my husband brought him to me as a tiny babe."

"And his own mother?" Jane asked eagerly, wanting to hear what she had always believed — Tom was the son of some nobleman, rejected by his father on account of family shame.

The old woman sniffed.

"He was the result of unchastity before marriage by the daughter of my husband's master. The man was a farm labourer who was lucky to escape with his life, and the girl — she was no more than fifteen years old — died in childbirth."

Already, Jane was beginning to know a great fondness for the old countrywoman, after but a week beneath her roof; and all through the long sunny afternoons, as Mother Benson worked at her lace-making, she talked to her, of the customers at the apothecary's shop, of her father and mother and of her talkative, merry sister, Mary.

And of Tom who stayed when he could have gone away to set up on his own. Spending his money recklessly, frequenting the riverside taverns with his friends, then creeping back into the Silver Still as they lay sleeping.

Her voice softened as she spoke of him, and her eyes clouded over with dreams, but if the old woman saw she said nothing, merely bent her head even closer over her work.

As time passed, Jane's white hands grew calloused and red. She wore, without a murmur, a homespun dress. Her face lost its pink and white city colouring, taking on a golden glow from the sun, and she wore her long yellow hair imprisoned and concealed by one of Mother Benson's caps.

In the long evenings she sat on her stool learning the craft of lace-making, working and listening to Mother Benson's tales of Tom …

Within the claustrophobic atmosphere of William Verney's hot, gloomy house, every nerve of every person imprisoned there had been alive and jangling since Mary died.

Who will be the next? their eyes asked. Will it be me? Or you?

"I will take your own broom to you if you do not stop that wailing," Tom told Prue.

Then he was immediately ashamed when he saw how Prue was stunned instantly into a shocked silence, mouth agape. She was sweating, but then they were all sweating, closed inside this airless house with the scent of death in every corner.

She was shivering. But then they all trembled with fear most of the time. But this time it was different.

Suddenly Tom knew the truth. Prue was sick. As he moved towards her, she recoiled, her hands immediately going with a protective gesture to her throat. It took all his strength to hold her whilst he ripped with his free hand at the fastenings of her bodice, tearing it apart and exposing the tokens of death … How would he ever forget the way she fought and screamed!

The fever possessed her so that they had to tie her down to her bed, yelling obscenities, with Mollie O'Malley sitting by her side, hour by hour.

Long, heat-filled days of listening to Prue dying loudly, all the horrors she had foretold attacking her with cruel ferocity. Seeing her knock the feeding cup from Mollie's hand, screaming that she would rather die than be served by a wicked wanton. And watching patient, warm-hearted, once voluptuous Mollie dispensing the same open-hearted affection she used to show to the courtiers who visited her little house.

And when the end came, it was to Mollie that Prue turned, holding fast to the plump be-ringed hand as she fought for every last gasping, rasping breath. And it was Mollie O'Malley who sobbed the loudest when the dead-cart came and took Prue away.

Then there were the days and nights of waiting, their only contact with the world outside through the watchman at the door.

All conversation kept to a minimum between five frightened people who eyed each other warily, watching for signs that the sickness had crept from the walls and claimed another victim.

For Tom, there were nights of dreaming soft

dreams; of walking with Jane through meadows, lying with her in the grass, holding the softness of her in his arms.

Oh, Jane, my Jane. I dream of thee as if one day that dream could be reality ...

"Bring out your dead!"

That was reality.

Algernon, William Verney's young apprentice, died in his bed, just three days after Prue. He was one of the lucky ones, with the disease catching him by the throat as he lay sleeping in a wine-sodden stupor.

"I will tell the watchman," Tom said, feeling a lethargy that was as much of the spirit, as of the body. By now they only spoke when it was necessary, passing each other on the stairs, or in the passageway, and forcing themselves to eat the bread passed to them through the shutters by the grumbling watchman.

Then, waking to another sweltering day, Tom put his feet down on the boards and saw them rise up and bend as if they would hit him straight between the eyes. When he shook his head to try to clear the mists from his eyes he was suddenly and violently sick.

And he knew he was touched with plague ...

For this he had left Jane. For this he had put duty above all else. To die like a dog yelping with pain. Clinging to the wall which slid away from his grasp, calling out in a voice which came from his burning throat with the ponderous groan of a sleeper caught in a terrifying nightmare.

"Stay away from me! Help me! Stay away, for God's sake, stay away!"

He never knew how he got back up the narrow stairs and on to his own bed, but William was there, piling covers over him. There was a face bending over him, and at first he thought it was Jane's, then waveringly it turned into the bloated features of the nurse, Mollie O'Malley.

John Warren, the doctor, was shouting at Mollie to hold his arm high as he lanced the buboes under his armpits.

"Keep still, Tom Baxter! You are going to live. Do you hear me? You are one of the lucky ones, me laddo."

And so it was. But he was weak, so weak that Mollie had to spoon the broth into his mouth.

"You and me, the lucky ones," she told him. "Shows how the good Lord does not always see fit to shine only on the righteous."

"I love you, darlin' Mollie," he whispered, and she kissed him soundly on his bristly cheek.

"Aye, so you do, Tom Baxter. But mine was not the name that has been on your lips these weeks past."

"Weeks? Did you say weeks?"

He tried to sit up, but she pushed him back none too gently.

"Many's the time I've seen you, young Tom, roistering and wenching in the river taverns." She

shook her head sadly. "And poor dead Prue, so virtuous ..." She turned her head aside and he saw a tear roll down a flabby cheek. "And your Mistress Verney. I wager she has known but one man in all her pious God-fearin' days, and yet she went, dying as quietly as I've no doubt she lived."

Tom lay back and closed his eyes, feeling the tears well up beneath them. Then when he could cry no more, she stayed with him, holding his hand and comforting him. And talking ...

"If you want my opinion, she died not so much of the plague, but because her heart was broken. I watched that poor woman just lie her down and die, and when her time came she went with the name of her little one on her lips."

Tom raised himself with an effort on to one elbow, then as the low ceiling dipped towards him, lay back again.

"There is another daughter," he whispered.

"Aye, and her name is Jane," Mollie said. "You have no need to be a-telling me that, Tom Baxter!" And her face creased into a rueful smile.

# Chapter 6

All day it had seemed to Jane as if she could hear Tom calling her name, and that night, she went outside the cottage after darkness had fallen.

It was a night of stars with a sliver of a moon, and the air was full of the scent of a summer almost gone, and with the promise of crisp cold days to come.

It was strange how in spite of the country smells, she could still sense the rotting stench of the plague in her nostrils. And particularly in the past few weeks ...

"You must not dwell so, my dear," Mother Benson would say. "Trust in the Lord. Always."

She must try to find out what was happening in London ... she could not stay here for ever, not knowing ... Tomorrow, or next week, when they walked to market with lace to sell, she would accost a stranger demanding news.

But even as she decided, she knew she could not and would not endanger Mother Benson. For such was the fear of contamination, that if they knew Jane had come from London, they would refuse to buy the lace. No, she would do nothing that could harm the kind and gentle old woman, who asked for nothing but a roof to cover her head and one meal a day.

It was true, as Tom had said, that the country was divided, with one set of values for the rich and another for the poor. She began to walk slowly back to the cottage. Never again would she take the material things of life for granted. She would be a changed person, she told herself, speaking her thoughts aloud as usual.

Never again would she fret and complain about

the set of a gown, or because her hair was not the shade she wished it to be.

Then the day came when Jane heard at market that the merchants were meeting again in the Exchange, and the butcher told her that his brother in London had taken the shutters down from his shop windows, and had called his apprentices back to him.

If it were true that the plague was almost over, Jane thought, her heart sinking, then where was Tom?

She was across the long meadow and back on to the road, about halfway home, when she heard the sound of horses' hooves coming up behind her.

Instinctively Jane stepped back into the hedgerow, averting her face, and drawing the hood of her cloak closer. Then as the rider drew rein, pulling in beside her, she felt her heart begin to beat with dull and heavy thuds.

Fearfully she peered up at the rider, not recognising his voice when he leaned forward and spoke to her.

"Jane! 'Tis you" he said.

And it was Tom ...

He lifted her up to sit the horse in front of him, and his voice held the remembered teasing laughter as he said. "Jane, sweet Jane. Do not look at me as if I were a ghost. I told you I would come back for you."

Blue eyes wide, she twisted round and stared at him, so close that she could feel his breath, and still she could not believe it was he.

"'Tis thee," she whispered, using Mother Benson's way of speaking, and as she patted his cheek with a touching, childlike gesture, he felt the roughness of her fingers, and as she traced the outline of his mouth he saw that her cheeks were the shiny red of a countrywoman's. And yet he had never seen her lovelier.

"No questions yet; not a single one till we are back at the cottage, and no tears either!"

Then with his arm holding her tightly, he urged the horse forward. Oh, God! How to tell her what had passed? And how, knowing what he must tell her, could he feel this singing happiness, so that the rain, sweeping down from a grey marbled sky, was like a blessing on his face?

If he had loved her before, he worshipped her now, this girl he had known as a friend, a sister, the daughter of his master, still trothed to another, but *his*, dear Lord. As surely his as if they were of one flesh.

"I'm afeared to ask you," Jane was saying at that very moment, waiting at the door of the cottage as Tom tethered the horse to the stoop. "I know I have to know, but oh Tom, I'm so afeared."

Gently Tom led her to the fire; gently he took both her hands in his own.

"All dead," he said quietly. "Your mother, your sister Mary. Prue and Algernon. But your father

lives. He lives and waits only for you to return."

At first he thought she had not heard.

"No," she said softly, then louder, "No! It cannot be ..."

She put her hands over her ears, like a child who tries to shut out the thunder, but she was trembling so much she could not hold them there.

Then he sat down in Mother Benson's chair and pulled her down on to his knee, holding her, smoothing her hair away from her face, talking to her softly, but telling her how it had been ...

"Winter is coming early," Tom told Mother Benson, "and with it will come the end of the plague. And what's to become of ye?" he asked, lapsing into the countryman's way of speaking as he often did when deeply moved. "It is obvious," he went on, "those hands of yours will not be able to work with your lace bobbins for much longer. Tomorrow, before we leave for London, I will ride over to the big house to speak with the master. I will use my influence ..." Then he looked away from her, knowing that the circumstances of his birth was a forbidden subject. "There are almshouses near to the village and the master can wield his power and have you installed in one of them. And Mr Verney has said that I will be made free of the Society of Apothecaries, so I will be able to send you money."

Next morning, damp-eyed, Mother Benson said her farewells to them and waved until they had ridden away.

Hours later, as they approached the outskirts of the city after riding the last miles in silence, Tom slowed the horse down to a walking pace.

It was strange to see so many houses with the shutters thrown back, letting in the air to rooms so long cloistered, and now Jane saw that most of the crosses on the doors of infected houses were white. London was coming back to life again.

"*I* wish," Jane said suddenly, "I wish we could turn the horse and ride back this minute to Mother Benson's cottage. I am afraid of that dead house, Tom ... When I was away I could pretend that it would be the same when I came back. I could pretend that Mary would run in from the garden, and that my mother would be there, sitting in the parlour with her embroidery on her lap ..." Her voice broke.

"You will not be in the house for long," Tom said gruffly, and before she could ask him to explain, he was climbing down from the horse, leading it by the bridle, and they were turning into the familiar street.

She was home ...

Fearfully she glanced around her, conscious of the steadying touch of Tom's hand on her arm.

"Your father will be in the side parlour, sweet love," he whispered, forgetting in his sympathy for her that he was supposed to be treating her with coolness. "I saw him at the window as we came up to the door."

Then Jane was in her father's arms, and his

tears were on her face; their tears mingled, and when he held her away from him she saw how he had changed. This wizened, shrunken little man was a shadow of the father she remembered.

"Tom has told me the way it was, Father," Jane whispered. "Do not distress yourself by talking about it. There will be time ..." Then she kissed him again. "I will never leave you, Father, now that I am all you have."

William Verney shook his head. "Come and sit by me, dear child, there are things to say, and little time in which to say them. Samuel will be here on the hour to collect you."

"Did you say *Samuel* will be *here*?" She stared at him in disbelief.

William nodded. "You did not think I would let you stay in this house? Even for one night?" He passed a hand wearily over his face. "They are still here, Jane. They linger round corners, sad ghosts, with footsteps that fade as they approach. Oh, no, I would not want you to hear them, my daughter. For you there is life to be lived."

"With *Samuel*?"

"It is all arranged. He will take you away and the wedding will be from his mother's house. His father has bought him a country practice not a mile away from where they live. I only wish your mother could know how happy you will be ... she often spoke of Samuel before she ..." He bowed his head, unable to go on.

Getting up, Jane walked over to the window. She was at a loss how to tell him that what he had so carefully arranged could not be.

She turned towards him. "Father. You know that Samuel did not once try to contact me all the time I was with Mother Benson in the country?"

William nodded. "He did not know where you were, my dear. He tells me he was frantic, having heard on good authority that we were infected and the house and shop closed up. For all he knew you might have succumbed to the distemper and died. He tells me he was scarce able to make sense of his book learning, and that his fellow students found him a melancholy fellow indeed."

"And he is Doctor Reeves now, you say?"

"With the beginnings of a thriving country practice."

William Verney had taken up his familiar stance, short legs splayed wide as he went on: "This house is to be sold, and I am to take up an appointment as assistant to the apothecary of the College of Physicians at the headquarters at Amen Corner, and I will live in nearby rooms serviced by a good woman by the name of Mollie O'Malley. A woman fallen from grace, I know, but redeemed by the good works she has performed as a nurse-keeper and I feel that we may therefore show proper Christian charity to her."

Jane stood back, aghast. Her father had not changed all that much after all. She recalled how he had always made his plans without consulting

her mother, and now he was setting out her life in the way he felt it should go.

It was impossible that he could have done all this without waiting to see, without wondering, if she was still willing to marry Samuel. It was impossible, and yet it was true ...

"And so if I refuse to marry Samuel, then I have no home," she said softly, so softly that he did not hear. "And what is to become of Tom?" she asked.

William nodded in a satisfied way. "Tom will be made free of the Society of Apothecaries three days before Christmas, and I have settled enough money on him to start up on his own. I think the shop he has in mind is in St Martin's-in-the-Fields, the apothecary having died there of plague. So many of us, Jane. And yet I, who do not deserve to live, live on."

Tom knew all this and did not tell me, Jane told herself. He knew that I was to marry Samuel; that my father had arranged it all, and yet he did not tell me.

She walked over to the window and looked out into the street. She turned back to the room and it was as if the walls were closing in on her.

And when Samuel came down the street, his boots echoing loudly on the cobbles, swinging his cane as if he strolled down some country lane, Jane saw him and went to stand by the fireplace, head held high, hands clasped in front of her in an attempt to hide their trembling.

"Well, Samuel?" Jane said, and her gaze was so direct, so challenging that he stepped back a pace, and the arms he held out to her dropped to his sides.

This was a Jane he did not know; a serene and beautiful woman.

He did not know what to say and Jane knew it. When he would have moved towards her she put up her hand.

"Stay where you are, Samuel. What I have to say will not take long. I would have said it many weeks ago, but I could not come to Cambridge to find you, and you ... you did not think to inquire what had become of me.

"What would you have done, Samuel, if I had died along with my sister and my mother? Would you have mourned me and told yourself it was meant to be?"

He smiled with uncertainty. "I know how you must be feeling, dear heart. This house is filled with memories of what used to be. That is why I am taking you away this minute. Just as you are. I pledge the rest of my life to you, dear Jane."

The pale bulbous eyes glittered with sincerity. He felt no end of a fine fellow as he held out his hand towards her.

And still there was something in the way she looked at him that made him hesitate.

"I will take your hand, Samuel," she was saying. "But it will be to say farewell. I do not love you. I can never be your wife."

Samuel opened his mouth to speak, then closed

it again. He fumbled with his untidily knotted cravat, then blinked his eyes, the thick white eyelids with the gingery fair stubs of lashes. He hadn't expected this at all.

His mother would be pleased. That was his first coherent thought, that his mother would be pleased. She had never approved of Jane. Had thought her flighty.

"I know not what to say," he said at last, his voice stumbling even over the saying of that. "Dammit, Jane, you *cannot* do this! I love you ... I love you."

"Please go now, Samuel," Jane said. "Before my father comes downstairs again. Don't be afraid, I will explain it was all my fault."

She came and touched his cheek. "There will be another love for you. You will see."

Then she was walking towards the door, holding it open as she spoke and, protesting mildly, still unable to accept what was happening, Dr Samuel Reeves, newly graduated from Cambridge, found himself being shown politely but firmly out of the house. It had all happened so quickly he could scarcely believe it.

Telling her father could wait. He would have to be told, and he would have to listen, but now all Jane desired was to sit quietly, alone, to gather the chaos of her thoughts, to still the beating of her bewildered heart.

To sit. And be still.

Suddenly, she had to be out of this house, so stifling, so filled with dreadful memories. So, picking up her skirts, she ran out of the room down the stairs and into the rose arbour by her herb garden.

What the future might hold for her she did not know. What she did know was that she was homeless, bereft of family and friends, of everything she had held most dear ...

She closed her eyes, too saddened for tears, too anguished for prayer. Hearing but dimly the sound of iron wheels on cobblestones as a cart went by on the other side of the wall. Not hearing at all the sound of Tom's footsteps as he came up behind her, then lifting her head to see him standing there beside her, bareheaded in the thin sunshine of that autumn afternoon, the thick black hair curling to his shoulders.

"Well, Jane?" he said, coming to sit beside her. "Samuel Reeves seemed to be in a mighty hurry just now." And the teasing laughter sparkled in his dark eyes as he touched her nose with the tip of his finger.

"I sent him away. He has gone away for ever," she told him. Then as Tom's arms came round her, her composure shattered into a thousand wavering pieces, and the tears of mingled joy and sorrow came at last.

"Do not leave me, Tom," she sobbed, all pride gone. "Oh, I beg thee, do not leave me ever again. I am so afeared, so very much afeared."

And there, in the rose arbour, hidden from the silent brooding house, he held her close and kissed her, gently at first and then with passion. And she returned his kisses, murmured of her love, and heard him swear that never would he leave her again, not if all the Samuels in the world lined up outside the door and claimed her for their own.

"You will marry me, sweet Jane," he told her. "And there will be hard times ahead when you will have to work with me, and toil with me, for I intend to repay the money your father has settled on me ... I will cherish thee, and I will slave for thee, and there will be times when we fight, for we were born to fight and to love as no other man and woman have fought and loved since time began."

Jane lifted her head, looked deep into his eyes and saw her future mirrored there, knowing with certainty that with this man nothing would be certain.

For he was Tom ... very dear Tom and, oh God, it was wonderful to be alive. In a weeping city of sadness, a London with whispering dead sighing from every corner of every twisting street, it was oh, so very good to be alive ...

THE END
© Marie Joseph, 1977

---

*Ring a ring o' roses*
*A pocketful of posies*
*Atishoo! Atishoo!*
*We all fall down!*

*With the passage of time even great disasters diminish, transformed into the language of every day — sometimes into nursery rhyme ... And so it is with "Ring a ring o' roses", which dates from the reign of Charles II. Though England prospered two great blows fell — the plague in 1665 and in 1666 the Great Fire of London which razed two-thirds of the capital to the ground. In some senses the fire was providential for it cauterised from the city all traces of plague. Before that, at the time of our novella, a wise man carried a pocketful of posies to disinfect the air and the ring o' roses signified the circle of inflamed sores that meant the plague. Some survived, but others succumbed to fever, and wheezing, sneezing, all fell down — and died.*

# 25 WAYS TO LO

**Try our zippy fashion and beauty tricks for last-minute pick-you-ups**

**1** A SCARF ADDS STYLE ...
Nattily knot a colourful square round a simple sweater; glamorise a party number with a floaty narrow stole

**2** EYES BRIGHT ...
So you've no time for the full works? Well, just apply mascara to your lashes, then brush up brows with an old wand that has just enough dry colour left on it to create a subtle sensation

**3** BE CHIC ...
To update your classic cardi, wear it with the 'V' at the back. Then simply add a wide belt and a long string of beads to complete a swish switch

**4** SPEED SCRUB ...
If you haven't much time to spare, skip the cleanse-and-cleanse-again routine — wash instead with a rinsable make-up remover

# OK GREAT FAST

## 5 LEG IT ...
Give a tarty-smart lift to an elegant skirt with a pair of seamed tights or stockings. They'll show off your pins to perfection

## 6 OFF THE SHOULDER ...
Why not wear your bag across your body for a touch of trim continental chic? That way you can keep both hands free and deter the snatchers too!

## 7 CURL UP IN SECONDS ...
Squirt on hairspray before using heated rollers — the result will be almost instant success

## 8 NEW SHAPE FOR OLD ...
Take a comfy-cut smock and blouse it over a low-slung studded belt to achieve the long, lean, laid-back look. Turn the sleeves up to elbow length to complete the effect

## 9 QUICK LIP TRICK ...
No need to fiddle with pencils — a lip styler can outline, colour and glamorise all in one go

## 10 A PEARL OF AN IDEA ...
Just knot two long ropes together and sling them round your neck — big beads give the very best effect

## 11 BONE UP ON STRUCTURE ...
Slim down those chubby cheeks in mere minutes with artfully applied face shaping blushers

## 12 NOT SUCH OLD HAT ...
Dress up a plain titfer with this designer trick — a matching coloured bow at the back

## 13 FACE SAVER...
Touch up day-long make-up to look like new with crafty cream concealer — nobody will ever know

## 14 CHEAP AND CHEERFUL ...
Wear bright bangles en masse for a technicolor treat. They'll jazz up the plainest outfit

## 15 TAKE A A BOW ...
Racy ribbons do wonders for a simple white shirt

## 16 JUST A LINE ...
Dot a creamy eye pencil along lashes and smudge-shape into an eyeline with a cotton bud

## 17 IT'S A CINCH ...
Don't let your waist go to waste — pull in a loose top with a wide, contrast-colour belt that'll show off your shape beautifully

**18** HIGH-LIFE HAIR ...

Fancy combs turn a day style into a night style in no time at all

**19** DIAMANTE IS A GIRL'S BEST FRIEND ...

Pile on the fake sparkles at party time for that flash with dash million dollar look

**20** IN THE PINK ...

Use one pretty pink colour crayon on your eyes, cheeks and lips for fast face flattery

**21** STREAKS AHEAD ...

Wake up your everyday hair with streaks of spray-on colour

**22** THE GRACE OF LACE ...

Pin a square of pretty lace into a deeply plunging V-neckline for that quietly sexy touch of class

**23** NAIL MAGIC IN MOMENTS ...

Slick off chipped polish in record time with a handy dip-in remover pot

**24** SKIP TO IT ...

Looking for an exercise routine that won't take all day? Get back on the ropes!

**25** RED ALERT ...

For a discreetly wicked look, be a scarlet lady from the very tips of your fingers right down to your toes

# IT'S A GLITTER-KNIT!

Don't pay a fortune for evening elegance. Our sequinned stunner will come to your aid for *any* party!

**MATERIALS** Lister/Lee Motoravia 4-ply, 6 [7:8] 50-g balls. One pair each of 2¼ and 3mm OR nos. 13 and 11 knitting needles. A 4·00 crochet hook. 13 [15:17] strings of 8mm sequins obtainable from Ells & Farrier, 5 Princes Street, London W1R 8PH.

For best results it is essential to use the recommended yarn.

For stockists send SAE to:

George Lee & Sons Ltd, PO Box 37, Whiteoaks Mills, Wakefield, Yorkshire WF2 9SF.

**MEASUREMENTS** To suit bust 81 to 86 [91 to 97:102 to 107]cm OR 32 to 34 [36 to 38:40 to 42]in, length from shoulder 60·5 [61·5: 62·5]cm OR approx 23¾ [24¼:24½]in, sleeve seam approx 18·5cm OR 7¼in.

**TENSION** 27 sts and 36 rows to 10cm OR 4in measured over patt on 3mm OR no. 11 needles.

**ABBREVIATIONS** K = knit; P = purl; st(s) = stitch(es); g st = garter stitch; patt = pattern; rep = repeat; beg = begin(ning); tog = together; yfd = yarn forward; sl = slip; dec = decrease; alt = alternate; rem = remain(ing); S = sequin: to place a sequin in position K next st, but as you work it push a sequin through the centre of st to right side of work; cm = centimetres; in = inch(es).

**NB** Instructions for the larger sizes are in [ ]; where one figure is given, this applies to all sizes.

**Back and front (alike)**

Thread 2 strings of sequins on each ball of yarn, adding more sequins when necessary. With 2¼mm OR no. 13 needles cast on 131 [147:163] sts. Work 8 rows g st.

Change to 3mm OR no. 11 needles.

**Row 1** (Right side) (K2 tog, yfd, K14) to last 3 sts, K2 tog, yfd, K1.

**Row 2 and every following wrong-side row** P.

**Row 3** K1, S 1, (yfd, sl 1, K1, psso, K11, K2 tog, yfd, S 1) to last st, K1.

**Row 5** K1, S 2, (yfd, sl 1, K1, psso, K9, K2 tog, yfd, S 3) to end, but finish last rep S 2, K1 instead of S 3.

**Row 7** K1, S 3, (yfd, sl 1, K1, psso, K7, K2 tog, yfd, S 5) to end, but finish last rep S 3, K1.

**Row 9** K1, S 4, (yfd, sl 1, K1, psso, K5, K2 tog, yfd, S 7) to end, but finish last rep S 4, K1.

**Row 11** K1, S 5, (yfd, sl 1, K1, psso, K3, K2 tog, yfd, S 9) to end, but finish last rep S 5, K1.

**Row 13** K1, S 6, (yfd, sl 1, K1, psso, K1, K2 tog, yfd, S 11) to end, but finish last rep S 6, K1.

**Row 15** K1, S 7, (yfd, sl 1, K2 tog, psso, yfd, S 13) to end, but finish last rep S 7, K1.

**Row 17** K1, S 7, (K2 tog, yfd, S 14) to end, but finish last rep S 8, K1.

**Row 19** K1, S 6, (K2 tog, yfd, K1, yfd, sl 1, K1, psso, S 11) to end, but finish last rep S 6, K1.

**Row 21** K1, S 5, (K2 tog, yfd, K3, yfd, sl 1, K1, psso, S 9) to end, but finish last rep S 5, K1.

**Row 23** K1, S 4, (K2 tog, yfd, K5, yfd, sl 1, K1, psso, S 7) to end, but finish last rep S 4, K1.

▷

# IT'S A GLITTER-KNIT!

◁ **Row 25** K1, S 3, (K2 tog, yfd, K7, yfd, sl 1, K1, psso, S 5) to end, but finish last rep S 3, K1.
**Row 27** K1, S 2, (K2 tog, yfd, K9, yfd, sl 1, K1, psso, S 3) to end, but finish last rep S 2, K1.
**Row 29** K1, S 1, (K2 tog, yfd, K11, yfd, sl 1, K1, psso, S 1) to last st, K1.
**Row 31** K1, K2 tog, yfd, K13, (yfd, sl 1, K2 tog, psso, yfd, K13) to last 3 sts, yfd, sl 1, K1, psso, K1.
**Row 32** P.
These 32 rows form the patt.
Rep them 4 times more. Work should measure approx 46cm OR 18¼in.
**Shape armholes** Keeping patt correct, cast off 10 [12:14] sts at beg of next 2 rows, then dec one st at beg of every row until 101 [109:117] sts rem.
Work straight until 6 complete patts from beg have been worked.
**Divide for neck Next row** Patt 34 [37:40], turn and leave rem sts on a spare needle.
Work on first set of sts as follows:
* Dec one st at neck edge on every row until 18 [20:22] sts rem.
Work 3 [6:9] rows, so ending at armhole edge.
**Shape shoulder** Cast off 7 sts at beg of next and following alt row. Work 1 row.
Cast off *.
With right side facing join yarn to inner end of sts on spare needle, cast off 33 [35:37], patt to end of row.

Work 1 row, then complete as for first side from * to *
**Sleeves**
With 2¼mm OR no. 13 needles cast on 99 sts.
Work 8 rows g st.
Change to 3mm OR no. 11 needles.
Work in patt as given for back and front until 32nd [30th:28th] row of 2nd patt has been worked.
**Shape top** Cast off 10 [12:14] sts at beg of next 2 rows. For 1st and 2nd sizes only, dec one st each end of next 4 [2] rows, then for all sizes, dec one st at beg of every row until 63 [57:51] sts rem. Cast off 3 sts at beg of every row until 15 sts rem.
Cast off.
**Neck border**
Join right shoulder seam. With right side facing join in unsequinned yarn and, using a 2¼mm OR no. 13 needle, K up 160 [170:180] sts evenly all round neck. K3 rows.
**Dec row** K7, K3 tog, (K13 [14:15], K3 tog) 9 times, K6 [7:8]. 140 [150:160] sts.
K 3 rows.
Cast off.
**To complete**
Do not press, but pin out work and leave under a damp cloth until dry.
Join rem shoulder and neck border seam.
Set in sleeves, then join side and sleeve seams. Using 4 thicknesses of yarn, crochet drawstrings for required length to thread through holes of diamond patt at waist and sleeves.
This garment can be washed by dunking it gently in lukewarm soapy water.

## KNITTING WITH SEQUINS

With a single knot tie cotton holding sequins to the working yarn; now slip sequins from cotton on to the working yarn. Move one threaded sequin up close to the yarn that is being wound round the needle in the process of knitting the next stitch, then push the sequin through the loop to the front of the work as the stitch is being completed, as shown in illustration.

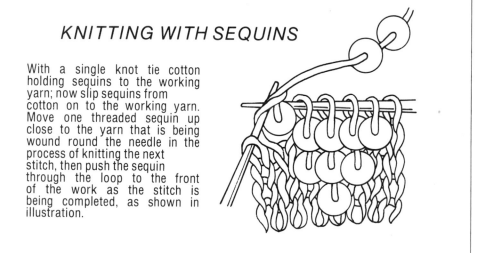

# Keep your flowers daisy-fresh

**If flowers have a habit of wilting
as soon as you put them in water, don't despair.
Here are a few tricks you can follow
to make sure they last for days instead of hours**

The first rule is to keep everything as cool as possible. It's no good proudly placing your vase of flowers in direct sunshine, on the mantelpiece, over the fire or near a radiator.

Before arranging the flowers, harden them off. This means treating the stems to allow water to get to the leaves and petals quickly. To do this expel air bubbles and expose the inner tissue to water by splitting the ends of the stems for $\frac{1}{2}$ in, or longer, according to stem length. The longer the stem, the longer the split should be.

After you've done this, stand the flowers in water up to their necks,
foliage and all, for an hour or so. It's a good idea to use tepid water — about 21°C (70° F) — rather than cold.

Sounds brutal but some flowers, shrubs especially, will absorb water more successfully if the ends of the stems are placed in a couple of inches of boiling water until quite firm.

Once you've arranged them, some flowers, like carnations, mimosa and violas, will last longer if sprayed with a fine mist spray.

Some flowers — bluebells and narcissi — give off sap when cut, become slimy and affect other flowers unless you change the water often.

Unless flowers are sap-giving it's not necessary to change the water daily but do keep an eye on it to ensure it doesn't discolour or get too stale. Always strip the leaves from the part of the stem that is going to be under water and top up water level each day. If you have a water butt in your garden, fill your vases with rain water from it — it's ideal!

Don't crowd too many flowers into one pot.

Finally you'll find that flowers will stay fresher in metal containers than in glass. If placed in sunlight a glass vase will attract light which encourages bacterial activity in the water.

# SUFFER THE LITTLE

**And Sue Papworth has certainly suffered, trying to save them from themselves. Until dawned the day of The Great Tricycle Accident Discovery ...**

WHEN he was feeling particularly philosophical, Father always used to say that The Good Lord Watches Over Drunks and Little Children, and, after extensive field research, I eventually came to the conclusion that He *must*. Drunks I don't have all that much experience of (though I did once witness a pretty convincing display of tightrope dancing on the white line down the middle of the road at rush hour); but the ability of babes of tender years to come up smiling out of mayhem, like the chap in the silent movie who blithely stands there as the house falls about his ears, seems to have no other possible explanation.

Small children seem to put so much concentration and diligence into attempts to annihilate themselves. Their inventiveness can be pretty mind-boggling too, and very bad for the nervous system. My blood pressure has never recovered from the number of times I have seen small persons do their level best to incinerate, flatten, fillet or otherwise slay themselves, and they've all emerged unmarked from experiences that would have done for your average Para.

They do it *just* out of reach, too, which is why practically all adults are always in a state of exhausted mid-gallop. The slightly older child does it at speed, and no one but the Deity has much chance of intervening in cases of bicycle-jousting with sharpened clothes-props, or all manner of things involving old prams, roller skates and steep hills with main roads at the bottom of them. But the little ones are really the heart-stoppers; they can launch into auto-destruct suddenly, or with slow and earnest concentration, or time and time again. *Usually* time and time again, which means you're kept constantly on your toes. And yet the disaster that's ever imminent never actually seems to strike ...

As it happens, I wasn't there when a neighbouring two-year-old launched himself off the landing under the nose of his entire bodyguard and bounced down two flights of stairs, *boing-boing-boing*, one step at a time, on his head, and came up smiling. But I did do the hundred-yards dash a bit later when I chanced to notice him and a teeny chum playing tug of war with a *scythe*, amid gales of innocent infant laughter. You get such heartrendingly wounded looks for horridly spoiling their nice game, too, after you've checked up on the presence of the right number of fingers and started breathing again. The thing was like a razor, but it had done no damage at all.

I was galvanised into full canter once more when little Willie next door decided to eat a broken milk bottle, whipping it from his little fist with a whinny of alarm three seconds after take-off at the other end of the drive. His disappointed shrieks would have got me carted off by the NSPCC instantly, if they'd chanced to be around, but it

## "A two-year-old launched himself off the landing and came up smiling"

would have been nothing to the withering four-year-old scorn that accompanied the information that he'd been doing that *all morning* and he was quite all right thank you very much and could he have his nice bottle back now? And not a drop of blood anywhere — except where I cut myself on the thing.

There was never any blood, either, when the little lad with such a fascination for lawn mowers attempted, about once a week, to see what would happen if you shoved it downhill whilst lying on it with your hand inside the nice interesting bit that went round and round. After several sprints, I learned to face the other way, shut my eyes, heave my shoulders up around the ears and cringe. He mows the lawns now, with the full complement of fingers, and probably has no idea why I leap three feet in the air every time I see him get the mower out of the garage.

It's probably because of their charmed

# CHILDREN!

lives that children enjoy adult disasters with such relish. The entire streetsworth of kiddies really loved it when I set fire to the chip pan and people got the chance to run about shouting and dialling 999 and *three* fire engines rolled up one after another, full of men in helmets with hoses and choppers and radio sets. I expect it's pretty good going that only one little dear tip-toed off home and set about doing precisely the same thing, in order to get her own private visitation. She did all the things I did, but her house stubbornly didn't catch fire. There seems no earthly reason for that.

The ladders possibly gave her little sister the idea of shinning out on to the window-ledge, shutting the window, and promptly falling asleep three floors up, cosily bedded down on three inches of concrete. A batallion of white-lipped adults crept up the stairs, silently prised open the window... and she quietly rolled off the ledge. Into the room, still snoring gently!

It was all very different, of course, when I used to climb out through the safety railings on my third-floor bedroom window and back in again, and mountaineer up the drain-pipes: I was quite safe, because I knew what I was doing. (I've no *idea* why my parents had fits.) But present-day kids, I felt, *didn't* know what they were doing — they were unknowing innocents in their daily dice with death. That's what I thought — until the day that I witnessed the Great Tricycle Accident Discovery...

It chanced that I spotted him fall off his new tricycle whilst negotiating a particularly difficult section of rockery next door but three. He emitted a howl of outrage and, before I could blink, Mrs Rockery galloped out, disentangled tricycle and knees, fed him a ginger biscuit — and he pedalled off, beaming. On the third circuit, he took a kerb too fast, and ended up upside-down under the machine, this time outside an empty house. He sat up, and cast a shrewd glance around. And then he picked up self and trike, trotted along to the pavement outside Mrs Rockery's, upended the trike, crawled under it — and howled. Out she hurtled: up trike, up kiddy, pat-pat, biccy, beam-beam, pedal-pedal... I sat up, electrified.

I watched him, after that, with even more care. Sure enough, when life grew tedious, a neat little traffic accident was constructed, under the wreckage crawled the victim and, *yell*, PING! — out shot the lady with the ginger biscuit, like three lemons coming up on the fruit machine.

And that's when I began to wonder. Maybe it's all a great elaborate *bluff*. Maybe kiddies are on the whole *not* launching themselves innocently to their doom beneath the wheels of a milk float, but actually monitoring parental reflexes, IQ, and ability to stand up under stress — or take to the bottle ... So could it be that they want to test out whether, as Father maintained, The Good Lord really *is* watching over drunks, too?

# 'Happiness is a well chosen pet'

## says JAMES ALLCOCK, our resident vet

KIPLING is unfashionable now, but these telling lines from "The Power of the Dog" could have been written today:

*There is sorrow enough in the*
*    natural way*
*From men and women to fill our day;*
*But when we are certain of sorrow*
*    in store,*
*Why do we always arrange for more?*
*Brothers and sisters, I bid you*
*    beware*
*Of giving your heart to a dog to*
*    tear.*

And not only a dog. Cats, budgies, hamsters, goldfish, all tear at hearts, and I have little doubt that there are even some well loved stick insects.

Not every pet is a satisfactory one, though, and failure occurs usually when the wrong one is chosen. Wrong in the sense that it does not fit a particular household or lifestyle. So the owner gets little pleasure from his pet and the animal leads a bored, ill-kept, ill-cared-for existence.

Let's divide house pets into two groups: caged and uncaged. Dogs and cats can live in the house, but almost all other pets have to be caged or confined in some way. A more basic divide is that cats and dogs are the only pets that can be toilet trained and so live in our houses with us. Budgies and small finches may fly freely around the living room, but pictures and light shades need a regular clean afterwards. The children's pet rat or gerbil might join the family circle for a gallop around the hearth rug in the evening, but a dustpan and brush should accompany him.

Any of the larger animals just cannot come indoors. Ducks and lambs can be delightful companions, but whenever either becomes excited — such as at the sight of food or their owners' return — this excitement produces side effects, semi-liquid in the case of ducks! I've kept both and never convinced either that they should not come indoors, but whenever they did it was a disaster!

Caring for any animal involves finding time, and the time needed varies. Dogs are most demanding. They need much more than food, grooming and a walk. They need company. I don't think anyone should take on a dog if the house is empty all day five days a week. It's not unreasonable to leave a dog alone in the house for three or four hours every morning or afternoon — he could enjoy the chance of an uninterrupted snooze — but no dog can sleep for eight hours each night and then nine hours each day. When he's finished his sleeping needs (about 15 hours a day, but partly cat-naps) every dog needs company and relief from solitary confinement.

Cats are much more independent beings. Two cats (that's why I used the plural), with a cat door so that they can come and go at will, may have a very enjoyable life if owned by a family that is out all day. But if you're single and spend a few nights each week out on the tiles, any pet will become fed up with waiting for your return — and his supper. So with that lifestyle, a goldfish might be the only pet you could be fair to.

Once you have decided on the type of pet that you can keep in the manner which he deserves — and the type you like — there are further choices to be made. What breed of dog suits you? The obvious is to choose a toy dog for a flat, a small dog for a small house, medium dogs for pre-war semis, biggish dogs for the detached house with half an acre, and giant breeds for the country mansion. Not so. The dog's activity is much more important than it's size.

A 12-pound Jack Russell wants to do something all day and if he can't roam in the hedgerows or dig holes in the garden, he will dig holes in the furniture if he is confined throughout the day. Working dogs — collies, spaniels, retrievers — have been bred to spend many hours doing their daily work. In contrast, some giant breeds — St Bernards and Irish wolfhounds, for instance — are bone idle. Twice around the block and they're tired out. They need limited occupation, but a lie down is one of their major pleasures. Those breeds that hunt by sight — whippets, borzois, Salukis, for example — limit their activity to intensive 10-minute explosions of energy, and then are prepared to rest for a few hours before the next gallop which fits in well with many domestic routines.

Coat length is another factor that should influence choice. Long-haired dogs need grooming and that takes time. Many Old English sheepdogs are a matted mess, and miserable dogs because their owners will not give them this time.

WHICH sex should you choose? Decide in advance — don't just take what's there. My own choice is a bitch. Gentler, kinder with children, less inclined to wander. Try and find the dog's breeder, so you can see the mother of your puppy — there is a reasonable chance that pups will grow to be like Mum.

Puppies are ready to leave Mother at seven to eight weeks of age, but there's no reason why you should not select your pup younger than this. The "middle" pup of a litter is often the best. The one that comes forward first is the bossy, dominant, self-assertive pup. The one that hangs back might grow up to be a shy, nervous adult.

Much the same considerations apply in choosing a kitten, except the kitten's early life experiences seem to be all important. The kitten that meets human hands at two or three weeks old is always a gentle kitten and relaxed when he's picked up, while those that are born on farms and don't meet humans until they are eight or 10 weeks old become "spiky" kittens when handled.

Smaller pets might be obtained from their breeder and the budgie that has been handled while in the nest is a much more confident bird than the one that saw only parent birds before he was feathered. Home-bred gerbils, guinea pigs, rats or mice may be quieter to handle than those born in larger establishments.

Pet shops can be a good source of small pets, and perhaps the only source of goldfish, tropical fish, terrapins, snakes, small finches and the larger parrots. Choose your pet shop carefully though. Look for clean, tidy cages with all the animals and birds looking well. Check for adverts about Cage Bird Shows, Rabbit Club Meetings, Aquarius Society outings. These adverts tell you two things: first, that enthusiastic, specialist pet-keepers use this pet shop — and they are reliable judges — and second, the address of the particular club or society. You should join the appropriate club, or at least go to their show before starting to keep your pet. Finding out first means good caring later.

Whatever pet you choose, pick one that is free from blemishes. Don't take on the coughing pup, the lame kitten, the sickly mouse or the fish that swims on his side. There will be ill health later. Because they cannot demand it of you, can I ask, on behalf of all caged animals, that you keep more than one? Even the goldfish all alone in a bowl can be lonely.

Family planning isn't difficult. Two of the same sex cannot breed. Two males might fight, but neutering will prevent this and, of course, unwanted litters if one of each live together. Don't be afraid of asking your vet about this.

Kipling was wrong. Hearts are torn when our pets depart (one hopes from old age) but there is much more enjoyment than sorrow in pet keeping. And this pleasure is greatest when the well-chosen, well-kept pet obviously enjoys being with you.

# Cook of the Realm

*Mrs Betty Clark, from Lerwick, Shetland Isles, finds this supper dish a godsend*

## SAVOURY MEATBALLS AND PASTA

*"This is one of my family's favourites. I also whizz it up if friends drop round for supper. I find it freezes well — but don't add the grated cheese until you actually serve it."*

**Preparation time: 20 min. Cooking time: 35 to 40 min. Serves 4**
**8 oz (225 g) minced beef**
**8 oz (225 g) pork sausagemeat**
**1 tbsp (15 ml) plain flour**
**Salt and ground black pepper**
**3 tbsp (45 ml) oil**
**1 onion**
**4 oz (100 g) mushrooms**
**1 clove garlic**
**1 red pepper**
**3 tbsp (45 ml) tomato purée**
**¼ pt (150 ml) dry cider**
**¼ pt (150 ml) beef stock**
**1 tsp (5 ml) sugar**
**8 oz (225 g) tagliatelle**
**4 oz (100 g) Cheddar cheese, grated**

Place beef and sausagemeat in a bowl with flour and season with salt and pepper. Mix until evenly combined. Pinch off walnut-sized pieces of mixture and roll into balls with floured hands. Place oil in a pan and add meatballs, fry for 10 min until evenly browned. Remove from pan, reserve. Peel and chop onion; wipe and slice mushrooms; skin and crush garlic; core, deseed and slice pepper. Add to pan and fry for 5 min. Add tomato purée, cider, stock, sugar and stir well. Return meatballs to pan, reduce heat; simmer uncovered for 25 to 30 min. Cook tagliatelle in boiling salted water for 10 min. Drain tagliatelle. Serve meatballs and sauce with tagliatelle, sprinkled with cheese.

*Mrs Hull from Wantage, Oxon, makes this super dessert to round off Sunday lunch*

## APPLE MACAROON TART

*"I make this as a change from the usual apple pie. It's delicious served with scoops of softly whipped cream."*

**Preparation time: 25 min. Cooking time: 45 min. Serves 4 to 6**
*Filling:*
**1 lb (500 g) cooking apples**
**2 tbsp (30 ml) water**
*Pastry:*
**6 oz (175 g) plain flour**
**Pinch of salt**
**3 oz (75 g) vegetable shortening**
*Topping:*
**3 oz (75 g) caster sugar**
**2 oz (50 g) ground almonds**
**1 egg**
**Glacé cherries**

Set oven at 350°F, 180°C (Mark 4).
**To make the filling:** peel, core and roughly chop apples. Place in a pan with the water and cook over a low heat for about 15 min, stirring occasionally until soft.
**To make the pastry:** sift flour and salt into a bowl. Rub in shortening until mixture resembles breadcrumbs. Stir in enough cold water to mix to a dough. Roll out on a lightly floured work surface and use to line a 7-in (18-cm) fluted flan dish or flan ring placed on a baking sheet. Trim edges, reserve trimmings. Spoon apples into dish, smooth over.
**To make the topping:** place the sugar, almonds and egg in a bowl and mix well. Carefully sprinkle over apples. Roll out reserved pastry trimmings and cut into strips. Arrange in a lattice design over top of tart. Bake in oven for 30 min. Remove from oven and cool slightly. Cut glacé cherries into quarters and arrange around edge of tart.

READERS' RECIPES!

Judging from Christine France's postbag, our readers must be among the most imaginative cooks in the land! Here are just a few of your own favourite recipes

*Mrs Thomas from Sheffield, South Yorkshire, sent in this mouthwatering main meal*

## PORK CHOPS IN GINGER BEER

*"This dish is simple enough to make an every-day meal and special enough for a dinner party. I often use it when I am entertaining — and a little extra cooking time won't spoil it if my guests are late. It can be prepared and cooked in advance, to give me time to get ready, and reheated when they arrive."*

**Preparation time: 15 min. Cooking time: 1 hr. Serves 4**
**4 pork chops**
**2 tbsp (30 ml) oil**
**1 large onion**
**2 carrots**
**2 sticks celery**
**1 oz (25 g) plain flour**
**11.6-oz (330-ml) can ginger beer**
**1 chicken stock cube**
**¼ pt (150 ml) hot water**
**½ tsp (2.5 ml) soy sauce**
**½ tsp (2.5 ml) lemon juice**
**2 tbsp (30 ml) tomato purée**
**Salt and ground black pepper**
Set oven at 350°F, 180° (Mark 4). Snip rind of chops with scissors to decorate edges. Place oil in a large frying pan and heat. Fry chops in hot oil until browned on both sides (about 10 min). Transfer to cas-serole dish. Peel and slice onion and car-rots. Slice celery, add to remaining oil in pan and fry for 8 min until onion is soft. Stir in the flour and remove from heat. Gradually add the ginger beer, stirring well between each addition. Add stock cube to water and mix into pan. Return to heat and bring to the boil stirring until liquid thickens. Stir in soy sauce, lemon juice, tomato purée and salt and pepper to taste. Pour sauce over chops, cover and bake for 45 min. Serve with new potatoes.

*Mrs Jones from Torquay often whisks up a dream of a dessert to tempt her guests*

## LEMON CHIFFON RING WITH FRUIT

*"This is a well-worn recipe from my scrap-book. I must have been using it, with differ-ent fruit fillings, for the last 20 years! It's a success every time and always looks most impressive on the dinner table."*

**Preparation time: 15 min (plus standing time). Cooking time: 10 min. Serves 6 to 8**
**2 lemons**
**1 pt (500 ml) water**
**2 oz (50 g) cornflour**
**2 eggs**
**6 oz (175 g) sugar**
**Oil**
**3 kiwifruit**
**14-oz (397-g) can cherries**
Pare the zest from the lemons and place in a pan with the water. Bring to the boil and boil for 5 min. Remove from the heat. Strain, reserving the liquid. Place the cornflour in a bowl and separate the eggs. Add the yolks to the cornflour. Squeeze the juice from the lemons and add with the sugar to the cornflour. Mix well. Gradually stir in the lemon-flavoured liquid to the cornflour mixture until smooth. Place in a pan and return to the heat. Bring to the boil, stirring, until mixture thickens. Remove from heat. Lightly oil a 2½-pt (1.4-l) ring mould. Whisk the egg whites until they form soft peaks and fold into the lemon mix-ture. Pour into the prepared ring mould and chill in the refrigerator until set. **To serve:** turn lemon chiffon ring onto a serving plate. Peel and slice the kiwifruit and mix in a bowl with the drained cherries. Pile the fruit mixture into the centre of the ring and serve.

'VE JUST counted up in my diary. One hundred and twenty two nights and I'm no nearer to getting my wicked way than I was — well, one hundred and twenty two nights ago. They say God hates a coward! If that's true, he must be feeling pretty murderous towards me by now.

I sometimes wonder, the way men who employ blonde, long-legged secretaries must, whether I would have been so keen to rent out my room if my prospective lodger had been short, dumpy, bespectacled and balding. The answer has to be a straightforward no. I hadn't even planned to have a lodger. My spare bedroom was to be a workroom where I could paint and keep my sewing machine, and a folding bed for when aunts came to stay. And then, one evening in the pub after the badminton class (where I'd been admiring him through the nets for some time, causing the instructor to tell me more than once to keep my eye on the shuttlecock), he told me he was being turned out of his flat in a week and had nowhere to go. So I said, purely instinctively (and whoever said you should rely on your instinct ought to be shot) that I had a spare room; there wasn't room to swing a mouse in it and the bed was just a narrow folding one, but he was welcome to it, temporarily. He thanked me and said he'd bear it in mind and I thought no more (or rather, not much more) about it. And then a few days later he rang and asked, very shyly and politely, whether he could take me up on my offer, just for a couple of weeks or so until he found somewhere, and I said — I hope there wasn't a tremor in my voice, that I didn't sound too keen — that he could move in tomorrow if he wanted. So he did.

Let me attempt to describe him: he hasn't a lantern jaw or craggy features, nor does he have twinkling blue eyes or a sardonic smile. He is quite simply the most attractive man I've ever met. He is tall and very young, and his body's hard and firm, though that's just a guess as I've never seen him any way other than fully dressed (he wears a tracksuit for badminton), apart from a weeny bit of chest I once spotted when he hadn't done his dressing gown up properly.

He is from the North and has recently taken to calling me "Pet". I suspect his mother — who rings him every Sunday at seven — molly-coddled him. He lives on take-away Chinese curries which create little washing up and, although I can no more picture him wielding a duster or vacuum cleaner than I can picture myself wielding a torque wrench, he is nevertheless very considerate, creeping in so as not to wake me when he comes in late, always cleaning the bath after himself and never taking the last of the milk or cornflakes. Oh, I forgot to mention that he's got a baby face — no, that's not quite right; it conjures up a picture of chubby cheeks and baldness and toothlessness ... More a shy, vulnerable, little-boy-lost look, but at the same time the kind of face that makes women wonder what he looks like without clothes. Well, when I say women I really mean me, though friends have commented on his friendly brown eyes and nice smile. He is eight years younger than me, by the way (I am thirty-two and he is twenty-four), he shaves every other day and wears a grey leather jacket and one earring when he goes out with the lads on a Saturday

# THE MAN WHO CAME TO STAY

**A short story by Sally Sheringham**

night. He is partial to strong beer and the *Beano*, has a degree in chemistry, and had a serious two-year relationship with a girl (very pretty, according to a photo he showed me of her and not like me at all), but she left him and there followed, in his words "a very promiscuous six months". He fancies a woman at work but she's married, and apart from that, as far as I know, there's no one.

I don't want to give the impression that I'm some horrendous lecherous woman with a *penchant* for young boys; nor, indeed, desperate to ensnare a man in marriage. I am perfectly happy as I am — or rather was, before he came to live here. I have many friends and interests, and a fulfilling job. Falling in love and marrying would be the icing on the cake, but the cake itself is perfectly adequate.

My lodger isn't a long-term prospect. At least, I don't think he is. I mean, I don't fantasise about us sitting either side of the fire in old age. Nor, indeed, about us walking down the aisle, friends and relations in tears because we make such a lovely pair. No, I'm afraid my fantasy revolves purely round taking him to bed. By the way, talking of relatives, my mother wouldn't approve. Oh, dear me no, not with the age gap and his Northernness and the weekend earring — especially not the weekend earring! No, what's required here is simply a nice, friendly, warm, sexual relationship to see us through the winter, or for as long as he lives here. In theory that

sounds simple enough, but in practice there are two major stumbling blocks: 1) I have no idea whether or not he fancies me; and 2) if he does, how do we go about making the transition from flatmates to lovers?

The only indications I've had about 1) are that twice he's glanced fleetingly at my bust and once when I told him about a man who'd asked me out he said he had good taste. Oh, and once when he walked in on me when I was in the bath. "Goodness, you gave me a fright," I said laughingly afterwards, and he laughingly replied, "Not nearly such a fright as you gave me!" Whichever way you look at that, it has a distinctly uncomplimentary ring to it.

And 2) is even more difficult. I mean, how can we one minute be watching "Sergeant Bilko" in our dressing gowns and slippers and the next, well, turning our minds to thoughts of love? And yet, if we're both sitting there feeling the same, what a terrible waste …

WE WOULD have made ideal flatmates if only passion (a much more acceptable word, I think, than lust) hadn't raised its ugly, irrational head. We talk openly on any subject. Sometimes we go out alone, sometimes together. We like each other's friends. Sometimes we play Scrabble or go to the cinema. Sometimes I go to the pub with him and his mates. There's something nice about sitting in a pub surrounded by shy, impressionable young men. It makes me feel rather woman-of-the-worldish. I am keen for them to like me and find me attractive,

# THE MAN WHO CAME TO STAY

so I can imagine them saying to him: "How on earth can you live under the same roof as her and not take advantage?" And he will reply (this is pure fantasy, of course): "With extreme difficulty. In fact it's slowly driving me crazy."

It's certainly beginning to drive *me* crazy.

"I'll tell you what it's like," I told my colleagues in the canteen one day. "It's like being on a strict diet and having a chocolate eclair constantly waving underneath your nose."

"Except that you're not on a diet," Ros pointed out. "I can't see what the problem is. Just cook him a candlelit dinner, get him blind drunk and then proposition him." Ros is stunning and has never had to proposition a man in her life.

"I've tried that. The words won't come out," I said. "Besides, I'm not accustomed to propositioning. He should do it."

"That's just where you're wrong, right?" said Norma. Norma is a feminist from California where, according to her, everything is more laid back, cool and together than it ever will be over here. "We're living in liberated times, okay? This guy's English, shy, insecure and young. So? He's scared stiff of you! He has no trouble picking up some dolly bird in a disco because he sees her as an inferior being. But a woman like you is outside his experience. You've housed him, right? You're his intellectual equal, right? He enjoys your company, right? You're the experienced older woman, right? He's petrified he's going to blow the whole scene, so he's hanging in there keeping cool but praying you're going to make the first move. Right?"

"No, it's not right, it's all wrong," said Jean fiercely, turning on me. "Why on earth is a nice girl like you wasting your time with a — a *lout* like him? You've said yourself that he drinks, never buys toothpaste or washing-up liquid and only pays £10 a week rent. It's blatantly obvious he's taking advantage of your good nature. *And* there's the age difference. I may be old fashioned, but the idea of a relationship based purely on — on lust, I find most distasteful. I'm surprised, a well-brought-up girl like you. Where's the *romance* in it all? What you want to do is find a financially secure man your own age. With prospects." Jean is married to a financially secure man with prospects. He's called Eric. He is also stout and boring and never laughs. I said to Jean, rather severely in retrospect, that if she didn't read so many romantic novels maybe she would have a more realistic view of the world in general and relationships in particular. I said that many sexual relationships were based on far less than he and I had. Besides, how could she, a married woman with a husband to keep her warm in bed, possibly understand what it was like to be a single woman, to wake up each morning with a cold water bottle for company?

"If you must know," she replied frostily, "Eric and I prefer twin beds," and she stood up and left without finishing her jam roly-poly and custard.

"Wow!" said Norma. "That is one hung-up lady, right? A real yesterday lady. But you are a today lady and you've got every right to exploit that situation. Look, just hang in loose and say to the guy straight: 'You turn me on and I'd really appreciate it if our living-together relationship expanded to incorporate sex.' Right?"

I nodded, knowing that I would no more say that than do as Ros now suggested; accost him when he got home from work wearing nothing but a short black see-through nightie and a pair of high heels.

I am beginning to see Jean's point of view more and more, and part of me very much wishes that I too were a "yesterday lady", living in a world where women experience only love, where men do all the asking. And the thing is, however much advice I'm given, it all boils down to one thing: me (and I can see it has to be me) saying, "Would you like to sleep with me tonight?" It should be easy. Nothing *that* serious can happen — I mean, the ceiling won't fall in. The best that can happen is that he'll say yes; the worst is that he'll say no. But there's also a third possibility. He could laugh. He could say, "You must be kidding!" and *laugh*. And it's that, ridicule, not rejection, that I'm afraid of.

SO THE weeks flash by and every evening I try to summon up the courage to say something, and every evening I lose my nerve. It's getting bitterly cold and snow is forecast. My bedsocks and hot water bottle are in full use, and he, apparently, wears an old jumper in bed ... THIS IS THE WINTER OF MY DISCONTENT I write in capitals in my diary.

Curiously, with all this going on, I've been asked out by three different men. Jean says it's the sparkle in my eyes. Norma says it's a "kinda karma" I give off. I suspect it's a sort of hungry look that I've acquired over the last few weeks, noticeable only to men.

All three are quite charming but sadly they pale beside the physical beauty of my lodger. (I'm hoping that one day looks will cease to be important, that I'll be quite happy with a Jean's Eric lookalike — as long as he makes me laugh. But I'm afraid I haven't yet reached that stage of maturity.) I asked all three men back for a coffee, not to make my lodger jealous but to make him aware other men find me attractive.

At Christmas he went north to his family and I went south to mine. I busied myself with homely, wholesome activities and, oh, the joy of being back on an even keel, of being absorbed by domestic family trivia. Only at night did I sometimes think about him, but, because he was hundreds of miles away and quite unobtainable, it was easy to smother any longings with one of my mother's Agatha Christie's. I returned to my flat, refreshed and happy that he was to be away another two weeks. The storm had passed, everything was back to normal. I had friends round for supper, spring-cleaned my flat, painted a picture and made a dress. The chocolate eclair was well out of sight and mind. I was at peace with the world, suffering only a temporary hiccough when he rang long-distance to see how I was.

But it was the lull before the most raging storm of all. As soon as I heard his key turn in the lock, saw his beautiful smiling face peering round the kitchen door as he said, "Hello, Pet, have you missed me?" all the old churnings and yearnings and achings started chugging away again.

It's worse than it ever was before. Some nights I cry myself to sleep. At work if I don't keep my emotions on a tight leash they are liable to break out all over the place. And this morning, I couldn't even bring myself to speak to him, and went out slamming the door so hard a picture fell off the wall.

I must put a stop to this once and for all. Today. It's a bleak January Saturday afternoon. The flat is freezing and the sky threatens snow. He's at a football match. Spurs v Sunderland. It's being televised but I refuse to watch it to see if I can spot him in the crowd. As soon as he comes in I'm going to say, "You're going to have to leave. Tomorrow, if possible."

He's back now but he's gone straight into the bathroom, so I don't have a chance. My heart's thumping like a drum. He emerges, wearing his best black cords, leather jacket and earring and announces he's off to a party. "I'm feeling optimistic tonight," he says, brandishing his blue toothbrush as if it's a symbol of his virility. (He pauses and, yes, I *know* I could have said it then but my mouth's gone dry.) "See you then. Have fun."

It is now one-fifteen. I have watched an entire Edward G Robinson film without taking in a word and have drunk a whole bottle of Sainsbury's medium dry sherry without tasting a drop. I am past the stage of imagining — or caring about — the hair colour and stature of the girl with whom he has chosen to spend the night; I am now considering my future in this modern world, where single women are expected to be careerists, have mortgages, be strong, fearless, tough, single-minded, be able to fend for themselves, be the initiators of sexual relationships, and at the same time be good cooks, vulnerable and sexy.

I trust I'm drunk enough to go straight to sleep. The snow has started to fall and my teeth are chattering slightly, but I'm not going to cry. I'm just over by the sink filling my hot water bottle, when two rather unexpected things happen. One is my hot water bottle springs a leak. The other is I hear his key turning in the lock. I swear and tell him about the leak and then, without hesitation — are these really *my* words? — I say, "I suppose you wouldn't like to be my hot water bottle substitute for tonight?"

THERE is the most dreadful silence, and he's looking at me the way a fishmonger might if asked for a pound of curtain material, filleted. Then he says, "Are you serious?" Oh, God, he's going to laugh and I'm so tempted to say no, I was only joking, but my neck muscles, controlled by some outside force, are making my head nod. And then — is this fantasy, am I dreaming? — he gives a kind of schoolboy whoop and picks me up and swings me round and round and his hair's all snow wet and he's saying, "I thought you'd never ask!"

So far, so good. We're both undressed and lying together in my bed and his arms are round me and his body's all warm and muscular and — comforting, if you know what I mean. The snowflakes are flapping about like crazy outside and I hope they drift, particularly round the front door so that it'll be impossible to go out tomorrow, even for the Sunday papers.

So here we are all warm and curled up and the happiness I feel, the sheer relief that it'll all been sorted out, is overwhelming. But there's still one more hurdle to go: is he or isn't he going to make the transfer from being hot water bottle to lover? Not that it matters really — it's so blissful just having him here to cuddle. But already he's gently kissing my face and neck, which in my experience is far from normal hot water bottle behaviour, and now he's kissing my ear and he's whispering. "I've been fantasising about this since the day I moved in."

My thanks must of course go to faulty hot water bottles and good old British winters, though what I can't help wondering in passing is how Californians, without either of these useful devices, ever "get their act together". Perhaps that's why they're always telling each other to stay cool. But as if it matters what they do or say in California. What's going on right here is far more interesting...

THE END
© Sally Sheringham, 1984

# IF I WEREN'T ME...

... who would I like to be? That's the question we asked a few famous faces to answer — and were in for some surprises!

"I'd like to be one of the Muppets because everything they do seems to be such fun — and they meet all the stars!"
**BONNIE LANGFORD**

"A well-fed tom cat, beautifully groomed, sitting on a cushion all day long just watching the world go by."
**LES DAWSON**

"I'd like to be ... 20 per cent the Rev Sydney Smith (for the humour and the passion) ... 3 per cent Dennis Norden, for his voice. He cannot sing in a much more interesting way than I cannot sing ... 25 per cent my father. He died when I was young, but was marvellously equable and multi-talented. Being an ex-marine engineer, he could turn his hand to anything. I particularly admired his skill at cutting his own hair and tap-dancing ... 5 per cent Andrew Carnegie (for the money) ... 5 per cent Arthur Wellesley, First Duke of Wellington. (It would be nice, just now and then, not to give a hoot for other people's feelings.) ... 15 per cent Molière (for his ability to speak French) ... And 27 per cent Arthur Marshall, for his charm and joie de vivre!"
**FRANK MUIR**

"I'd like to have the brain of Golda Meir and the looks of Marilyn Monroe!"
**FAITH BROWN**

"Ginger Rogers — to have been able to dance like her, partnered by Fred Astaire, and wear those romantic evening gowns. I can't think of anything more wonderful!"
**DANA**

"I'd like to be my wife — because I'm such a fantastic husband to her!"
**ROY CASTLE**

"I'd like to be Prime Minister because I think we should spend more money on ourselves — on health and education. Mrs Thatcher is spending too much on armaments and fighter planes while hospitals are having to close through lack of money. People shouldn't have to collect money in the streets to pay for kidney machines."
**RODNEY BEWES**

"Who or what would I like to be if I weren't me?
Roger Moore, handsome, famous and rich?
Margaret Thatcher, a clever, powerful head?
No — a being from some far-flung planet
Sent down to observe and
Help mankind to a future without wars
And without disease.
Mind you, at times I wonder if I am ·
Me."
**STRATFORD JOHNS**

"Myself in a thousand years — because I'd like to see what happens in the future."
**ISLA ST CLAIR**

"My greatgrandson, — future world golf champion and Nobel Peace Prize holder!"
**TIM BROOKE-TAYLOR**

# THE PATCHWORK QUILT YOU'LL TREASURE

**Patchwork quilts cost a small fortune to buy. So why not follow our simple step-by-step instructions and stitch your own, full of family memories?**

Patchwork, or pieced work as it is often called, is closely associated with the early American settlers, whose pioneer womenfolk recycled the family's old clothing to make warm quilts. They evolved the patterns as they worked and, as the quilts were handed down, so too were the patterns — with many memories woven in.

Our machine-sewn quilt is based on one of those early designs, a nine-patch pattern called The Ohio Star. This version is quick to stitch and quilt, and if you use favourite family fabrics, it too could become an heirloom to treasure.

## CHOOSING FABRICS

The best fabrics are dress-weight cottons, poly-cottons and light furnishing fabrics. Choose patterns and colours carefully. The Ohio Star, for example, needs dark and light shades to make the star stand out.

## MAKING TEMPLATES

Cut templates (your patterns for cutting the fabric) from thick card that will keep its shape and is easy to draw round.

## MARKING AND CUTTING

Draw round templates on wrong side of fabric with a pencil. Cut out with an extra 6 mm (¼ in) all round for turnings. The pencil marks will be your sewing line.

## MAKING THE QUILT

**Materials:** co-ordinating cottons or poly-cottons; calico or curtain lining for backing; 2½-oz polyester wadding; bias binding; two 10-cm (4-in) square templates.
**Method for one star square:** make 2 10-cm (4-in) square templates, divide 1 into 4 triangles and cut 16 fabric triangles, 8 dark, 8 light. Cut 4 matching dark 10-cm squares for corners and 1 10-cm square of contrasting fabric for centre. With right sides together sew 1 dark and 1 light small triangle together to make 1 large triangle. Make 8 large triangles in this way. Press seams to one side. Join large triangles together, dark to light to form 4 squares. Join these to dark corner squares in rows of 3 with a square of contrasting fabric at the centre. This makes 1 30-cm (12-in) square. Make 4 more.
**Method for main pattern:** cut 4 30-cm (12-in) squares from light cotton, allowing 6 mm (¼ in) for seams. Sew to pieced squares in rows of 3 (see right). Your work should now measure 90 cm (36 in) square. To enlarge quilt, continue adding 5-cm (2-in) borders and rows of 10-cm squares until the quilt will fit your bed.
**Making up and quilting:** cut backing fabric and wadding 5 cm (2 in) larger all round than the patchwork. Sandwich wadding between patchwork and backing, and tack through all layers to secure it. For hand quilting start in the centre and work outwards with small running stitches round the shapes. Or machine stitch along seam lines. The large squares can also be quilted in the Ohio Star pattern. Finish the quilt by trimming raw edges and binding with bias binding.

**Piece together family memories with our quilt — step-by-step diagrams on page 143**

# MEET
# DOLLY DAY-DREAM

Our traditional rag doll would
be a dream come true for most little girls — and
quite a lot of big ones too!
To find out how to make her, and her wardrobe of
clothes for every occasion,
turn to page 139

One basic wardrobe
takes Dolly from
morning to bedtime

First things first.
Bloomers no rag doll
should be without

Then the prettiest
petticoat in fine
lawn edged with lace

The demure day dress
would be equal to
any social occasion

The stylish coat,
hat and muff will
always cut a dash

And there's a cosy
flowered nightie
for sweet dreams

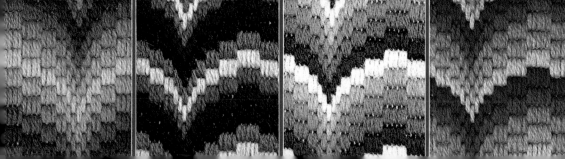

Vary the colour combinations of your tapestry to harmonise with your overall scheme

# TAPESTRY FOR BEGINNERS

### Tapestry is a lovely hobby — soothing, and always handy to work on. If you've never yet put thread to canvas, why not start with our stylish cushion cover in bold Bargello stitch?

Bargello (or Florentine) stitch takes its name from the Bargello Palace in Florence, because the pattern of the stitch mirrors the architectural design of the palace colonnades. The stitch is straight, simple and, as it is worked within 5 vertical holes, is very fast growing.

## MAKING THE CUSHION

**Materials:** 5 hanks of 2-ply crewel wool in toning colours; 46 cm (18 in) of single thread canvas (14 to 1 in), 66 cm (26 in) wide; size 20 tapestry needle; sharp scissors; thimble; 1 extra hank of wool for cord and tassels.

**Starting off:** cover raw edges of the canvas with tape to prevent it from fraying. Fold the canvas into 4 to make a centre crease.

**Working the stitches:** cut wool into 81-cm (32-in) lengths. Thread needle with 4 strands of the darkest colour and knot end. Work the first foundation row from the middle of the canvas outwards to each edge to get the pattern central. All subsequent rows are simply repeats with a change of yarn colour. Leave a 5-cm (2-in) margin of plain canvas all round. Begin the work

with a knot on the right side of the canvas about 4 cm (1½ in) away from the starting point. When this part of the work is complete, the knot is cut off. Bring the needle up on the centre fold line and work the first block of 5 stitches within 5 vertical holes as shown on chart (below). Step down 2 holes and work the next block of 4 stitches. Continue along the row, following the chart, finishing about 5 cm (2 in) away from the edge. Start other rows at edge of canvas, repeating pattern from the row above and changing colour of yarn. When the length of yarn is almost finished, darn in about 5 cm (2 in) neatly through the worked stitches on the wrong side of tapestry.

**Making up:** cut a piece of backing to the size of the canvas. With right sides of backing and canvas together, sew round three sides where embroidery finishes. Turn right side out. Insert feather cushion pad, fold in raw edge and hand stitch to close opening. Stitch cord round edge and sew a tassel onto each corner.

Now turn the page for our step-by-step instructions to make the tassels and cord ▷

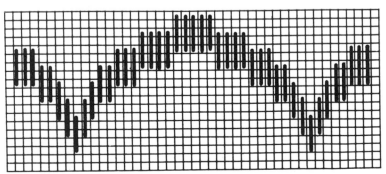

Each stitch of the Bargello pattern is worked within five vertical holes

## MAKING THE TASSELS

1. Cut a piece of card 9 cm (3½ in) in depth. Wind the wool round the card 62 times. Thread a length of wool and slip it under all the strands on the card and take the thread round once more. Slip the hank carefully off the card, pull the thread up very firmly and tie securely. Do not cut off these ends of thread. They will be used to sew the tassel onto the corners of the cushion.

2. Take another very long length of wool, double it and thread it through a tapestry needle. Place the thread round the hank to make a "waist" for the tassel, 2 cm from the top. Slip needle through the looped end of the thread, pull it quite firmly, wrap wool round the tassel once more and secure it firmly with a small stitch.

3. Still using the same thread, proceed to work your first row of button-hole stitch into the thread that you have tied round to make the "waist". Do not pull the stitches too tight or work them too closely. Work approximately 8 stitches around the "waist".

4. Continue working rows of button-hole stitches round head of tassel, always putting your needle into the bar formed by stitch of preceding row. Continue until you have very nearly reached the top of the tassel. To close in your stitches, start working into every alternate bar only, thus reducing the number of stitches until you've completely covered the head of the tassel.

5. To finish off the thread, push the needle down from the top through the centre of the tassel. Cut off thread at the level of loops. Cut through the loops and trim the end of the fringe.

Attach the four tassels to each corner of the cushion after stitching on the cord.

## MAKING THE CORD

1. To make the long cord to edge your cushion, you require two people each holding a pencil with a distance between them of approximately 426 cm (168 in). Wind wool 10 times around the pencils, making 20 strands in all.

2. Keeping the thread taut, spin one of the pencils round and round until the thread is twisted tightly against the pencils.

3. With a third person to grip the middle of the cord, fold from this centre point bringing both pencils together. Do not release the tension. One person must hold the pencils while the second person grips the cord near the looped end. Gradually release the cord from the two pencils to form its natural twist. Secure the ends together by winding thread round the cord and stitching. Stitch cord to cushion.

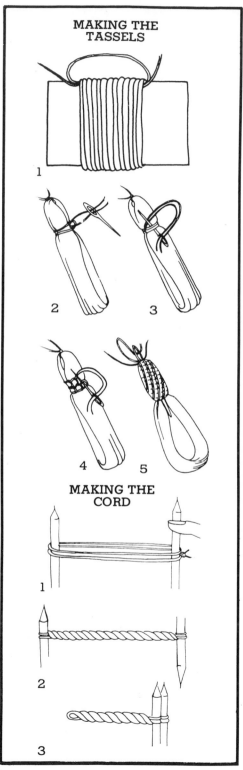

MAKING THE TASSELS

MAKING THE CORD

# HOW TO MAKE
# DOLLY DAY-DREAM

◁134 Made in the traditional way from creamy unbleached calico, our rag doll has embroidered features and thick, wool hair. She's nearly 2 ft tall with jointed arms and legs to make her easy to dress.

## MAKING THE PATTERNS

To enlarge the grid patterns for the doll (on p 140) and her wardrobe (on p 142) draw 15-mm squares on large sheets of paper, then transfer the pattern by plotting the outlines with small markers, starting at the widest points of the top, bottom and side edges. Join them up and mark on instructions. Allowances have been made for seams, hems and facings.

## CUTTING OUT

Lay patterns on fabric and cut out. Follow the cutting instructions marked on patterns, reversing one shape to make a pair where indicated.

## MAKING UP

Pin and baste edges together before stitching. Machine all seams on wrong side of fabric unless otherwise stated. A 6-mm seam allowance is included except at lower edge of body where it's 1.5 cm.

## MAKING THE DOLL

**Materials:** 50 cm of unbleached calico, 91 cm wide; 500 g polyester toy filling; 2 50-g balls of double knitting wool; 1 pair child's white ¾-length socks to fit 6 to 8½ shoe; 1 pair doll's shoes, size 4; Coats Anchor stranded embroidery cotton (colours 0137, 0136, 019, 0308, black and white); sewing cottons; tracing paper; pink and brown crayons; narrow ribbon.

**Arms:** stitch Arm shapes together, leaving open between dots. Turn to right side, smooth seam around hand and push a little stuffing down. Stitch along lines to make fingers. Stuff arm to elbow, stitch across joint line then stuff rest of arms. **Legs:** for each leg, stitch together calico Lower Leg shapes down centre front seam, E to F. Repeat in sock fabric. With wrong side of sock to right side of calico, baste the two pieces together round all edges. Baste calico soles to sock soles. Stitch Upper Leg to Lower Leg, G to E to G. Stitch together back seam of Lower Leg only, G to H. Baste and stitch Foot Sole to Lower Leg, F to H. Complete stitching back seam of Upper Leg, G to J. Turn leg to right side, stuff to dotted line at knee. With centre front matched to centre back seam, make 2 rows of stitching along dotted lines. Complete stuffing leg and baste open end. **Face:** stay stitch all round seam line of calico Front Head. Trace outline of full-size face features (below). Transfer onto fabric by putting Front Head on a board, covering it with tracing and pricking through paper with pin to mark outlines. Pencil in features lightly along pinpricks. **Eyes, nose and mouth:** with a single strand of 2 shades of blue embroidery cotton, work eyes in straight stitches radiating from the centre to give a shaded effect. Fill in the white eye corners and red mouth with vertical straight ▷

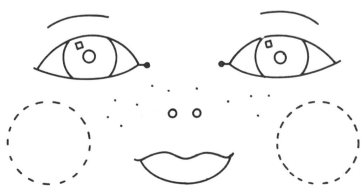

**Trace Dolly's full-size features to embroider**

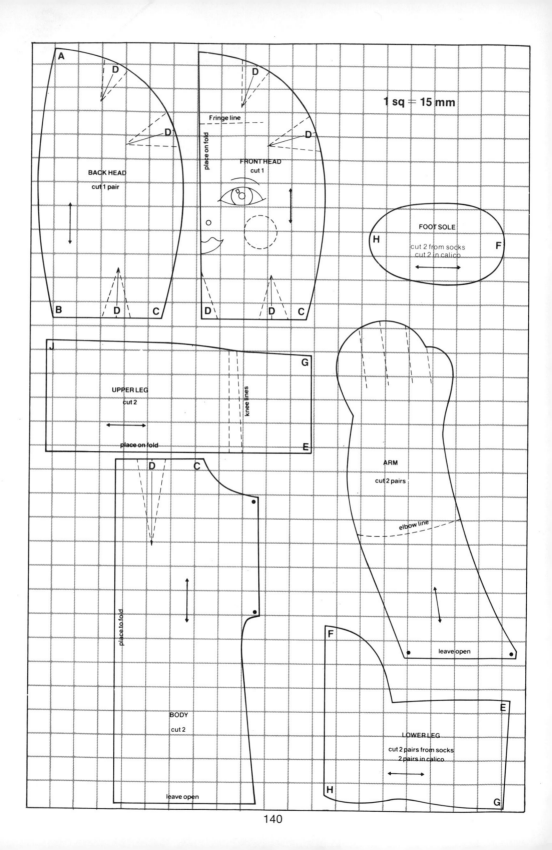

1 sq = 15 mm

BACK HEAD
cut 1 pair

FRONT HEAD
cut 1

Fringe line

place on fold

FOOT SOLE
cut 2 from socks
cut 2 in calico

UPPER LEG
cut 2

place on fold

knee lines

ARM
cut 2 pairs

elbow line

leave open

BODY
cut 2

place to fold

LOWER LEG
cut 2 pairs from socks
2 pairs in calico

leave open

leave open

140

satin stitches, using 2 strands of embroidery cotton together. Outline eyes and eyebrows with a single strand of brown in chain stitch. Stitch pupils and nose in single strand of black, stitch a white highlight in each eye. Mark cheeks lightly with pink crayon, dot on freckles. **Head and body:** join Back Heads together, A to B. Make darts around Front and Back Heads and at neck edges in Body shapes. Baste arms to right side of one Body piece between dots. Stitch Front Head to the Body piece at neck, matching Cs. Repeat for Back Head. Match and stitch both sides of Head and Body together (enclosing arms in body) in a continuous seam, leaving open at body base. Turn to right side and stuff evenly. Turn under raw edges of body and insert legs, leaving gap in centre. Top stitch legs and body through all fabrics with several rows. **Hair:** to make fringe, cut a 7 by 2-cm strip of paper. Lay flat, cover with 10-cm lengths of wool placed centrally. Enclose wool with another strip of paper, machine through centre. Tear away paper, fold fringe at machine line and sew on dotted line indicated on pattern. Trim to just above eyebrows. For plaits, cut paper strips, 16 cm long, and strands of wool, 61 cm long. Stitch as for fringe. Sew

to centre seam line of head and hold individual strands in place around the head with stitches. Stitch wool to face below cheeks. Gather to each side of head, plait and tie with ribbon.

## HOW TO MAKE HER WARDROBE

Try clothes on the doll as you make them to check for fit. Different fabrics and the amount of filling will affect her shape.

### PANTS AND PETTICOAT

**Materials:** 1 m white cotton lawn; 3.5 m of 1 cm lace; 60 cm white bias binding; 70 cm very narrow elastic; 2 small press fasteners; sewing cotton.

**Method for pants:** stitch centre front and back seams. On right side stitch 3 rows of lace across one side for back of pants. Stitch leg seams, F to G to F. Make 1 cm hem at waist and legs, leaving gap to thread elastic. Stitch lace around legs on seam line. Cut elastic to fit doll's waist and legs, thread through and fasten. Sew up gap.

**Method for petticoat:** cut a piece of material 88 by 25 cm for petticoat skirt. Stitch seam leaving 6 cm open at waist. Neaten opening. Hem lower edge and sew 3 rows of lace. Join Bodice Back and Bodice Front at shoulder, D to E. Stay stitch round neck and armholes. Stitch 4 rows of lace to Bodice Front. Bind neck and armholes and cover armholes with lace. Join side bodice seams. Gather waist of skirt and stitch to bodice. Neaten centre back opening and stitch lace round neck. Sew on press fasteners.

### DRESS

**Materials:** 1 m cotton lawn; embroidery silk and dots for smocking (optional); shirring elastic; 3 buttons; 3 press fasteners; sewing cotton.

**Method for dress:** join Front Bodice to Back Bodice at shoulders, H to J. Stay stitch round neck. Cut strip 35 by 4 cm for neck frill. With right sides together, fold in half and stitch across the short edges. Turn to right side. With raw edges together, pin frill around neck, from dot to dot at centre back, making a pleat every 2 cm. Stitch and neaten raw edges. Top stitch close to seam. Cut 2 pieces of fabric 35 by 30 cm for Skirt Back and one piece 74 by 30 cm for Skirt Front. Stitch Skirt Backs leaving top 5 cm open. Match Front and Back Skirts together and use pattern guide to shape armholes, K to L. Either smock, or gather top of Skirt Front and Back with rows of shirring elastic. Stitch Skirt Backs to Bodice Backs between □s. Stitch Skirt and Bodice Fronts together. Gather upper ▷

**1 sq = 15 mm**

PETTICOAT BODICE BACK
cut 1 pair

place on fold

lace placement lines

PETTICOAT BODICE FRONT
cut 1

PANTS
cut 1 pair

place to fold of fabric

fold line

fold line

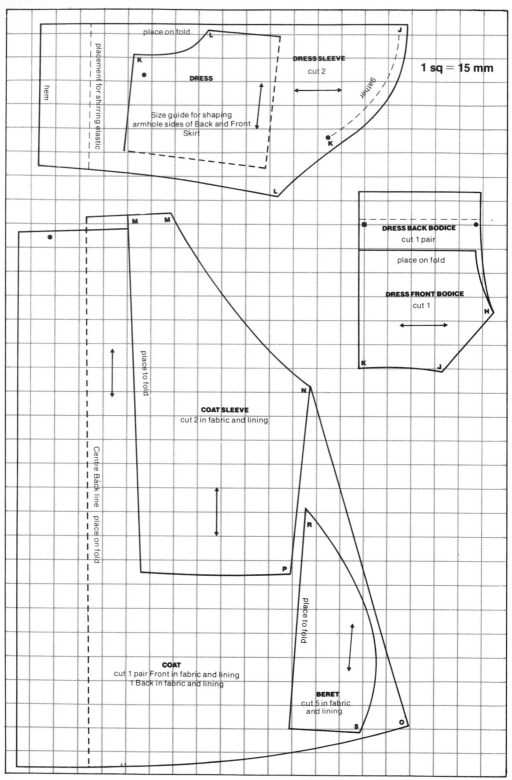

place on fold

L

K

**DRESS**

**DRESS SLEEVE**
cut 2

1 sq = 15 mm

J

gather

K

hem

placement for shirring elastic

Size guide for shaping
armhole sides of Back and Front
Skirt

L

M  M

**DRESS BACK BODICE**
cut 1 pair

place on fold

**DRESS FRONT BODICE**
cut 1

H

place to fold

K  J

**COAT SLEEVE**
cut 2 in fabric and lining

N

Centre Back line  place on fold

R

place to fold

P

**COAT**
cut 1 pair Front in fabric and lining
1 Back in fabric and lining

**BERET**
cut 5 in fabric
and lining

S  O

◁ edges of sleeves between dots, K to J. Hem the wrists. Stitch 2 rows of shirring elastic along pattern line. Fit sleeves into armholes matching J to K to L. Cut and sew sash strips 40 by 6.5 cm. Press flat and baste to Skirt Backs just below shirring.. Join skirt sides and sleeves together enclosing sashes. Neaten back opening, sew on press fasteners and buttons. Hem skirt and make bow for front of neck.

## COAT, BERET AND MUFF

**Materials:** 60 cm needlecord, 112 cm wide; 60 cm lining fabric, 112 cm wide; 32 cm narrow cord for muff; fur fabric for collar, beret and muff; 3 press fasteners; 3 buttons; sewing cottons.

**Method for coat:** with right sides facing, stitch Sleeves to Fronts and Back, M to N. Stay stitch round neck. Stitch underarm and side seams, P to N to O. Repeat for lining. Press seams.' Cut strips of fur fabric 36 by 5 cm. Fold in half with fur sides together. Stitch across short ends. Turn to right side, stitch to right side of coat around neck from dot to dot. Press hem and front facings to wrong side on both fabrics. Turn up sleeves and tack. Fit lining into coat, wrong sides together and slip stitch into place. Sew on press fasteners and cover with buttons.

**Method for beret:** stitch each Beret Section R to S. Repeat for lining. Cut 7 cm circle of fur fabric, gather round the edge, add a little filling, pull up gathers tightly to make a bobble and sew to beret. With wrong sides together, fit lining into beret and baste raw edges together. Cut strip of needlecord 36 by 5 cm for band. With right sides together, join short edges. Turn to right side and stitch one edge to beret, folding in raw edge as you do so. Fold band in half, turn in raw edge and sew to lining.

**Method for muff:** cut fur fabric and lining 18 by 10 cm. Join short edges of fur together. Turn to right side and turn in raw edges. Repeat for lining. With wrong sides together, fit and slip stitch lining into muff. Sew on narrow cord.

## NIGHTDRESS

**Materials:** 80 cm fine cotton; 1.5 m lace edging; 70 cm narrow ribbon; shirring and narrow elastic; sewing cotton.

**Method for nightdress:** cut 2 pieces of fabric 48 by 43 cm. Use dress guide to shape armholes. Cut 2 sleeves from Dress pattern. Stitch front and back shoulders. Make hem at neck edge. Sew on lace. Turn up sleeves and stitch a row of shirring elastic. Fit sleeves into armholes. Stitch side and underarm seams. Thread elastic through neck to fit doll. Hem lower edge and stitch on lace. Add a ribbon at neck.

## HOW TO MAKE THE
# PATCHWORK QUILT

*Continued from page 132*

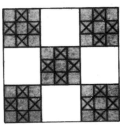

1. Make 2 10-cm sq templates. Cut 1 into 4 triangles. Cut out fabric with extra 6 mm border all round for seam allowance

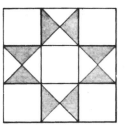

2. To make 1 30-cm square sew dark and light triangles together into 10-cm squares. Join plain and patterned squares in rows of three

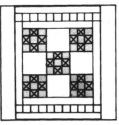

3. For the top of the quilt sew 5 30-cm patterned sq and 4 light 30-cm sq into 3 rows. Press seams. Sew rows tog to make 1 90-cm sq

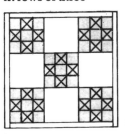

4. Enlarge quilt with 5-cm strips of fabric to top and bottom then along sides, to make 1 100-cm sq. Press seams

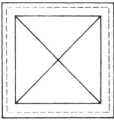

5. Extend with rows of 10-cm sq and 5-cm strips to make quilt 130 by 100 cm. Sandwich wadding between lining and quilt

# Family fun

Your bank balance won't stretch to expensive entertainments? So what! There's loads of family fun to be had for free if you know where to look. Just start with Linda France's A to Z of painlessly penny-wise pleasures

*A* is for ACTING and AMATEUR DRAMATIC SOCIETIES. There's bound to be one in the area where you live — and if there isn't, why not start one up? And, no, you don't have to be "terribly theatrical, darling" — if you're not keen to tread the boards, your help might be welcome backstage in the wardrobe, make-up or publicity departments. Encourage little ones to take part in school plays and volunteer your services when it comes to stitching angel wings and halos. Keep suitable old clothes for children to dress up in at home.

*B* is for BOOKS and sitting in your living room curled up on the sofa reading a jolly good novel. I'm sure it is one of life's greatest pleasures and costs nothing but a trip to the local library. Make a habit of noting the best sellers' lists published in the Press and reading one of the books mentioned. B is for BIRD-WATCHING too. Scatter cake and bread crumbs and watch the variety of birds which visit your garden. Buy the family an *I Spy* book — they won't all be starlings and sparrows. If you want

more information, send an sae to The Wildfowl Trust, at Slimbridge, Gloucester GK2 7BT.

*C* is for COMPETITIONS. Look out for all the fabulous free-entry competitions in *Woman's Realm*, or for groceries with competition labels. Many of the latter will need research from either your book shelves or the library. Often there's a slogan to write and it's worth making an effort to find a catchy phrase. Ask the children to help as they have a knack of being able to say something apt and witty in an original style. C is also for CATHEDRALS and walking

through the interiors to admire stained glass and architecture, and for CLIMBING the towers for a gargoyle's eye view over the city. And C is for your parish CHURCH. Your could endeavour to find out more about its history or merely sit quietly and CONTEMPLATE.

*D* is for DREAMING of either the fantastic, like being discovered in the local supermarket and becoming a stage and screen superstar, to the more realistic dreams like walking the Pennine Way or climbing the Brecon Beacons — and DOING something about it!

*E* is for EXERCISE. If your living room is as tiny as mine you won't be able to do armsstretch and knees-bend with all the family. However, I'm sure it must be more of a giggle if you can. Perhaps you should all gather in the back garden. I guarantee that your children won't need any persuasion to take part, but your partner probably will. You need to be pretty fit to EXPLORE, on foot or by bicycle, nearby towns and villages. Scour the local paper for news of any EXHIBITIONS too.

144

# for FREE!

**F**is for FIRST AID. The degree to which we are protected at home depends on how aware we are of the dangers involved in everyday activities. The British Red Cross Society offer useful training schemes in first aid to people of all age groups, starting from five years upwards. For more information, get in touch with your local branch headquarters — you'll find their address and number in your local telephone directory. Then you can try out your techniques on one another!

**G**is for GAMES. Keep a drawer reserved for playing cards, snakes and ladders, drafts and dominoes — then when the kids get bored, you'll know how to cheer them up. These games are all long-term favourites with simple rules that children can learn easily. Board games seem to bridge the gap between the age groups and teach us how to be GOOD sports and GOOD losers.

**H**is for HOBBIES, and there's nothing better than looking back through past editions of *Woman's Realm* to get ideas from the "Get Crafty" series. Materials don't have to be expensive, especially if you keep a bits-and-pieces box for fabrics, threads, buttons, beads and empty packaging. Appliqué, patchwork and collage can all be tried with oddments that you've collected. The children will have many hours of fun making pictures from scraps of materials and they will soon learn how to use fabric adhesive sensibly. It's nice to keep one wall free somewhere prominent in the house to pin up their pictures or, better still, why not have a go at framing them yourself? You'll find that they'll brighten up a blank wall considerably.

**I**is for INDULGING yourself by splashing on a favourite fragrance on a mundane Monday instead of keeping it only for those really special occasions, and having your hair styled and coloured completely free of charge or for just a nominal fee at a local hairdressing school. Alternatively I is for IMMERSING yourself in a bath full to the brim with warm water that has been laced with a sachet of scented bath oil, lying back and eating one piece of exotic fruit such as a mango or a passion fruit while you leisurely twiddle the taps with your toes.

**J**is for JUMBLE SALES. Spend an afternoon rummaging through the clothes and maybe you'll be lucky and pick up a real bargain for pennies. Look for any clothing which, however crumpled, can be laundered and altered to make something stylish, and labels denoting manufacturers famed for their good quality.

**K**is for KNITTING. As wool tends to be expensive, look out for special offers and baskets of oddments. Remember that sons might enjoy plaining and purling besides daughters. (And if you want to know how to teach them, see page 66!) Multicoloured scarves can be made quickly by children anxious for a final result, or simple squares can be used to make a cot blanket. Spend time making mittens, dolls' clothes, tea cosies, to put aside for presents.

145

# Family fun for FREE!

**L** is for LEARNING another LANGUAGE. Borrow a book from the library, write cards stating, for instance, *la porte* (the door), *le lit* (the bed) and *la chaise* (the chair) and pin them on the appropriate items around the house. The neighbours will think you've finally flipped, but don't worry! Replace the cards once a week after you and the family have tested each other on your vocabulary. If this inspires you, enquire about evening classes at a local college or listen for news of language broadcasts on the television and radio.

**M** is for MUSIC. You like Barry Manilow? Try Bach or Beethoven instead. Your greatest love is symphonies? Replace them with syncopated jazz. Boogie-woogie while you vacuum, sing while you spring clean and beat time when you stir a sauce. Encourage the children to take advantage of music

lessons by learning to play a school musical instrument. Don't wince when they come home to practise but join in with them. Let them teach you how to play the note. Just think! You could become an expert on the euphonium or a concert pianist, thereby adding another string to your bow!

**N** is for NATURE TRAILS. Even in the very busiest cities and towns there are parks abundant with trees, plants and wildlife. Plan beforehand the route you will follow and on the day remember to take a basket for collecting pine cones, leaves, twigs and stones. On your return ask the children to write a story on what they've seen and done. Let them set up a nature table in their own bedrooms.

**O** is for ORIENTEERING. Anyone who is fit can have a go at navigating their way on foot between two points on a large-scale map. All one needs is comfortable shoes and suitable clothing for walking through the countryside and common land, a red pen, a whistle and a compass. Discover what is happening in your area by sending an sae to the British Orienteering Federation at 41 Dale Road, Matlock, Derbyshire DE4 3LT.

**P** is for having a PARTY and making sure that everyone who is invited brings along something good to eat. In New Zealand this is a common occurrence which is simply called bringing a PLATE. Real friends will join in the spirit of the event and won't be affronted, and all you have to provide is one dish such as a quiche or a pie plus the knives and forks.

**Q** is for QUESTION and QUIZZES and it's your starter for 10. Everyone seems to enjoy watching television panel games, but how many of us actually sit down with a notepad and try to beat the panellists? If you think you can do as well as, if not better than, the contestants in front of the camera, then why not drop a line to the television company? Thousands of people write to them each year, but — who knows? — you could strike lucky and rise to stardom yet!

**R** is for ROLY-POLY PUDDING. It's delicious and won't cost much to make. Sift together 12 oz of plain flour and 2 rounded teaspoons of baking powder in a bowl. Add 6 oz of finely-chopped suet and a pinch of salt. Mix the ingredients with sufficient water to make a soft, but firm dough. Turn dough out onto a work surface and roll into a rectangle about $\frac{1}{4}$ in thick. Spread with jam of your choice almost to the edges. Damp the edges with water and roll up dough lightly. Seal edge. Wrap pudding tightly in a scalded, well-floured cloth; tie up the ends securely. Put the pudding into a pan of fast boiling water. Simmer for around 2 to 2½ hours ... And, regretfully, R is for REDUCING your weight and replacing ROLY-POLY PUDDING with RADISHES.

**S** is for SPORT, which should be part of all our lives. You don't have to be an expert to STRETCH, SKIP and STRENGTHEN your muscles to make you look and feel so much better. The Sports Council will send you information about sports courses going on in your town if you send them an sae. The address to write to is 16 Upper Woburn Place, London WC1H OQB. However, if you feel that participating in sport *really* isn't for you, S is for being a SPECTATOR instead.

**T** is for TEACHING YOURSELF TOPIARY, TAPESTRY and TYPING. The first will find you trimming bushes and trees into ornamental shapes, the second will produce a stylish cushion cover to be proud of (turn to page 136 and find out how!), and the third might enable you to earn the money to buy the shears and thread, and other things besides.

**U** is for UNFINISHED. Make a list of all the jobs which you've started and left unfinished. Resolve to paste the last strip of wallpaper in the corner of the landing, to undo the half-knitted cable-stitch sweater which you've stuffed in a carrier bag and restart the neckband, and to unpick the velvet skirt which you stopped making when you discovered the pile on the back and front were running in the opposite direction.

**V** is for VOLUNTARY WORK. You need never be lonely or bored if you are prepared to give a few hours of your time to voluntary work. Somewhere there is some organisation or charity looking for someone just like you and your family to give them help. There are literally hundreds to choose from: you could help the handicapped, deliver meals to the elderly, be trained to counsel people whose problems seem to them insurmountable, or you could initiate the formation of new groups. Read the Directory of Community Services which you will find in the reference room of your library.

**W** is for WRITING. It's said there's a book inside all of us — so now might be an ideal time to begin writing it. If you feel you need help, you could join a writers' circle or a creative writing class. You will be invited to take along your work, whether it is poetry, short stories or plays for the television and radio, and it will be discussed by all the members of the group. This might be just the spur you need, and in the process you'll be making many new friends with a common interest.

**X** is for never being lazy by writing XMAS in place of Christmas on the yuletide cards which the children have made themselves. Home-made cards are such a pleasure to make and a joy to receive. The children could print with potatoes and poster paint; you could stitch scenes with embroidery thread and sequins onto slips of material, sticking the fabric onto the card with adhesive.

**Y** is for YES instead of no, and making the effort to tramp out on a wet Sunday with your family. Y is for yelling YUK when the children splash through the puddles and for being YOUNG enough in spirit to wade through the water behind them.

**Z** is the last but very far from the least... It's for ZEST, which is still possible even if you aren't zooming off in a hang-glider or zipping around the world on a yacht. In a hurry-scurry world we need pastimes for relaxation and physical wellbeing. Fortunately, what we don't need is oodles of pennies before finding something that catches our enjoyment and interest. Have fun!

# YOUR GUIDE TO
# HIGH-SPEED STAIN REMOVAL

*It only takes a drip and a drop and — curses! — there it is: a red wine stain on your beautiful new blouse, candlewax on your favourite tablecloth, or felt tip pen on a white school shirt... We know the problems — and here are the solutions!*

## ANIMAL STAINS
**Washables:** be quick! Scrape off solids, blot with white paper towels, soak in biological detergent, rinse and wash.
**Non-washables:** scrape, blot and dry clean.

## BALLPOINT PEN
**Washables** (except acetate or triacetate): soak mark in methylated spirit. Soak in biological detergent, rinse and wash.
**Non-washables:** treat with methylated spirit or dry clean.

## BEER
**Washables:** blot, sponge with warm water and washing-up liquid. Soak in biological detergent, rinse and wash.
**Non-washables** (except acetate): treat with 1 part white distilled vinegar to 5 parts water.

## BLOOD
**Washables:** mop up with white tissues, then soak immediately in strongly salted cold water. Keep changing salt water solution until clear. Soak in biological detergent then wash with same detergent, making sure all stain has gone as the slightest heat will seal it in. With wool, don't rub the stain, just let cold water run through the fabric to stop felting.
**Non-washables:** sponge the mark with cold water. Blot dry. Dry clean if necessary.

## BUTTER, MARGE, FATS
**Washables:** scrape off solids. Work in neat washing-up liquid. Repeat with washing-up liquid and warm water. Wash in hottest water fabric will tolerate.
**Non-washables:** try a proprietary grease solvent or dry clean.

## CANDLEWAX
**Washables:** scrape off solids. Put item in the freezer or fridge to harden wax. Ease off as much as you can, remove rest by sandwiching fabric between sheets of clean blotting paper and applying a warm iron to melt wax. Keep moving paper to a clean patch as wax melts. (Take care not to melt material!) Use a branded stain remover to remove last traces, wash on hottest setting the fabric will take.
**Non-washables:** use the freezer-and-iron method described above, then stain remover.

## CHEWING GUM
**Washables:** pick off solids. Put fabric in fridge, or hold a plastic bag of ice cubes on gum to harden. Use a branded stain remover then wash as usual.
**Non-washables** (except acetate or rayon): freeze as above and pick off solids. Treat with methylated or white spirit.

## CHOCOLATE
**Washables:** scrape away solids. Sponge with warm water and washing-up liquid. Wash in biological detergent.
**Non-washables:** scrape off solids. Treat with branded grease solvent.

## COFFEE
**Washables:** mop up. Sponge with warm water and washing-up liquid. Rinse with cold. Wash.
**Non-washables:** mop up and sponge with warm water. Try branded solvent or dry clean.

## JUST THE TRICK

If you stain a dry-clean only garment or something precious and delicate it's best taken to the experts — with a full description of what caused the stain. But in an emergency, many stains can be removed from non-washable fabrics by a proprietary solvent or an aerosol cleaner, provided you:
* Deal with it at once
* Check for colour-fastness
* Follow pack instructions

148

## DYE
**Washables:** dab splash at once with cold water (warm water will set the stain). If the stain is large, put material in a cold rinse in your washing machine, then soak in biological detergent.
**Non-washables:** dry clean immediately.

## EGG
**Washables:** scrape off solids. Rinse in cold water, soak in biological detergent. Wash.
**Non-washables:** scrape off solids. Dab with washing-up liquid or try a grease solvent.

## FELT TIP PEN
**Washables:** rub in soap, wash as usual.
**Non-washables** (except acetate or triacetate): sponge with methylated spirit or dry clean.

## FRUIT
**Washables:** rinse at once in cold water. Loosen dried fruit stains before washing with equal parts of glycerine and warm water.
**Non-washables:** sponge at once with cold water then use a branded stain remover.

## GRASS
**Washables** (except acetate): try methylated spirit before washing and rinsing. Or work washing-up liquid into stain and wash.
**Non-washables:** use a branded stain remover.

## HAIR COLOURANTS
**Washables:** treat at once. When stain has dried you won't be able to remove it. Soak in cold water, rub in liquid detergent, dab on white distilled vinegar. Soak and wash in biological detergent.
**Non-washables:** rub in washing-up liquid, rinse well; or dry clean.

## INK
**Washables:** rinse really well in cold water under a running tap. Then treat with liquid detergent from the back of the stain. Rinse again, wash normally.
**Non-washables:** wetting will spread mark. Use branded stain remover or dry clean.

## IRON-MOULD
**Washables:** rub light stains with lemon juice and salt. Leave for an hour then rinse well. Then use a proprietary iron-mould remover.
**Non-washables:** dry clean only!

## JAMS, MARMALADE, HONEY
**Washables:** scrape off solids, blot with white tissue. Sponge with warm water and washing-up liquid or with biological detergent. Wash.
**Non-washables:** scrape off solids. Rinse with cold water, rub with washing-up liquid.

## LIPSTICK
**Washables:** scrape off solids. Treat with washing-up liquid, wash as usual.
**Non-washables:** use a branded spot remover.

## NAIL VARNISH
**Washables** (exept acetate or triacetate): blot as much as you can. Use a non-oily nail varnish remover, working from the back of the fabric. Wash as usual.
**Non-washables:** dry clean only!

## SIX TIPS
- Never use coloured cloths for removing stains. Use clean white cloths or tissues
- Remove solids or semi-solids
- Use two cloths — one behind the stain and one where it went in
- Work from behind the stain to get it out the way it entered
- Don't rub. Transfer solvent (with stain) to the right side
- Rub from outside the stain to its centre, and keep turning your cloths so the cleaning surface near the fabric is clean

## PAINT
**Washables:** be quick! For **emulsion** stains: blot or scrape off excess. If it's fresh, flush with cold water. If it's dried, try a stain remover. For **gloss** (oil-based) paint stains, except on acetate or triacetate: mop up. Treat at once with white spirit or brush cleaner. Sponge with cold water, wash and follow up with a branded stain remover.
**Non-washables:** blot or scrape then dry clean.

## PERSPIRATION
**Washables** (except acetate): fresh stains should come out easily . For old stains, try sponging with 1 tbsp white vinegar to $\frac{1}{2}$ pt warm water. Wash then hang out to dry.
**Non-washables:** try vinegar solution above or sponge gently with a solution of warm water and washing-up liquid. Or dry clean.

## SPIRITS
**Washables:** mop up with white tissue; sponge with warm water and wash as usual.
**Non-washables:** blot with white tissue, sponge with warm water and washing-up liquid.

## TAR
It's very difficult to clean up tar stains.
**Washables:** scrape away solids. Soften with a little glycerine. Work in warm water and washing-up liquid or use a branded tar remover. Wash in hottest water fabric can take.
**Non-washables:** scrape off excess, soften with glycerine, try a stain remover.

## TEA
As for coffee stains.

## URINE
**Washables:** mop up, rinse under cold running water. Soak in biological detergent and wash.
**Non-washables:** sponge with warm water and washing-up liquid. Rinse with cold water.

## WINE
**Washables:** mop up. Pour ordinary kitchen salt over. Soak in cold water and wash. For emergencies: pour white wine on red stains to take out colour.
**Non-washables:** blot with talc, dry clean.

# Memories are made of this...

Why not take a time-trip with our show-biz quiz? Though if you do <u>too</u> well, you could be showing your age!

**1** A ventriloquist's act on radio seems like a Monty Python joke. But there was one in the Fifties: can you remember the name of the show, the ventriloquist, the dummy and the schoolmaster?

**2** No prizes for guessing who ... But in which Marilyn Monroe film did this famous shot appear?
a) <u>Gentlemen Prefer Blondes</u>
b) <u>The Seven Year Itch</u>
c) <u>Some Like It Hot</u>

**3** Who played BBC TV's original Robin Hood? And, for a bonus point, who was Robin's Maid Marian?

**4** In April 1954 TV's very first soap opera was created to rival radio's <u>The Archers</u> and <u>Mrs Dale's Diary</u>. What was it called — and can you name the characters pictured right?

**5** In 1961 a husky-voiced 15-year-old sang <u>Don't Treat Me Like a Child</u>. Who was she?

**6** Whose catchphrases were?
a) "Wakey, Way-kee!"
b) "Not you, Momma, sit down!"
c) "My name's Julian and this is my friend Sandy..."

**7** What did the initials <u>TW3</u> stand for?

**8** Who is this — and what did he have us all doing in the early Sixties?

**9** Who said the following — and in which film?
a) "You ain't heard nothing yet!"
b) "After all, tomorrow is another day..."
c) "If you want anything, just whistle ..."

**10** Two of the most famous faces on TV in the Fifties. Can you name them?

**11** These two fresh-faced lads were top of the pops in 1961 and brought a secondary European glory to Britain. Can you remember who they were and what their triumph was?

**12** Who was "your quiz and quizzitor"?

*Turn to page 189 for the answers*

# THE NO-PANIC

**Feeding guests famously need not mean hours spent in the kitchen. Follow our menu and you'll have time to relax and enjoy yourself!**

## CARROT AND CORIANDER SOUP

*Crushed coriander seeds give this soup its slightly spicy flavour. If you use your own home-made stock the flavour will be even better, so when you have time make the stock and freeze in handy quantities*
**Preparation time: 10 min. Cooking time: 27 min. Serves 4**
**1 lb (450 g) carrots**
**1 medium onion**
**1 oz (25 g) butter**
**1 tsp (5 ml) dried coriander seeds, crushed**
**1 tsp (5 ml) caster sugar**
**1 pt (600 ml) chicken stock**
**Salt and ground black pepper**
**2 tbsp (30 ml) fresh soured cream**
**Carrot curls to garnish**
Peel and dice the carrots; peel and chop the onion. Fry vegetables over a low heat in butter until the onion is soft (about 5 min). Crush the coriander seeds and add with the sugar, chicken stock, salt and black pepper. Bring to the boil, cover and simmer gently for 15 min. Liquidise or sieve. Reheat gently; transfer to tureen. Top with soured cream and carrot curls.

## POUSSINS WITH ASPARAGUS

*Most freezer food stores sell poussins, and the frozen food cabinets in most supermarkets have them too. Baste often during cooking for a really succulent result*
**Preparation time: 15 min. Cooking time: 1 hr 3 min. Serves 4**
**4 poussins, fresh or frozen, thawed**
**1 oz (25 g) butter**
**15-oz (425-g) can green asparagus spears**
**¼ pt (150 ml) chicken stock**
**Salt and ground black pepper**
Set oven at 400°F, 200°C (Mark 6). Wipe the poussins well and dry with kitchen paper. Place them in a medium-sized roasting tin and dot with the butter. Place in the oven and cook, basting occasionally, for 1 hr, or until tender and the juices run clear. Place in a serving dish and keep warm in a low oven. Drain excess fat, from the tin. Drain the green asparagus spears. Cut off tips and reserve. Sieve

or liquidise the remaining asparagus and add to juices in pan with the chicken stock. Bring to the boil, stirring. Season with salt and pepper. Spoon some sauce into dish with poussins and add reserved tips. Pour remaining sauce into a jug and serve separately. Accompany with buttered sweetcorn, whole baked tomatoes, jacket potatoes with butter and salt.

## BLACKBERRY APPLE MERINGUE

*If you can't get hold of fresh blackberries, use frozen instead — they won't spoil the result. In fact you can vary the soft fruit according to taste and what's in season*
**Preparation time: 20 min. Cooking time: 18 min. Serves 4**
**1 lb (450 g) fresh blackberries**
**1 lb 8 oz (700 g) cooking apples**
**6 oz (175 g) granulated sugar**
**2 tbsp (30 ml) water**
**Finely grated rind and juice of ½ lemon**
**2 egg whites**
**4 oz (100 g) caster sugar**
Set oven at 400°F, 200°C (Mark 6). Wash and dry the fresh blackberries. Peel, core and slice the cooking apples. Put in a saucepan with the granulated sugar, water, grated lemon rind and juice. Cover with a lid and cook very gently for about 5 min or until the blackberries are just tender. Remove from heat and transfer apples and blackberries to a glass, ovenproof dish, put into oven for 10 min. Meanwhile, whisk the egg whites until stiff and standing in peaks. Whisk in half the caster sugar and fold in the rest. Spoon into a piping bag fitted with a medium star nozzle and pipe 8 large swirls of meringue around the edge of the dish. Return dish to the oven for about 5 min to brown. Serve hot or cold.

**From top, left: Blackberry Apple Meringue; Jacket Potatoes; Whole Baked Tomatoes and Sweetcorn; Poussins with Asparagus. Bottom, from left: Carrot and Coriander Soup; Asparagus Sauce**

# DINNER PARTY

Clockwise from centre:
Cherry Glazed Gammon;
Celebration Cake; Fresh Fruit Salad; Turkish
Salad; Poached Salmon; French Dressing;
Lemon and Dill Mayonnaise; Red Salad; Green Salad;
Creme Vichyssoise; Prawn and Melon Cocktail

# STYLE

For that special occasion you want everything to be perfect. Here's the answer — our sumptuous spread

*(Turn to page 159 for the recipes)*

# WHEN THE CROWD COMES ROUND

**Tell them to bring a bottle and you'll provide the eats. And it's all so easy for you with our informal, make-ahead party plan**

## FRENCH BREAD PIZZA

*Prepare in advance and freeze. Cook from frozen in a moderate oven for 15 min*
**Preparation time: 15 min. Cooking time: 9 min. Serves 6**
**1 large French stick**
**14-oz (396-g) can tomatoes**
**1 tsp (5 ml) oregano**
**Salt and ground black pepper**
**8 thin slices salami**
**1 oz (25 g) butter**
**1 onion**
**1 green pepper**
**3 oz (75 g) Cheddar cheese, grated**
Cut French stick in half lengthways, cut each half in 3. Drain tomatoes, chop. Mix with oregano, salt, pepper. Spoon over bread. Cut salami into quarters, place over tomatoes. Melt butter in pan, peel, chop onion, halve, deseed, rinse and dice pepper, fry 3 min. Spoon onto salami, sprinkle with cheese. Grill for 5 min until golden.

## POTATO SALAD

*New potatoes in a creamy dressing which is really best made on the day itself*
**Preparation time: 15 min (plus standing time). Cooking time: 15 to 20 min. Serves 6**
**1 lb 8 oz (700 g) new potatoes**
**Salt and ground black pepper**
**6 oz (175 g) back bacon**
**6 tbsp (90 ml) mayonnaise**
**2 tbsp (30 ml) natural yoghurt**
**6 spring onions**
Scrub the new potatoes and cut any large ones into quarters. Cook them in boiling,

salted water for 15 to 20 min, or until tender. Meanwhile, derind the bacon and grill for 5 min or until each side is crispy. Chop. Drain the potatoes and then leave to cool. Put into a bowl with the chopped bacon. Mix the mayonnaise and natural yoghurt together and season with ground black pepper. Stir half into the cooled potatoes. Trim and thinly slice the spring onions and add half to the mixture. Spoon remaining dressing into a dish and serve immediately garnished with the remaining spring onion.

## SAUSAGES WITH TOMATO DIP

*You can make this deliciously tangy dip in advance and keep it covered in the refrigerator, but the sausages are best cooked on the day*
**Preparation time: 15 min. Cooking time: 20 min. Serves 6**
**1 lb (450 g) pork chipolata sausages**
**1½ oz (40 g) butter**
**1 large onion**
**3 sticks celery**
**2 oz (50 g) mushrooms**
**10½-oz (298-g) can condensed tomato soup**
**¼ pt (150 ml) water**
**2 tsp (10 ml) Worcestershire sauce**
**½ tsp (2.5 ml) caster sugar**
**Ground black pepper**
Grill the pork chipolata sausages for 20 min, turning during cooking. Meanwhile, melt the butter in a pan. Peel the onion and finely chop. Wash and chop sticks of celery and mushrooms. Fry vegetables for 7 min, or until soft. Stir in the condensed tomato soup, water, Worcestershire sauce, caster sugar and black pepper to taste. Simmer for 5 min. Cool. Serve with the grilled sausages.       ▷

Back, from left: **Strawberry Trifle; Summer Pudding; Cider Cup; Mutton Pies. Centre, from left: Sausages with Tomato Dip; Potato Salad; Potato Salad Dressing; Green Salad. Front: French Bread Pizza**

## CIDER CUP

*If you have room in your refrigerator, chill the drinks for 24 hr before mixing*
**Preparation time: 5 min. Makes 2½ pt (1.4 l)**
**1½ pt (850 ml) dry cider, chilled**
**3 tbsp (45 ml) lime cordial**
**½ pt (300 ml) orange juice, chilled**
**½ pt (300 ml) ginger ale, chilled**
**1 orange**
**1 lemon**
**1 small bunch mint**
Mix cider, lime, orange juice and ale. Slice orange and lemon and add. Pour into a chilled jug. Serve decorated with mint.

## GREEN SALAD

*Serve a crisp green salad to offset the richer dishes on the menu*
**Preparation time: 15 min. Serves 6**
**1 cos lettuce**
**1 bunch watercress**
**1 small carton cress**
**Salt and ground black pepper**
**1 tsp (5 ml) whole-grain mustard**
**¼ tsp (1.25 ml) caster sugar**
**2 tbsp (30 ml) lemon juice**
**4 tbsp (60 ml) oil**
Wash lettuce and dry. Shred and place in a bowl. Wash watercress and cut off thick stalks. Wash and drain cress. Add watercress and cress to lettuce. Put salt, pepper, mustard, sugar, lemon juice and oil in a bowl. Whisk, pour over salad before serving.

## MUTTON PIES

*Mint gives these pies a lift, or add 1 tbsp (15 ml) Garam Masala curry powder instead*
**Preparation time: 30 min. Cooking time: 1 hr. Makes 8**
**1 tbsp (15 ml) oil**
**1 small onion**
**12 oz (350 g) lean minced lamb or mutton**
**6 tbsp (90 ml) best stock**
**2 tbsp (30 ml) fresh chopped mint**
**Salt and ground black pepper**
**1 lb (450 g) plain flour**
**4 oz (100 g) margarine**
**4 oz (100 g) lard**
**Egg to glaze**
**Watercress to garnish**
Place oil in a pan, peel and grate onion. Fry for 3 min. Add meat and fry for 3 min, stirring. Add stock, bring to boil, cover and simmer for 20 min. Stir in mint, salt and pepper. Cool slightly. Set oven at 375° F, 190° C (Mark 5). Sift flour and a pinch of salt into a bowl and rub in fats. Add enough cold water to make a stiff dough. Roll out on a lightly floured surface and use half to line 8 4-in (10-cm) tartlet tins. Divide filling between tins. Dampen edges of pastry. Roll out remaining pastry and cut out rounds for lids. Cover filling with lids. Seal edges. Brush with beaten egg, make 2 slits in each lid and bake in centre of oven for 30 min. Serve garnished with watercress.

## SUMMER PUDDING

*An absolute must for soft fruit lovers. If you use frozen fruit, omit the water*
**Preparation time: 15 min (plus standing time). Cooking time: 10 min. Serves 6**
**12 oz (350 g) blackcurrants**
**4 oz (100 g) raspberries**
**5 oz (150 g) granulated sugar**
**2 tbsp (30 ml) water**
**8 slices white bread**
Pick over fruit, rinse and drain. Place in a pan with sugar and water. Cover and cook gently for 10 min. Cut crusts from bread and use to line a 1½-pint (850-ml) pudding basin. Pour in fruit and juice and cover with remaining bread. Put a saucer on top and add a heavy weight. Refrigerate overnight. Turn out onto a dish and serve with whipped cream.

## STRAWBERRY TRIFLE

*Prepare the day before and chill. Decorate with cream and strawberry before serving*
**Preparation time: 20 min (plus standing time). Cooking time: 5 min. Serves 8**
**2 jam Swiss rolls**
**3 tbsp (45 ml) sherry**
**2 tbsp (30 ml) orange juice**
**12 oz (350 g) strawberries**
**3 oz (75 g) caster sugar**
**2 tbsp (30 ml) custard powder**
**¾ pt (400 ml) milk**
**¼-pt (142-ml) carton double cream**
Cut the Swiss rolls into ½-in (1-cm) slices and use to line base and sides of a trifle dish. Mix the sherry and orange juice together and spoon over. Reserve a strawberry for decoration and hull and halve the rest, tossing in 2 oz (50 g) of the sugar, and spoon over Swiss roll. Blend the custard powder with a little milk. Heat remaining milk; whisk into custard powder until smooth. Return custard to pan, bring to the boil, stirring until thickened. Stir in remaining sugar. Cool. Pour over strawberries and leave to set. Whisk double cream until just stiff. Place in a piping bag fitted with a star nozzle and pipe around edge of trifle. Decorate with reserved strawberry.

CELEBRATE IN STYLE

Continued from p 155

## PRAWN AND MELON COCKTAIL

*Prepare this refreshing starter the day before and chill in the refrigerator*
**Preparation time: 30 min. Serves 25**
**3 honeydew melons**
**4 oz (100 g) stem ginger**
**2 lb (900 g) peeled prawns**
**1 lb 8 oz (700 g) whole prawns in shells**
Cut melons in half and scoop out pips. Cut into thin wedges lengthways; cut crossways at ½-in (1-cm) intervals down to skin. Cut with a sharp knife as close to skin as possible. Tip chunks of melon (with any juice) into a bowl. Finely chop ginger and add to bowl with the peeled prawns. Mix well. Cover and chill until required.
*To serve:* spoon cocktail into individual glasses and garnish with whole prawns.

## CHERRY GLAZED GAMMON

*A spectacular centrepiece for any table, this gammon tastes as good as it looks!*
**Preparation time: 25 min. Cooking time: about 4 hr 50 min. Serves 25**
**10 lb (4.5 kg) gammon joint**
**Whole cloves**
**Clear honey**
**Demerara sugar**
**Fresh bay leaves**
**Glacé cherries**
Soak gammon overnight in cold water. Weigh after soaking to calculate cooking time. Allow 25 min per lb (450 g) plus 25 min. Place gammon in pan, cover with cold water and bring to boil slowly. Cover and reduce heat so that it cooks at a slow simmer for 2 hr 30 min. Set oven at 350° F, 180° C (Mark 4). Remove from pan and wrap in foil. Bake for 1 hr 50 min. Increase oven temperature to 425° F, 220° C (Mark 7). Remove foil from joint and skin. Score diamond pattern on exposed fat. Stick cloves in at each point. Brush with honey, sprinkle well with sugar. Return to oven for 15 to 30 min, basting occasionally with honey. Remove from oven. Garnish with bay leaves and cherries, securing leaves with cloves, cherries with cocktail sticks. Cool.

## TURKISH SALAD

*A colourful rice salad with almonds. Delicious on its own or with French dressing*
**Preparation time: 15 min. Cooking time: 25 min. Serves 25**
**Salt**
**2 lb 8 oz (1.1 kg) long grain rice**
**2 tbsp (30 ml) turmeric**
**2 oz (50 g) butter**
**8 oz (225 g) whole blanched almonds**
**6 oz (175 g) raisins**
**6 oz (175 g) stuffed olives**
Bring a pan of salted water to the boil. Add rice and stir once. Cook according to instructions on packet. Drain and rinse with boiling water. Return to the pan and add turmeric. Mix well until evenly coloured. Melt butter in a pan and add almonds. Fry gently until almonds are golden brown. Allow to cool. Add the almonds and raisins to the rice. Slice the olives and add to the rice. Mix well and turn into a serving bowl.

## CREME VICHYSSOISE

*A classic soup to serve either hot or cold as you please. Make up in advance and freeze to save you time on the day*
**Preparation time: 20 min. Cooking time: 35 min. Serves 25**
**6 lb (2.7 kg) leeks**
**3 lb (1.4 kg) potatoes**
**6 oz (175 g) butter**
**3 pt (1.7 l) chicken stock**
**3 pt (1.7 l) milk**
**1½ pt (850 ml) double cream**
**Salt and ground black pepper**
**Ground nutmeg**
**Fresh chives**
Trim the leeks and peel the potatoes. Thinly slice the leeks and rinse well to remove any grit. Drain well. Dice the potatoes. Melt butter in very large pan, add the sliced leeks and the diced potatoes and fry for 5 min. Stir in the chicken stock and the milk. Bring slowly to the boil, cover with a lid and simmer for 25 min, or until the vegetables are soft. Remove from the heat and allow to cool slightly. Liquidise until smooth. Return the soup to the pan and add the double cream. Season to taste with salt, ground black pepper and ground nutmeg to taste. When reheating the soup, be careful that you do not boil it as this will curdle the cream.
*To serve:* chop the fresh chives and sprinkle over the soup.                              ▷

## POACHED SALMON

*A surprisingly easy dish to prepare, so make up for it by taking extra care with presentation. Poach the fish with some white wine for extra flavour and freeze the leftover reduced stock to use on other occasions*

**Preparation time: 30 min. Cooking time: 48 min. Serves 25**

**6 lb (2.7 kg) whole salmon**
**1 tbsp (15 ml) whole black peppercorns**
**1 lemon**
**4 sprigs fresh parsley**
**2 bay leaves**
**1 onion**
**2 tsp (10 ml) salt**
**Watercress**
**Cucumber slices**
**Lemon slices**

Clean the salmon (if not already cleaned). Rinse under cold water. Place the salmon on the trivet inside the fish kettle. Cover with water. Add the peppercorns, cut the lemon into wedges and add to the fish kettle with the parsley and bay leaves. Cut the onion into quarters and add to the kettle with the salt. Place over heat. Bring to the boil, cover with lid and simmer for 42 min until the fish flakes when tested with a fork. Lift fish out of the liquid on the trivet and allow to cool. Boil the liquid until reduced by two thirds. Cool. When the salmon is cool, carefully remove the skin and discard, then take a small knife and carefully scrape away the thin layer of dark meat over the fish, following the grain of the fish to expose the pink meat on both sides of the fish. Arrange on serving platter. Carefully spoon some of the reduced cooking liquid over the fish to keep it moist. Keep remaining liquid for stock. Garnish with watercress, cucumber and lemon slices.

## FRENCH DRESSING

*A straight dressing to add zip to any salad. Olive oil gives a good flavour but you can substitute corn oil for economy. Don't dress the salad too soon, or it may lose its crispness*

**Preparation time: 5 min. Serves 25**

**½ pt (300 ml) olive oil**
**¼ pt (150 ml) white wine vinegar**
**2 tsp (10 ml) salt**
**Ground black pepper**
**1 tbsp (15 ml) dry mustard powder**
**4 tsp (20 ml) caster sugar**

Place the olive oil and white wine vinegar in a large screwtop jar and sprinkle in the salt, ground black pepper, dry mustard powder and caster sugar. Shake well until evenly mixed. Check the seasoning. Chill in refrigerator until required. Just before serving, shake vigorously.

## GARLIC AND HONEY DRESSING

*This slightly sweet dressing is an ideal and unusual way to perk up an ordinary tomato salad*

**Preparation time: 8 min. Serves 25**

**½ pt (300 ml) olive oil**
**¼ pt (150 ml) white wine vinegar**
**2 tsp (10 ml) salt**
**Ground black pepper**
**1 tsp (5 ml) dry mustard powder**
**3 tbsp (45 ml) clear honey**
**4 cloves garlic**

Place the oil and white vinegar in a large screwtop jar. Add the salt, pepper, mustard powder and honey. Crush the garlic cloves and add to the jar. Tighten lid on the jar and shake well until ingredients are evenly mixed. Chill until required. Shake vigorously before using.

## ORANGE SALAD

*A crisp salad with a tang of orange to liven up your palate. Sprinkle with a little French dressing just before serving*

**Preparation time: 30 min. Serves 25**

**4 iceberg lettuces**
**3 bunches watercress**
**3 large green peppers**
**1 lb 8 oz (700 g) frozen whole French beans, thawed**
**5 oranges**
**1 cucumber**

Rinse, drain and roughly chop the lettuce. Cut off main stalks from the watercress, rinse and drain. Core, deseed, rinse and thinly slice peppers, add to lettuce with watercress and French beans. Peel oranges and, using a sharp knife, cut on either side of the membranes to release segments. Add to salad. Toss lightly to mix. Divide between serving bowls. Thinly slice cucumber and scatter over the salad.

## RED SALAD

*A simple but effective way of arranging salad ingredients for a splash of colour*

**Preparation time: 25 min. Serves 25**

**3 lb 8 oz (1.6 kg) tomatoes**
**3 large red peppers**
**4 15-oz (425-g) cans red kidney beans**

Rinse and drain the tomatoes. Core, deseed, rinse and thinly slice the red peppers. With a sharp knife cut the tomatoes into thin slices. Drain the red beans. Arrange slices of tomato, red pepper and kidney beans in diagonal rows across the serving platter.

*To serve:* chill then add the garlic and honey dressing from the refrigerator, poured evenly over the ingredients to coat.

## LEMON AND DILL MAYONNAISE

*A delicious accompaniment to salmon and salads. If you have the time, leave it to stand for a full 24 hr so that the flavour can develop before using*

**Preparation time: 5 min. Serves 25**

**1½ pt (850 ml) mayonnaise**
**1 pt (600 ml) fresh soured cream**
**4 tbsp (60 ml) lemon juice**
**1 oz (25 g) fresh chopped or 1 tbsp (15 ml) dried dill weed**
**Salt and ground black pepper**
**¼-pt (142-ml) carton single cream**

Mix mayonnaise, fresh soured cream, lemon juice and fresh dill or dried dill weed together in a bowl. Season to taste with salt and black pepper. Stir in a little single cream to make the mixture of a thick pouring consistency. Pour into a serving dish.

## CELEBRATION CAKE

*Whether it be a wedding, christening or anniversary, this rich dark fruit cake will be the focal point of the table. Best made in advance to allow the flavour to mature*

**Preparation time: 30 min. Cooking time: 30 min. Makes: 9-in (23-cm) cake**

**5 oz (150 g) raisins**
**7 oz (200 g) sultanas**
**13 oz (375 g) currants**
**4 oz (100 g) glacé cherries, chopped**
**4 oz (100 g) chopped nuts**
**4 oz (100 g) chopped peel**
**2 tsp (10 ml) finely grated lemon rind**
**9 oz (250 g) plain flour**
**2 tsp (10 ml) mixed spice**
**8 oz (225 g) butter**
**8 oz (225 g) soft brown sugar**
**5 eggs**
**2 to 3 tbsp (30 to 45 ml) brandy or rum**

Set oven at 300°F, 150°C (Mark 2). Thoroughly grease and line a 9-in (23-cm) square cake tin. Tie a band of double thickness brown paper or newspaper around the outside of tin to prevent overcooking. Mix together the raisins, sultanas, currants, chopped glacé cherries, nuts, peel and finely grated lemon rind. Sift the

plain flour and the mixed spice together. Cream the butter with the soft brown sugar until light and fluffy, then gradually beat in the eggs. Fold in the flour and fruit alternatively. Stir in the brandy or rum. Spoon the mixture into the prepared tin and bake for 2 hr. Reduce oven temperature to 275°F, 140°C (Mark 1) and bake for 1 hr, or longer if necessary. The cake should be evenly risen, golden brown and firm. A skewer inserted in the centre should come out clean and the cake should be just beginning to shrink away from the sides of the tin. Leave in the tin for about 1 hr to cool, then turn out and finish cooling on a wire rack.

When the cake is cool, you can prick over the surface with a skewer and spoon over a few extra tablespoons of brandy or rum to enrich the flavour even more.

*To store:* wrap the cake tightly in a double thickness of greaseproof paper followed by a layer of kitchen foil. Leave to mature in a cool dry place for about one month before covering with almond paste and decorating with royal icing.

## APRICOT GLAZE

*This glaze is used to secure the almond paste to the cake. If you have any left over it will keep in a screwtop jar for several weeks*

**Preparation time: 5 min. Makes ½ pt (300 ml)**

**8 oz (225 g) apricot jam**
**2 tbsp (30 ml) water**
**2 tsp (10 ml) lemon juice**

Place the apricot jam and water in a pan. Heat gently until jam has melted. Sieve, add lemon juice and mix well. Apply quickly to the cake whilst warm.

## ALMOND PASTE

*For speed you can use a ready-made almond paste, but do allow it to dry out thoroughly before icing*

**Preparation time: 10 min. Makes 2 lb 8 oz (1.1 kg)**

**10 oz (275 g) icing sugar**
**10 oz (275 g) caster sugar**
**1 lb 4 oz (575 g) ground almonds**
**5 egg yolks, or 2 eggs plus 1 yolk**
**Few drops of almond essence**
**1½ tsp (7.5 ml) lemon juice**

Sift icing sugar and mix in a large bowl with caster sugar and ground almonds. Make a well in the centre. Beat egg yolks with almond essence and lemon juice, add to well. Mix until ingredients bind well together to make a firm paste. Store in an airtight container until required. ▷

## TO APPLY THE ALMOND PASTE

If the top of the cake is uneven, trim it until flat. Turn the cake so that the smooth base is used for the top. Measure the length and depth of the cake sides. Use ⅔ of paste for the sides, dividing in two. Roll out one piece on a surface lightly dusted with icing sugar, to twice the depth and once the length of one side. Trim the edges. Cut the rectangles in half lengthways. Repeat with the remaining portion, to make 4 strips. Brush the strips with apricot glaze and press each side of the cake onto one strip in turn. Trim off the surplus paste. Roll out remaining paste to fit the top of the cake. Brush with glaze, place cake on it top down, pressing evenly to seal. Trim off the surplus paste, turn the cake the right way up. Leave in a cool place to dry out for at least 24 hr before icing.

## ROYAL ICING

*To get a really bright, white appearance a tiny drop of blue food colouring can be added to the mixture*
**Preparation time: 10 min. Makes 2 lb 8 oz (1.1 kg)**
**5 egg whites**
**2 lb 8 oz (1.1 kg) icing sugar**
**4 tsp (20 ml) lemon juice**
**2 tsp (10 ml) glycerine**
Lightly beat the egg whites in a clean, dry bowl. Sift the icing sugar gradually into the egg whites with the lemon juice and glycerine until smooth and glossy, adding enough icing sugar until icing forms stiff peaks. Keep in an airtight container until required.

## TO APPLY THE ROYAL ICING

Place a blob of icing in the centre of a 14-in (35.5-cm) cake board. Place cake diagonally on board. Put a large spoonful of icing on top of the cake. Using a palette knife, spread it evenly over surface of the cake. Hold an icing ruler or long palette knife across one end of cake at an angle of 45°. With an even pressure, draw it across the icing towards you to smooth the surface. Repeat if necessary until smooth. Trim away any surplus icing from edges. Allow top to dry for 24 hr. Apply icing in same way to sides, one side at a time, but using a smooth icing comb or ruler to smooth surface. Allow to dry. Repeat the

process with a second layer of icing. Allow to dry for 24 hr.
*To finish the cake*: using a 5-in (12.5-cm) square of paper as a guide, mark a square diagonally on top of cake with a pin. Using a No 2 plain writing nozzle, pipe parallel lines in pairs across the square. Turn the cake and pipe similar lines at right angles over the first. Pipe a single line around the outside of the square. Pipe parallel lines across the corners of the cake board. Using a No 12 shell nozzle, pipe a line of overlapping shells around the top and bottom edges of the cake. Allow to dry for 24 hr before decorating.
*To decorate*: using a dab of icing, secure a silver cake ribbon around cake. With icing dots fix silver balls at corners of square and at ends of lines on board. Attach silver leaves, bells, etc, as desired.

## FRESH FRUIT SALAD

*A little time-consuming to prepare, but a worthwhile result. The different coloured fruits provide a really attractive dessert that appeals to most people, and a slight hint of alcohol in the syrup makes it an extra special treat*
**Preparation time: 50 min. Serves 25**
*Syrup:*
**1½ pt (850 ml) water**
**12 oz (350 g) caster sugar**
*Salad:*
**3 large pineapples**
**6 tbsp (90 ml) lemon juice**
**8 red apples**
**1 lb (450 g) black grapes**
**4 grapefruit**
**6 kiwifruit**
**¼ pt (150 ml) Grand Marnier**
*To make the syrup:* pour the water into a pan and add the caster sugar. Stir over a low heat until the sugar dissolves. Bring to the boil and boil for 5 min. Cool.
*To prepare the fruit:* slice and cut skin from pineapples. Cut into bite-sized chunks. Place lemon juice in a large bowl. Wash, core and roughly chop the red apples. Add to the lemon juice. Toss well to prevent discolouration. Wash the black grapes, halve and remove the pips. Add to the apples with the pineapple. Peel the grapefruits and using a sharp knife, cut on either side of the membrane to release segments, add to the bowl. Peel the kiwifruit and slice. Add to the bowl and gently mix the fruits together. Turn into serving bowls. Stir the Grand Marnier into the cooled syrup and pour over the fruit. Cover and chill in refrigerator.

# THE DRINK

Champagne, or sparkling wine, helps any celebration seem even more of a special occasion. The high price of champagne may be prohibitive, but you can use a sparkling wine in its place or just have a few bottles of the real thing for the toasts.

When you're choosing, make sure you always look closely at the label. Only the excellent sparkling wines made in the Champagne region of France are allowed to call themselves "champagne"! High quality sparkling wines may be made all over the world by the same method, but they will be labelled "méthode champenoise". Some good, often cheaper, sparkling wines are made in tanks under pressure. They will have a less delicate flavour than champagne proper and you'll find that the bubbles will not last so long! Serve lightly chilled.

To open a bottle of sparkling wine remove the foil and wire from the cork. Grip the bottle in one hand and the cork in the other, and gently twist the bottle, easing out the cork. Have a glass ready.

In addition to sparkling wines or champagne, you'll no doubt be needing ordinary wine to serve with the food. If you're buying large amounts, it's usually cheaper to buy 1½- or 2-litre bottles, or wine boxes. Many very acceptable Spanish and Italian wines — both red and white — are now sold in larger sizes. Alternatively, you can buy the wine by the case; many off-licences have a special discount price for wine bought this way.

You'll need to allow half a bottle per person, plus a little extra just in case. If the bottles are unopened, they can be kept for future use. Once opened, wine should be recorked or covered to exclude as much air as possible, then stored in the refrigerator. When you want to serve it again, it can be brought back to room temperature if necessary.

A good red wine should be brought to room temperature, so put it in the room where it is to be served several hours before it's needed. The ideal temperature is 65 to 70° F (18 to 21°C). White wines are best chilled, and two to three hours in the refrigerator is normally sufficient for this. If you're short on fridge space, find a cool place — a cellar would be ideal — to store the bottles until you need them.

And spare a thought for the non-drinkers among your guests; a varied selection of soft drinks, including mineral water and fruit juices, would be welcome.

# THE PLAN

There really is no hidden secret to successful entertaining. All it takes is good advance planning — especially if you are catering for large numbers.

Unless you want to end up in an exhausted heap, plan to do as much as possible well in advance of the party.

Choose dishes that need as little as possible in the way of last-minute attention, and, preferably, a few which can be frozen ahead and simply thawed and served on the day.

Buffet-style food is by far the easiest and the most sociable when you have a large number of guests to serve — you don't have to worry about seating plans and the guests can serve themselves.

Our "Celebrate in Style" menu caters for about 25 people, but will easily adapt to serving six or a 100.

# YOUR PERFECT PARTY CHECKLIST

1. What is the occasion? Is it formal or informal?
2. How many people do you think you will be catering for?
3. How much space do you have available? Would you be better off hiring a hall, rather than squeezing everyone into your not-so-big house?
4. Consider the time involved in shopping and preparing the food. Do you need any extra help?
5. Do you have enough equipment (cooking utensils, serving dishes, crockery, cutlery, glasses etc) and cooking facilities to cope with the number of guests?
6. Don't try and be over-ambitious — just stick to the dishes that you have prepared before and which you know will work. Practice makes perfect!
7. Plan your menu well ahead and spread out the work as much as possible, making full use of freezer space if you have one.
8. If you choose any hot dishes, make sure that they are the kind which won't spoil if kept hot.
9. Make yourself lots of lists so that you don't forget anything — shopping, equipment, cook-ahead timetable, number of guests, and your foolproof countdown on the big day. Then, once you have prepared all the food, arranged the table, welcomed the guests and the party's going with a swing, you can relax at last and enjoy yourself!    ▷

# COOKING BY NUMBERS

| Number of portions | 10 | 20 | 40 |
|---|---|---|---|
| **SOUPS**<br>*Hot or chilled* | 1.8 litres<br>(3-3½ pt) | 4.0 litres<br>(7 pt) | 8.0 litres<br>(13 pt) |
| **PATE**<br>*Allow 2 to 3 half slices of*<br>*toast per person* | 575 g<br>(1¼ lb) | 1.1 kg<br>(2½ lb) | 2 kg<br>(4½ lb) |
| **COLD MEAT**<br>*eg ham or salami,*<br>*sliced for salad* | 900 g<br>(2 lb) | 1.8 kg<br>(4 lb) | 3.6 kg<br>(8 lb) |
| **MEAT WITHOUT BONE**<br>*Rolled meat, bacon joint*<br>*or casseroles* | 1.1 kg<br>(2½ lb) | 2.2 kg<br>(5 lb) | 4.5 kg<br>(10 lb) |
| **MEAT ON THE BONE, ROASTED**<br>*Serve hot or cold, with*<br>*salad for buffets* | 1.8 kg<br>(4 lb) | 3.1 kg<br>(7 lb) | 6.3 kg<br>(14 lb) |
| **QUICHE**<br>*Can be served hot or cold* | Two<br>20-cm<br>(8-in)<br>quiches | Four<br>20-cm<br>(8-in)<br>quiches | Eight<br>20-cm<br>(8-in)<br>quiches |
| **POULTRY ON THE BONE**<br>*Oven-ready weight,*<br>*serve hot or cold* | 3.5 kg<br>(8-9 lb)<br>bird | 7 kg<br>(16-18 lb)<br>bird | 2 x 7 kg<br>(2 x 16 lb)<br>bird |
| **FISH, FILLETED**<br>*As part of made-up dishes* | 1.1 kg<br>(2½ lb) | 2.2 kg<br>(5 lb) | 4.5 kg<br>(10 lb) |
| **RICE OR PASTA**<br>*Uncooked weight* | 450 g<br>(1 lb) | 700 g<br>(1½ lb) | 1.1-1.5 kg<br>(2½-3 lb) |
| **GREEN VEGETABLES**<br>*Uncooked weight* | 1.7 kg<br>(3½ lb) | 3-3.5 kg<br>(6-7 lb) | 6 kg<br>(13 lb) |
| **POTATOES**<br>*For potato salad* | 700 g<br>(1½ lb) | 1.5 kg<br>(3 lb) | 3-3.5 kg<br>(6-7 lb) |
| **FRENCH DRESSING**<br>*or mayonnaise.*<br>*Smaller quantities will be*<br>*needed if salad is served*<br>*ready-dressed* | 300 ml<br>(½ pt) | 600 ml<br>(1 pt) | 1.2 litres<br>(2 pt) |
| **CHEESEBOARD**<br>*Allow 1-1½ oz per person* | 350-450 g<br>(¾ lb) | 900 g<br>(2 lb) | 1.1-1.5 kg<br>(2½-3 lb) |

What's the first step to
success when you're catering for crowds? Getting
the quantities right. So
here's our simple guide to basics ...

| Number of portions | 10 | 20 | 40 |
|---|---|---|---|
| **WINE**<br>*1 bottle serves 6 glasses*<br>*1 litre bottle serves 9 glasses* | Four<br>70-cl<br>bottles | Eight<br>70-cl<br>bottles | Sixteen<br>70-cl<br>bottles |
| **SHERRY**<br>*One bottle serves 12 glasses* | One-two<br>bottles | Three-four<br>bottles | Seven<br>bottles |
| **GROUND COFFEE**<br>*2 cups per person* | 2.2 litres<br>(4 pt)<br>water<br>200 g<br>(7 oz)<br>coffee | 4.5 litres<br>(8 pt)<br>water<br>400 g<br>(14 oz)<br>coffee | 9 litres<br>(16 pt)<br>water<br>800 g<br>(28 oz)<br>coffee |
| **FRUIT SALAD**<br>*Make sugar syrup and cool,*<br>*add fresh fruits of choice* | 1.6 kg<br>(3-4 lb)<br>fruit<br>1.1 litres<br>(2 pt)<br>syrup | 2.7 kg<br>(6 lb)<br>fruit<br>2.2 litres<br>(4 pt)<br>syrup | 5.5 kg<br>(12 lb)<br>fruit<br>4.5 litres<br>(8 pt)<br>syrup |
| **LETTUCE**<br>*Depending on size* | 1-2 heads | 4-5 heads | 5-6 heads |
| **CUCUMBER** | 1½ | 2-3 | 3-4 |
| **TOMATOES** | 700 g<br>(1½ lb) | 1.2 kg<br>(3 lb) | 2.3-2.7 kg<br>(5-6 lb) |
| **WHITE CABBAGE** | 700 g<br>(1½ lb) | 1.3 kg<br>(3 lb) | 2.3 kg<br>(5 lb) |
| **CELERY** | 2 heads | 4 heads | 5 heads |
| **ICE CREAM** | 1¼-1½<br>litres | 2½-3<br>litres | 4-6<br>litres |
| **CREAM FOR COFFEE** | 600 ml<br>(1 pt) | 1.1 litres<br>(2 pt) | 2.2 litres<br>(4 pt) |
| **BREAD** | 1 large<br>loaf | 2 large<br>loaves | 4 large<br>loaves |
| **MARGARINE** | ½ tub<br>125 g | 1 tub<br>250 g | 2 tubs<br>2 x 250 g |

# YOUR YEAR BOOK CROSSWORD

## ACROSS

**7.** A place of shelter about stuffy English (6); **8.** He keeps cattle in Marsh End, anyhow (8); **10.** From the apartment hurries back in a real panic (4, 4); **11.** Hey, this is a very fast tempo (6); **12.** Unofficially, it's not on disc (3, 3, 6); **15.** Has new American president come from Kentish Town? (7); **17.** Bird that could be a Virginia one? (7); **19.** As is written by the poet when he abandons standard English? (7, 5); **22.** She finds the French one odd, it's put about (6); **23.** You need two instruments to provide such dance music (8); **25.** It's quiet, I stress for a change, and goes on and on (8); **26.** After work, an attitude to resist (6).

## DOWN

**1.** Tuna in aspic? (9); **2.** Search in the bush until dusk (4); **3.** A place of worship ahead (6); **4.** Psalm-singer the car then damaged (7); **5.** Might you get caught going in and out through it? (8); **6.** Seasons for sailors (5); **9.** Veronica can drive fast in a satisfactory way (9); **13.** What terribly fast but inwardly fragile vessels have? (9); **14.** Girl gets job with old mail service (5, 4); **16.** Cavalier description of one from the Civil War? (8); **18.** Right, I take the box from the most wealthy (7); **20.** The waiter is a youngster from France (6); **21.** Pop group seen on board? (5); **24.** Makes a weasel noise? (4).

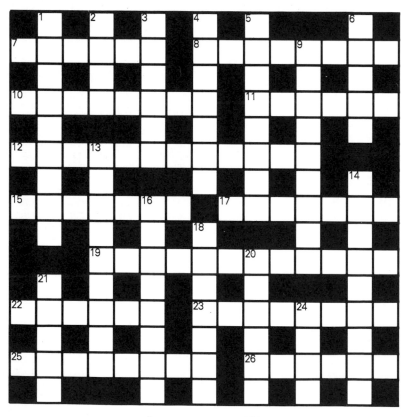

*Answers on page 189*

# WHAT'S THE MAGIC WORD?

## Charm, says Mary Bailey, is the Open Sesame to life

IN THE unlikely event of being assigned the role of Fairy Godmother at the christening of a little prince or princess, I'd settle for granting the gift of charm, waving my wand dismissively at brains and beauty. After all, if you've got charm, who could ask for anything more?

The Queen Mother has it. The man at Wandsworth Town Hall who explains my parking fines to me has it. So does Lord George-Brown — unlike any politician ever since. So, you can see, it has nothing to do with youth. And it is certainly not just a matter of clothes. The Queen Mother's dress is, to say the least, individual. Mr Putt at the Town Hall often wears odd socks and Lord George-Brown, well... And, though it's often allied to a golden tongue, charm must never be put down to mere flattery. The charmers of the world have no need to lie or exaggerate because everyone forgives them everything anyway.

It is the most durable of blessings, lasting as it does from birth to the grave. I remember when my father's wife, second wife and sister — ladies whom he had treated with financial carelessness, to put it mildly — decided to meet him together to confront him with the economic facts of life. I was more than a little alarmed — they *were* all over seventy! As visions of emotional scenes, heart attacks even, filled my mind, I made up my mind to join them. But when my aunt let me into her flat it was obvious how groundless my fears had been. Everyone had been there for some time and they were all drinking large gins.

"Do come in," beamed my father. "These naughty ladies are insisting on taking me out to lunch." My father might have aged, you see, but his charm had merely matured.

Can you learn it? I think not. It is by it's very nature an effortless attribute — and no respecter of intentions. It is bequeathed to the good and evil alike. Some young children have it. So do most animals — and there I think lies the answer.

"He makes me feel good," said a neighbour of his mischievous mongrel pup. And that, I thought, is it. Those with charm — for reasons never to be fully understood — make the rest of us simply feel better, and for that lift of spirit a grateful humanity rewards them by opening all doors.

Into customs they come with bottles and bottles of spirits, into the bank they drift just as the door is closing. And what happens? The customs officials wave them through and the bank manager prepares to extend their overdrafts with cries of understanding.

Unfair? Certainly! Irritating? Often! But where would we be without them? After all, it's all part of their charm...

# GILL COX

## Will they accept him?

I was divorced some years ago and have now met a man I'd like to marry. We have been seeing one another for some time and have a wonderful relationship. The only problem is my children. They are 12 and 14 now and can, at times, be quite hostile to my boyfriend. They're nice children really and I don't know why they have taken against him quite so much. We're really worried: if we marry, it could prove a disaster if the children never accept him. Do you think that in time they will get used to the idea? I don't want to hurt them — they went through enough when I and their father (who they still see) split up. I do so want some happiness myself, though.

⭐ Of course you do, and who can blame you? But I think you may have expected your children to be rather more mature than they are capable of right now. Their reaction to this new man in your life is most unlikely to be a logical, planned attack. They may feel that they would be disloyal to their father if they liked this "intruder". They may have cherished hopes that you and their father would get back together. They may feel that your love for this new man will in some way take away the love or attention you give to them. Their attack is a defence — so find out what they're defending and you may be able to ease the path to marriage. You might also buy your boyfriend a copy of Step Parenting by Brenda Maddox (Unwin paperback).

## Back to work

Now that my two children are at school I want to go back to work, for both financial and personal reasons. I used to be a secretary but I'm not sure I still want to do that. In fact I don't quite know what I want to do — or what I could do. I just don't know where to start. Is there anyone I could talk to about opportunities, or possible retraining for something quite different?

⭐ The Job Centre is the first place. They will know the type of work available in your area and will also be able to give you details of any retraining programmes. Think about training in new technology processes if you're looking for long-term prospects. It might help you keep up with your children's homework! The Job Centre's advice is free but you can also consult the National Advisory Centre on Careers for Women, who have to make a small charge for their services. They also publish a useful handbook, Returners. Write to them for guidance at Drayton House, 30 Gordon Street, London, WC1H 0AX. Happy job hunting — and good luck!

## Childbirth has changed

I'm pregnant with my second child. I know that things have changed a great deal on labour wards over the last few years and I'd really like to know what options are open to me. I would also like to investigate the possibility of having my child at home. Could you tell me the best people to advise me?

⭐ Speak first to your own GP who will know the maternity hospitals in your area — and their various policies. He or she may operate a shared-care system, which means that your GP can be the main doctor throughout your pregnancy. He or she will also advise about home births. If you feel that unnecessary obstacles are being put in your way, do seek the advice of

**Sharing a problem with someone who knows and cares is halfway to solving it. Here are a few which cropped up in Gill's postbag and which she feels might be of help to other readers**

your Community Health Council. And do read *Your Body, Your Baby, Your Life* an easy, informative guide to all aspects of pregnancy by Angela Phillips, Nicky Lean and Barbara Jacobs (Pandora Press, paperback). There's also the Birth Centre who can advise you how to negotiate the kind of birth you want. Their address is 101 Tufnell Park Rd, London N7 (please enclose an sae).

## She's starving herself

**We recently discovered that our 18-year-old daughter is anorexic. We made her go to the doctor because she kept wanting to diet, though she was well under her ideal weight. Admittedly, she did have a bit of puppy fat at one time but a short diet soon got rid of that. She wouldn't stop dieting though, and the doctor says that if her weight goes lower she will have to be hospitalised or she might die. I'm at an absolute loss and don't know what to do. I do everything I can to encourage her to eat but she feels that she's chubby. What on earth can I do?**

★ I think you have to consider that your daughter may be a very angry and frightened teenager who can't express her deepest emotions in any way other than by causing herself suffering and, as a result, pain to the family as a whole. Anorexics are often highly intelligent, critical of their own achievements to the point of perfectionism and articulate — except about expressing their own deeply felt emotions. Often the family background is one of emotional suppression, so that the only way an anorexic can protest is through destruction of the self. As the rigid dieting is her way of retaining control, any pushing, by

the family especially, may result in a yet more iron-like grip on her food intake. So you can see that your daughter's weight loss is by no means the whole problem; it's more a symptom of something much more complex, and the only way to overcome anorexia is for the anorexic to understand herself. Support and advice from fellow sufferers can certainly help. Try to persuade your daughter to contact Anorexic Aid at The Priory Centre, 11 Priory Road, High Wycombe, Bucks, or The Women's Therapy Centre at 6 Manor Gardens, London, N7 6LA (Tel. 01-263 6200).

## I'm a doormat

**I know what my problem is but how to get over it is something quite, quite different. I can never say no! If a neighbour asks me to get something while I'm out shopping I will do it even if I was intending to go in another direction. If someone asks for a lift I just can't say I don't feel like it. I'm the one who waits in for neighbour's deliveries. I seem to be at everyone's beck and call and they all take advantage of the fact. Sometimes I could scream but find myself saying no, of course I don't mind, only too happy to help...Please, how can I stop myself?**

★ Already you seem to realise what the problem is, so you're halfway there. If you got some satisfaction out of martyrdom there wouldn't be a problem — but clearly you don't. Well, nice people say no too, you know. You won't get rejected simply because you can't wait for someone's parcel

# GILL COX

or collect their prescription or whatever else. Being a good neighbour is one thing; being a doormat is taking it too far. It's practice you really need. The first time it will be a bit difficult, but once you've managed to say no once (and coped with the irrational guilt I'm pretty sure you will feel) it will get easier. Make it the next time someone asks you to do them a favour that will really put you out — don't delay taking the action you know you need. Politely but firmly say sorry, but you can't do that today because you're too busy, going the other way, have 101 things to do already or whatever. Remember that the thing about being a good old doormat is that people wipe their feet on you. Respect yourself and others will do the same.

---

## Plagued by Thrush

**For years now I have been plagued by recurring attacks of Thrush, the vaginal infection. In the middle of an attack it is impossible for me to have sex with my husband because I'm so sore. My doctor gives me treatment to cure the problem, but, really, I'd like to know how to prevent it happening at all.**

★ There are self-help tactics for the Thrush battle and I do know that is precisely what it is for some women. It's caused by a yeast imbalance which can be provoked or aggravated by heat — so wear cotton underwear for a start, stockings or crutchless tights and avoid trousers. Keep the sugar in your diet to a minimum. Avoid perfumed soaps and, during the middle of an attack, try just to use warm water to wash in and avoid baths (use a shower if possible). If you think an attack is imminent, and many Thrush sufferers know the signs, insert a tampon soaked in natural yoghurt. The bacteria in yoghurt can balance out the bacterial imbalance causing the problem. These and other self-help measures are detailed in a leaflet entitled *Self Help for Thrush* available from me on receipt of a large sae. But first-time sufferers and those in the throes of a fully fledged attack should always consult their doctor for a full diagnosis and treatment.

Everyone agrees health is precious, but a lot of us pay no more than lip service to the idea. Somehow, we're not prepared to make an effort.

To a certain extent, that's understandable. After all, what's right at one time rapidly becomes wrong. Milk was good for you — then we learnt that it carried TB and other infections. Milk was bad for you — then we learnt how to purify it. Milk was then so good for you that we gave it to all our schoolchildren. Then we discovered that heart disease was related to the amount of fat in our diets, and, hey presto, milk and other dairy products are not so good as they were!

So, what *is* good for you now? Perhaps the most important thing for health is that you need to feel good about yourself. Health is about "Do's" not "Don'ts". *Do* you take enough time off from the hurly burly of life to be fit and exercise as much as you would like? Do you keep yourself in the sort of shape you want to be in? If the answer to either is no, then what are you going to do about it?

Exercise is not harmful, but pushing untrained muscles too far too fast is just plain stupid. A regular programme of increasing exercise will make you painlessly fit. Exercise has to be geared to what you want to do and what you are good at — squash, tennis, golf or a private half-hour with an exercise tape. It is also important to keep up the good work.

Last year, for example, I was asked to see a very sick man with a probable heart attack. When I explained my fears he reacted with total astonishment. "But doctor, I've always played a lot of sport," he said. "I'm very, very fit." His last sport was rugby — some 20 years ago — and he now weighed over 20 stones!

Being overweight is not dangerous in

# 'Accentuate the positive' says DR PAT LAST

itself; it's just that overweight people have more chance than lighter folk of developing heart disease, high blood pressure and diabetes. Heavyweights are also more difficult to nurse and it is harder for them to recover mobility after an operation. So making sure that you are not carrying around too many extra pounds is not vanity but commonsense. However, you mustn't lose too much weight. People who are underweight have a slightly higher death rate than the normal or modestly overweight.

In the USA probably more people are obese than they are in this country but their rates for heart disease have fallen, mainly because they have changed other aspects of their life. For instance, smoking within the office environment is frowned upon by many American companies. How many of you have taken a head count of the number of smokers and non-smokers in your office, discovered non-smokers outnumber smokers and yet still tolerate a situation where everyone has to work in a smoky, polluted atmosphere? Not British Rail! There are more non-smoking compartments on trains and undergrounds than there ever were before.

Though the smoking rate among doctors has dropped dramatically over the past years as we have seen more and more of its adverse side effects, we have been slow to encourage patients to give up smoking. (I think we all realise that the effort and the desire must come from the patient.) But attitudes are becoming more aggressive. One doctor has suggested that people who are unwilling to give up smoking should not be considered for major arterial or cardiac surgery, and in Western Australia, doctors caring for children have ganged together to paint-spray hoardings carrying cigarette ads. These doctors are frustrated that all their dedication and skill in saving young lives is being invalidated by advertisements which encourage the young to smoke.

On to the next big "Do". When you are socialising, relaxing at home, enjoying good company, do have a good time, and drink a modest amount of alcohol, if you wish. But do consider how much. Do you really have a good time when you drink so much that you either feel sleepy, pass out, throw up or have such a rotten headache that you can't do your work next day?

Alcohol addiction is an increasing danger in our present society and with the advent of the drink shelves in the local supermarkets, it seems to be affecting women more. Alcohol appears to cause no problems when taken in moderation — in fact, it may have some benefit — but not if it's more than two glasses of wine, one large measure of spirits, or a pint of beer a day, with just the occasional episode of overdrinking. If you do go on a bender, it is important to remember that alcohol is cleared out of the body at a standard rate, and after a heavy or prolonged drinking spree your blood alcohol in the morning can still be well above the legal limit. In certain parts of the world, morning-after breathalyser tests are catching on.

Do enjoy your food. Eating is a great pleasure and we are fortunate in this country that the majority of foods are available to us. However, many of us spend money on foods that have little value, or are positively harmful.

As a child brought up in World War II, I can honestly say that I didn't see a sweet for five years of my childhood — and, you know, it really didn't bother me. I certainly wasn't deprived, and in all the years of rationing I don't remember ever being hungry. It is so easy to give in to the temptation of providing more than enough food in an attempt to be generous, and also to provide the wrong food which has got a high content of either fat or refined sugars which do the eater no good and soon dull the palate.

Do enjoy your health, and with this positive new approach to your lifestyle I wish you a happy and healthy 1985!

# LOOKS FAMILIAR

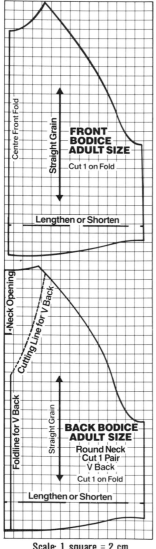

Centre Front Fold

Straight Grain

**FRONT
BODICE
ADULT SIZE**

Cut 1 on Fold

Lengthen or Shorten

Neck Opening

Cutting Line for V Back

Foldline for V Back

Straight Grain

**BACK BODICE
ADULT SIZE**

Round Neck
Cut 1 Pair
V Back

Cut 1 on Fold

Lengthen or Shorten

Scale: 1 square = 2 cm
Adult pattern ▷ 179

**Our loose and easy, drop-waisted, four-way frock really will flatter you all, from the little lady in the family right up to her great-granny**

**MATERIALS REQUIRED:** child's dress, using 90-cm wide fabric, takes 1.70 m; short-sleeved V-back dress, using 112-cm wide fabric, takes 3.20 m; basic adult's dress with full-length sleeves, using 112-cm wide fabric, takes 3.40 m; blue dress with ⅞ sleeves, using 112-cm wide fabric, takes 3.35 m. Sash (optional), using 112-cm wide fabric, takes 80 cm. Notions: lace collar, using 15-cm wide lace, takes 1.50 m. Bias binding, 1.5 cm wide, takes 50 cm for round-neck dress, 1 m for V-back dress. Velvet ribbon for child's dress, using 7-mm wide ribbon, takes 3.50 m. Purchased Peter Pan collar. Paper for squared up diagrams for bodice, sleeves and sash.
**Cutting instructions for the skirts (pattern pieces not needed):**

| Size | Cut two pieces |
|------|----------------|
| Child's (fits 5 to 8 year olds) | 38½ cm long by 90 cm wide |
| Adult's (fits sizes 10 to 18) | 66 cm long by 90 cm wide |

**GENERAL INSTRUCTIONS FOR ALL DRESSES:** seam allowance 1.5 cm (¾ in), hems 2 cm (1 in), neck edges .75 cm (½ in). Neaten raw edges with zigzag or oversew by hand. Press the seams apart as you work. Ease sleeves to fit armholes. Use hook and eye to close the back of the neck. To alter length, adjust on bodice and skirt.
**ABBREVIATIONS:** CB = centre back. RS = right side. WS = wrong side.
**TO MAKE THE BASIC DRESS**
**BODICE:** join CB seam to opening, press back turnings on opening. (There is no CB on V-back dress.) Sew front and back bodice to sleeve along armhole seams, ease sleeves to fit. Open one folded edge of bias binding. With bias at neck edge, RS together, sew along fold of bias. To neaten, fold in each end of bias. Turn bias under neck edge of WS of dress, sew along free neck edge of bias through dress. Bias should not show on RS of dress. Join front to back along underarm/bodice seam. Turn up 1.5-cm hem at cuff, machine or hand hem. On V-back dress, bias goes all round neck.
**Skirt:** join side seams on skirt panels. Gather top of skirt to width of bodice lower edge. Sew skirt to bodice matching side seams, making sure gathers are evenly spaced. Try on dress for length. Sew up hem by machine or hand.
**VARIATIONS**
**Child's dress** — When sewing on velvet ribbon, sew along both edges. Sew one row of ribbon 8 cm above the hem edge ▷178

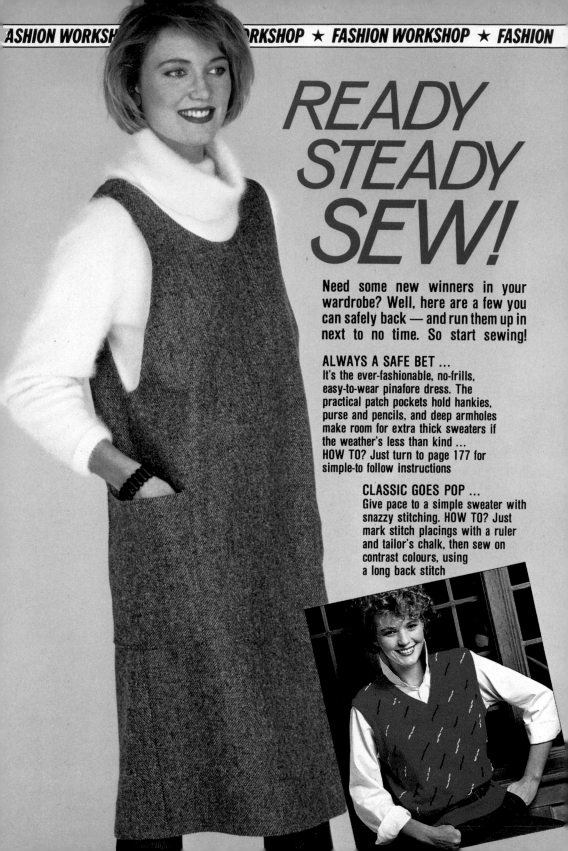

# READY STEADY SEW!

Need some new winners in your wardrobe? Well, here are a few you can safely back — and run them up in next to no time. So start sewing!

**ALWAYS A SAFE BET ...**
It's the ever-fashionable, no-frills, easy-to-wear pinafore dress. The practical patch pockets hold hankies, purse and pencils, and deep armholes make room for extra thick sweaters if the weather's less than kind ...
HOW TO? Just turn to page 177 for simple-to follow instructions

**CLASSIC GOES POP ...**
Give pace to a simple sweater with snazzy stitching. HOW TO? Just mark stitch placings with a ruler and tailor's chalk, then sew on contrast colours, using a long back stitch

## WAISTS GO RACY ...
Give bright new life to that little black number with a sash that says flash.
HOW TO? Just make the sash from our four-way frock (see page 179) in silk, satin, taffeta or lurex

## A CERT OF A SKIRT ...
Softly pleated from the waistband, it's as comfy-casual or as dressed up as you want it to be.
HOW TO? Just turn to page 177

# TIP FOR THE TOP

You don't have to splash the cash on a new winter coat. Why not wrap up wonderfully and be as snug as a bug in a rug – or rather, in a bright and beautiful blanket?

Blanket coverage makes a cosy cape... HOW TO? Just take a bright blanket 150 x 200 cm (60 by 80 in). Fold it in half lengthwise and mark fold line. With long edges towards you, cut away 2½ in up the centre of the top layer, to meet centre of fold line. Neaten raw edge, then turn under a ⅜-in hem and machine. Finally, wrap yourself up, throwing the opposite front corner over each shoulder for that cosy-cape look

## *PINAFORE*
### Continued from page 174

**MATERIALS REQUIRED:** 1.45 m of 114-cm wide fabric plus 2 m bias binding. (Pinafore will fit sizes 12 to 16.)

**TO MAKE THE PINAFORE:** with RS together, join the front piece to the back piece at shoulders and side seams. Neaten the neck and armholes with bias binding. To do this, open one folded edge of the bias binding and place the fold of bias along the wrong side of neck and armhole edges. Sew bias in place along the fold line, joining ends to neaten. Turn bias under neck edge so that it doesn't show on RS of the pinafore. Sew along the free edge of the bias through the pinafore. For the pockets, turn over 4-cm (1½-in) hem at the top, stitch along the edge of this hem and press. Then press under 1.5-cm (¾-in) hem round sides and bottom of the pockets. Place the two pockets in the correct position on the RS of the pinafore and machine stitch in place, 0.5 cm (¼ in) from edge. Try on the pinafore and adjust hem for length. Sew up the hem by machine or hand and then press the pinafore.

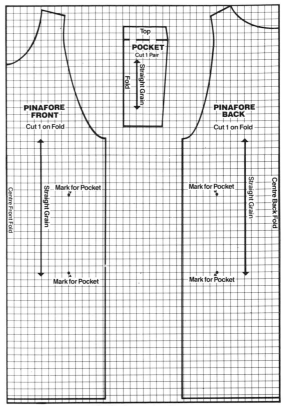

Scale: 1 square = 2 cm

### GENERAL INSTRUCTIONS

Seam allowance 1.5 cm (¾ in). hems 2 cm (1 in). Neaten all raw edges by hand. machine oversewing, zigzag stitch or with pinking shears. Press seams open as you go. and on completion.

**ABBREVIATIONS:**
WS = wrong side. RS = right side

## *SKIRT*
### Continued from page 175

This skirt is so simple to make that it doesn't require a pattern.

**MATERIALS REQUIRED:** choose a soft fabric that will fall into folds, 120 to 154 cm wide. Measure desired finished length of skirt, waistband to hem, double it and add hem allowance plus 30 cm. In all you will need approx 2.28 m of fabric, according to your size. You also need interfacing for waistband; matching cotton to top-stitch waistband and buttonhole; one button and one hook and eye.

**TO MAKE THE SKIRT:** cut off 30 cm (12 in) allowance for pockets and waistband. Cut remaining material into 2 lengths for back and front; allow for hem. Cut 4 pocket pieces and cut out the waistband (diag 1). RS facing, sew right-hand set of pockets together (diag 2). RS facing, sew left-hand set of pockets ▷

177

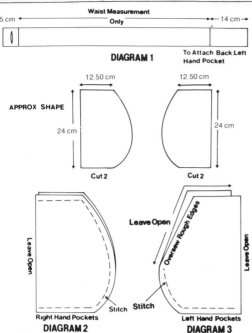

Waist Measurement
Only

2.5 cm ← 14 cm →

**DIAGRAM 1**

To Attach Back Left
Hand Pocket

12.50 cm          12.50 cm

APPROX SHAPE

24 cm          24 cm

Cut 2          Cut 2

Leave Open

Oversew Rough Edges

Leave Open

Leave Open

Stitch   Stitch

Right Hand Pockets          Left Hand Pockets

**DIAGRAM 2**          **DIAGRAM 3**

◁ 177 together (diag 3). Oversew the rough open edges of the left-hand pocket. RS of skirt together, attach straight sides of pocket edges to side seams of skirt. Turn and press. With RS together, join skirt side seams, overlapping join of pocket to side seam by 2.5 cm (1 in). Turn skirt to right side and press. Pleat or gather top edges of front and back skirt pieces to fit waist measurement. Interface the waistband and attach to skirt, stitching right-hand set of pockets under front waistband and left-hand set of pockets (diag 4) so that front left-hand pocket is stitched under front waistband and back left-hand pocket is attached to the rest of waistband. (When fastening skirt, front left pocket should lie over back left pocket.) Align left-hand pocket side seams and mark place for button and buttonhole (see diag 4). Sew on button. Sew hook and eye at either end of inner edge of left-hand pocket waistband. Press all seams, top stitch around waistband edge and buttonhole. Try on skirt for length and turn up the hem.

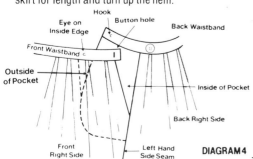

Hook
Eye on
Inside Edge
Button hole
Back Waistband
Front Waistband
Outside
of Pocket
Inside of Pocket
Back Right Side
Front
Right Side
Left Hand
Side Seam
**DIAGRAM 4**

## FOUR-WAY FROCK
### Continued from page 172

◁ 172 and another 13 cm above the hem edge. Sew on Peter Pan collar.

**Short-sleeved dress** — Puff sleeves with sleeves joined to dress; make cuffs, RS together, join ends, then fold cuffs in half, WS together, lengthwise. Gather sleeve edge to cuff. Sew double cuff to sleeve edge, matching underarm seam to cuff seam.

**Blue dress** — For collar, trim ends of lace to the shape of the pattern on lace. Thread narrow ribbon in and out of the holes on the plain edge of lace. Pull up lace to fit neck.

**Basic adult's dress** — For an extra touch of glamour, add a sash. For sash, unfold fabric and join centre seam. Fold again, RS together, sew all round edge, leaving opening. Trim edges, turn RS out. Sew opening. Press.

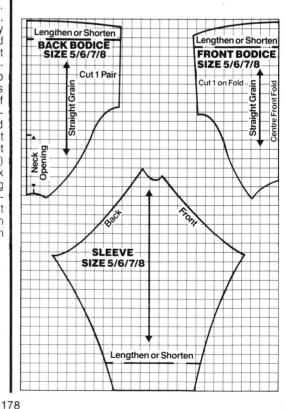

Lengthen or Shorten
**BACK BODICE
SIZE 5/6/7/8**
Cut 1 Pair
Straight Grain
Neck Opening

Lengthen or Shorten
**FRONT BODICE
SIZE 5/6/7/8**
Cut 1 on Fold
Straight Grain
Centre Front Fold

Back          Front

**SLEEVE
SIZE 5/6/7/8**

Lengthen or Shorten

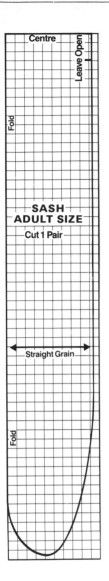

Centre

Leave Open

Fold

**SASH
ADULT SIZE**
Cut 1 Pair

Straight Grain

Fold

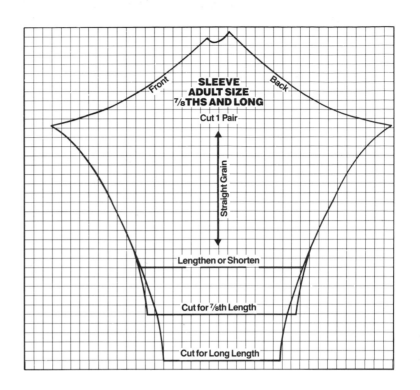

Front

Back

**SLEEVE
ADULT SIZE
7/8THS AND LONG**

Cut 1 Pair

Straight Grain

Lengthen or Shorten

Cut for 7/8th Length

Cut for Long Length

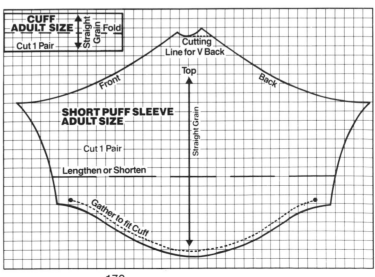

**CUFF
ADULT SIZE**
Cut 1 Pair

Straight Grain

Fold

Cutting
Line for V Back

Top

Front

Back

**SHORT PUFF SLEEVE
ADULT SIZE**

Cut 1 Pair

Straight Grain

Lengthen or Shorten

Gather to fit Cuff

**Scale: 1 square = 2 cm**

## Aries
### *March 21 – April 20*

**The good news** You're a natural leader, adventurous, ambitious and with a good chance of succeeding at almost anything you undertake. Physically you're likely to be lean and wiry, with a pleasingly compact frame.

**The not-so-good news** You tend to speak first and think later — and you loathe having to admit you're wrong. Physically, you're prone to eye problems: Ariens often have to wear glasses and suffer from headaches.

***Luck and love*** Your happiness lies with Sagittarians, Leos and Librans. Your lucky colour is red and your gemstone the diamond.

## Taurus
### *April 21 – May 21*

**The good news** You're faithful, patient and practical — and good with money! Your eyes are your best feature: they're likely to be large and dark, with a look of watchful sympathy that makes others confide in you.

**The not-so-good news** You can be pedestrian and plodding — obstinate too! You're probably on the solid side physically (built for comfort rather than speed) and could be prone to throat infections.

**Luck and love** You get on best with Virgos, Capricorns, and Scorpios; your lucky colour is red-orange and your gemstone the emerald.

## Gemini
### *May 22 – June 21*

**The good news** You're quick-witted, versatile and intellectual. Success is almost guaranteed in any area where you're called upon to teach, speak or write. You're likely to be tall and slim, with long elegant fingers.

**The not-so-good news** You tend to lose interest swiftly in pursuits and people, leaving others unhappy and bewildered when the warmth is switched off from your welcome. Your chest is the danger area physically.

**Luck and love** Sagittarians, Librans and Aquarians are a good match. Your lucky colour is orange, and your gemstone the topaz.

## Cancer
### *June 22 – July 22*

**The good news** You're sensitive to others and protective of them — your true talent is dealing with people. You're also open-minded, with a liking for change and variety. Physically, you're probably of small to average stature and quite sexily curved!

**The not-so-good news** You can be moody and prone to depression. Watch out for digestive problems — the stomach is your danger area.

**Luck and love** Those born under the signs of Scorpio, Taurus, Capricorn and Pisces will be your chosen companions. Your lucky colour is yellow-orange and your gem the moonstone.

## Leo
### *July 23 – August 23*

**The good news** You're affectionate, enterprising and a born organiser. You're extravagant and wasteful with money, but luckily you're never short of it. You are probably tall and quite big-boned, but with a rangy sort of figure.

**The not-so-good news** You're quick-tempered and can be overbearing — and yet you're wounded by even a hint of criticism from others. You could have trouble with your spine, so guard against back problems.

**Luck and love** Sagittarians, Ariens and Aquarians will love you. Your lucky colour is yellow and your gemstone the ruby.

## Virgo
### *August 24 – September 23*

**The good news** You're methodical, analytical, tactful, ingenious and alert — which should spell success in almost any career! You're also neat, small-boned, and will grow old very gracefully!

**The not-so-good news** Your natural reserve makes you undemonstrative, so others think you cold and calculating. You could be prone to digestive problems: a high-fibre diet could prove a wise decision.

**Luck and love** You'll find soul mates among those born under the signs of Capricorn and Pisces. Your lucky colour is yellow-green and your gemstone the peridot.

# *YOU* Your personality, your success, your looks, even, are all because you were born a star!

## Libra
*September 24 – October 23*

**The good news** You're sociable, romantic and artistic, and should succeed in any area calling for an eye for beauty. You probably have a graceful, well-formed body and large bright eyes.

**The not-so-good news** You are reluctant to act on impulse, which could mean missed opportunities. Librans are inclined to put weight on in later life, so be warned! Also, watch out for bladder infections: your kidneys could be a problem.

**Luck and love** Look for companions born under the signs of Gemini, Aquarius and Aries. Your lucky colour is green and your gemstone the opal.

## Scorpio
*October 24 – November 22*

**The good news** You're courageous, strong-willed and ambitious. You have a very real personal magnetism and could well be psychic. Your body is well formed and muscular, and you have the most arresting eyes.

**The not-so-good news** While love can bring out the best in you, it can also bring out the worst — you can be possessive and domineering. You need to guard against genital and bladder infections.

**Luck and love** Cancerians, Pisces and Taureans are your best bets. Your lucky colour is blue-green and your gemstone the turquoise.

## Sagittarius
*November 23 – December 21*

**The good news** You're optimistic, independent and enterprising, with a very real interest in other people, which makes you highly attractive to them. You're probably tall, loose-limbed and long-legged.

**The not-so-good news** You can be an exacting taskmaster, and intensely dislike having to play a subservient role. Your feet and hands are probably larger than you'd like — Sagittarians are seldom dainty. Health problems could lie with your liver, so watch out!

**Luck and love** Ariens, Leos and Geminis are most likely to succeed with you. Your lucky colour is blue and your gemstone the jacinth.

## Capricorn
*December 22 – January 20*

**The good news** You're ambitious, practical and persevering, with an attention to detail that makes you an excellent manager. Your determination may pay off in later life. Physically you're likely to be short, but pleasingly proportioned.

**The not-so-good news** If there is a black side you'll look on it, and you should try to develop your sense of humour. You could be prone to arthritis and rheumatism — your knees, in particular, could be a problem.

**Luck and love** You get on best with those born under Virgo, Taurus, and Cancer. Your lucky colour is indigo, your gemstone sapphire.

## Aquarius
*January 21 – February 19*

**The good news** You're inventive, idealistic, unconventional, and should succeed in any literary or artistic pursuit. Physically, you're well proportioned, probably with square, chiselled features.

**The not-so-good news** Though you choose to walk your own highly individual path, you envy others the material rewards they've opted for: remember you can't have it both ways! Health-wise, watch your blood pressure.

**Luck and love** Look to those born under Gemini, Sagittarius, Libra or Leo for true happiness. Your lucky colour is violet and your gemstones chalcedony — and glass!

## Pisces
*February 20 – March 20*

**The good news** You're sensitive, versatile and practical. Though you're adaptable and popular, you will nevertheless stand up for what you believe in. Physically you're pretty with melting eyes.

**The not-so-good news** You're tender-hearted to a fault and let others get away with murder. You'll stand up for principles but not for yourself. Your most vulnerable area physically is your feet — take care of them!

**Luck and love** You'll find the dearest companions among the Cancerians and Scorpios. Your lucky colour is red-violet and your gemstone the amethyst.

# SAY IT WITH

Your own hand-made crackers are such a personal, pretty way to package presents, decorate a table or transform any old day into a fun day. So why not get cracking!

## MAKING A BASIC 12-IN CRACKER

**Materials:** crêpe paper; lining paper; snaps; thin card; toilet and kitchen roll tubes; clear adhesive; thread.

**Method:** cut crêpe paper into oblong 12 by 8 in, grain running lengthwise. Cut lining 11½ by 7 in, card 7½ by 3½ in. Centre lining on crêpe paper, card on lining. Place snap between card and lining. Lay long and short tubes over papers, as shown. Glue crêpe paper edge.

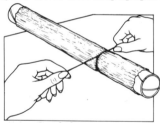

Roll papers tightly round tubes, hold until glue has stuck. Ease out short tube slightly. Wind thread round gap, pull tight and tie. Remove small tube.

Post a small present through long tube. Ease out tube and tie off second end. Then decorate cracker …

Crackers are simple to make, fun to decorate and special to give. You have to send for the snaps, and in bulk — 144 at a time — but you can always share them with friends or relatives. Stored in a dry place, your snaps will keep for years.

## DECORATING CRACKERS

**Papers:** keep them simple and inexpensive by using crêpe or tissue or go to town with the more elaborate foils or gift wraps.

**Presentation:** our basic crackers are decorated in a variety of ways to give you some ideas. We used doilies, glitter glue, sequins, ribbons, tiny flowers, lace edging, decorative stickers, and a ribbon which pulls up to make a bow. To make a centrepiece with the rose crackers, support them with thin sticks stuck in florists' foam and decorate with artificial ferns and baubles.

**Presents:** pick presents with care. They have to be small enough to post through the tube but don't have to be expensive to be appreciated. For example, a packet of seeds would go down well with a gardener, or for children a few favourite chocolates. You can see some of the presents we chose spilling out of our party cracker.

**Where to buy cracker snaps:** a pack of 144, 10-in cracker snaps are available from Stoneleigh Mail Order Co Ltd, 85 Princes St, Southend-on-Sea, Essex SS1 1PT. For current prices, phone (0702) 338053.

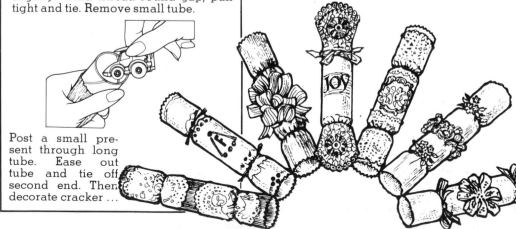

# CRACKERS!

## MAKING A ROSE CRACKER

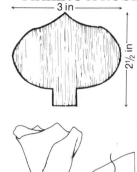

3 in

2½ in

Make a basic cracker with crêpe paper. Tie one end only and stiffen with thin card. Cut out 6 petals (see diagram left). Pop gift in open end, then squeeze to make stalk. Wire petals to stalk, over-·lapping them. Bind with green paper.

## MAKING A PARTY CRACKER

**Materials:** 2 empty 1-litre washing-up liquid bottles; gift wrap paper; thin card; clear adhesive; thin string.
**Method:** for cracker ends, remove necks and cut bottles in two. Base should be about 5 in high and tube 3½ in. Align base of bottle and tube together on gift wrap. Glue one edge of paper, roll round bottle pieces. Ease away tube from base end, tie string round. Tuck in ends of gift wrap. Repeat for other end of cracker. Cut card into an oblong 10 by 11 in, cover and roll to make central tube. Check cracker ends slide in, then glue. Make paper fan to decorate cracker. Fill ends with gifts, slip into tube.

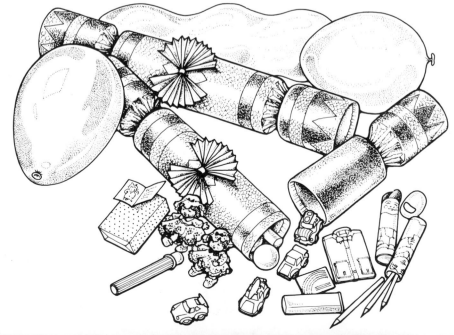

# A Christmas

## A short story by Mary Dugdale

I HATE, loathe, detest Christmas. I hate tinsel and turkey, carols and cake, presents and parties. The lot! I refuse to prance along in step to *Jingle Bells* from the first of October onwards. Given the choice, I would spend December the twenty-fifth on an uninhabited island, without TV or radio. Failing that, I'd retire to the uninhabited island of my own room, locked away with a sensible read like *Bleak House* or that Desert Island standby, *War and Peace*. On the twenty-seventh — and not a minute sooner — I would emerge, peaceful, rested, full of goodwill to all men, women and children, even — and this is the big test — even to my own family, even to my in-laws ...

And then what? I'll tell you. The same sad tears I shed every year, crying for Christmas Past. Running away wouldn't really help at all, cancelling my own Christmas wouldn't change the calendar. I'd know that magic and happiness wouldn't come my way, not this year, maybe not next year, maybe never. I may as well confess, perhaps you've already guessed, that it isn't really Christmas I hate at all. No ... it's the poor shadow of Christmas Present I can't bear, the cheat, counterfeit, parody, fake, the media event pretending to be peace on earth.

Behind my face, painted this year's colours, inside my body, dressed in this year's clothes, there's a little girl, woken by Christmas bells. She stands, barefoot, in her long white nightdress, seeing the shining stars and the crib, ox, ass and shepherds around the newborn child. She's still carrying her stocking, gazing in wonder at the parcels, wrapped in holly-strewn paper, under the tree. The room smells of pine, and tangerines. (No, not satsumas!) There are long thin boxes of dates on the sideboard, and sticky figs near a fruit bowl piled high with grapes and nuts. The room is gaudy with crêpe streamers, and the wireless is on, playing yesterday's carol service.

*Hark, the herald angels sing,*
*Glory to the newborn King ...*

And what has it all come to? Well, nothing much. Worse than nothing. If I didn't care, it wouldn't matter, would it?

Last year, Joe gave me exactly what I'd asked for, all I wanted for Christmas. He said, "I suppose you'll want a Christmas present?" And I said, "Well, I don't actually expect anything, but it would be nice."

Then he asked me what I'd like. I couldn't tell him, of course. But Joe expects answers, so I told him a book would be nice. Joe is practical, sensible. He pointed out that I wouldn't want just any old book, would I? Or any new book. He offered me a book token, twice as much as I'd dreamed of. Joe's generous, you see.

All the wonder and joy of that lumpy stocking, flattened into one brisk token! So I told him exactly which book I'd like, title, the author's name, the publisher, even the price, like ordering a book at the library. That's how I got what I wanted last Christmas.

In return, I gave Joe exactly what he wanted. Or rather, I gave him exactly what he said he wanted. It might be the same thing, I don't know. Another book. He thought it was all a bit pointless, wrapping them up and hanging on to them for five days, before the ritual exchange on the twenty-fifth, but I insisted, and he didn't object.

Last year, it was his family's turn. So we went there, Christmas morning, driving along empty roads. We ate what his mother calls, in nervous capitals, "The Meal", and stayed the night, after playing Monopoly and arguing with the others about what to watch. On Boxing Day, we went for a cold grey walk by the cold grey canal.

JOE'S sister spent the whole day preening for a party, the kind of exciting party you read about in pre-Christmas magazines. Her man arrived, and she left, a swan gliding away from dismal geese — and turkey of course! Boxing Day supper: cold turkey and more rows about TV. By the way, I kept out of them. The opposing armies were Joe's mum and his dad's sister, against their menfolk. I remembered, almost too late, that I hadn't wished my own mum and dad Merry Christmas. Then Scrabble — well, at least it was a change from Monopoly, and so to bed. Then, thank God, morning, and the drive home. End of Christmas.

So you see, I didn't smile back when Dr King finished squinting at his chart, and gave me that idiotic grin.

"A Christmas baby, then, Mrs David. My congratulations."

Maybe I muttered something, maybe he didn't hear. Anyway, I booked my next appointment and left. I walked out of that surgery haunted, like poor old Scrooge, by the Spirit of Christmas Yet-to-Come. Well, imagine it. Those dreadful newspaper pictures for a start, exhausted women looking exactly as if they've just had a baby while being dragged through a hedge backwards, and

# Carol

the babies — if you can see them at all — look barely human. Nurses, singing carols with their capes on, the way they do in all the hospital soap operas. Joe's mum, my mum, the bashful, boastful granddads, the whole lot of them. Christmas ... Bah ... Humbug, to coin a phrase.

No, it wasn't an accident, nothing like that. We wanted her all right. And in lots of ways, now seemed the right time. I mean, my contract was almost up, and Joe would be promoted next year, spending lots of time on trips abroad. It seemed a good idea to start a baby now, while he's around all the time. Joe was keen on doing everything right, coming along to classes with me, in at the birth, changing nappies, the lot — bar feeding her of course. Then we plan a second, when she's about eighteen months. That way, they'll be playmates, and I'll be able to get back to work quickly. I've organised myself some freelance work already, to get on with in all the long hours babies spend doing nothing. You know what I mean, don't you? Friends disappear to have their

# A Christmas Carol

babies, and then, when you see them again, they spend all the time telling you how exhausted they are, never a minute to themselves, and there's this tiny motionless bundle in the pram, sleeping.

Joe consoled me about the date. He went right out and bought five paperbacks — on breast-feeding, babycare, being a parent, seeing them through from orange juice to O levels, post-natal exercises. Babies don't arrive on time, he said. Two weeks, either side, rates as normal. And it's a myth, it seems, about them being born at night. Apparently, what happens is everyone remembers pains beginning at night, driving to the hospital through dark dramatic streets. You're as likely as not to give birth at half past two in the afternoon.

Well, December eleventh or January eighth sound normal enough as dates of birth go. Joe himself is a stickler for punctuality, but never mind that. There's always the risk of missing Christmas only to produce on New Year's Day but, not being a Scot, I don't care one way or the other about January the first. You don't get singers crooning about a baby born on New Year's Day, do you?

After the first week or so I was hardened, even quite witty. It was the only way to cope. "On or about December the twenty-fifth," I told everyone. "An angel whispered in my ear." And then, for a while, I managed to forget all about it. At work I was frantically busy, writing reports, interviewing, slogging away after hours, desperate to kill the myth about pregnant women losing interest in everything but the baby. I wasn't sick, and didn't look any different. No, that isn't quite true. Usually I'm a curvy 30A. Now, miraculously, I blossomed into a 32B. As Joe said, I was almost beginning to look like a woman.

By mid July, I was beginning to wonder if the whole thing was a mistake, still zipping up my jeans, when she began. Quickening, they used to call it. I remember one of those risqué scripture lessons, when we had to read that passage about "the child in my womb leapt for joy". Foetal movements, they said at the clinic, and wrote it down. Then it was goodbye, jeans. She was definitely growing, and moving like that spider the old woman swallowed, that wriggled and tickled and tickled inside her.

She. It isn't just bravado, that. At the clinic they say "he" as if women exist simply to produce men, as if the entire human race is single sex. I've noticed though that the latest trendy baby books refer to the infant as "she". Maybe it's something to do with the Equal Opportunities Act.

My friends are split: half think I'm whistling in the dark, the rest that I'm simply being trendy. The truth is that I've always wanted a daughter. So does Joe. We're agreed on that and, yes, I know it's whether they're healthy that matters.

Joe, like most men owning nothing statelier than a mortgage, isn't interested in a son and heir, Like the man in *Carousel*, he's overcome with the idea of *My little girl*. As for me, it's a bit harder to explain. Women's Lib is definitely part of it. There were three of us girls, before my brother was born, and I still remember, bitterly, the gloating, the triumph over a son and heir at last. Women's Lib? We were founder members. But there's more to it than that. I wanted a daughter — how can I put this? — happy to be herself. Knowing she's valued just as much as any son.

In September, we gave her a name, the day I wore my first maternity dress. Elizabeth. Safe, Joe thinks, dignified, a name that will last. Give Joe half a chance, and he'd produce a *Which* report on anything. Me ... I just like it. All right, I did have a crush on the head girl, and she was Elizabeth. But that was a long, long, time ago. Liz, Libby, Beth, Liza. You could go on for ever. And Elizabeth for best, for the christening, official forms, her wedding day.

In September I began to day dream like this, as if the growing bump came between me, clever, competent Mary, and Mrs David, you know, the one who's expecting a baby at Christmas.

Of course, I was exaggerating about *Jingle Bells* on October the first. Really, the shops didn't start with carols until Father Christmas arrived, in time for the school half term, the day before Hallowe'en. I had the afternoon off, for ante-natal, and at first I couldn't understand why there were so many children about, all over the place, and wearing ghastly masks. The mothers struggled around, somehow, trying to control wild boys of six or seven, little girls in witches' hats, and toddlers in pushchairs. And shopping at the same time — I don't know how they do it. It takes me all my time just shopping for the two of us. Next year, I'll be one of them, bustling about like Kanga in *Winnie the Pooh*, with my baby in one of those pouch things. (We gave up saying Elizabeth. After all, she might not be. Joe says it isn't even a fifty-fifty chance. There are more boys born, you see.)

OCTOBER, November. At the clinic, you compare bumps, and talk in a dreadful matey way about the extraordinary goings-on inside. A lot depends on how much water you carry. I was determined to work right up to the last minute, and the mental juggling it takes to switch from slick reports to how much I've gained in the last fortnight is incredible. I mean, it's hard enough to imagine a real live baby inside you. Add all the water, the placenta, the cord, and the mind boggles. I was a star pupil at the ante-natal, actually. Blood pressure normal, weight gain modest, no stretch marks, no puffy ankles, never smoked in my life. A real little goody-goody, teacher's pet. I even had Joe turning up, doing the breathing better than any of us.

December. So much time has passed. Life will never be the same again. Cliché, I know, but it happens to be true. I'm afraid of change. By now